2

The Disturbance Fee

By The Same Author

Roaring Boys
This Right Soft Lot
A Cack-handed War
Uncommon Entrance
Sorry, Dad
A Nest of Teachers
Shaky Relations
Lizzie Pye
Donkey Work
A Second Skin
The Outside Contributor

THE
DISTURBANCE FEE

by
Edward Blishen

HAMISH HAMILTON · LONDON

HAMISH HAMILTON LTD
Published by the Penguin Group
27 Wrights Lane, London W8 5TZ, England
Viking Penguin Inc., 40 West 23rd Street, New York, New York 10010, U.S.A.
Penguin Books Australia Ltd, Ringwood, Victoria, Australia
Penguin Books Canada Ltd, 2801 John Street, Markham, Ontario, Canada L3R 1B4
Penguin Books (N.Z.) Ltd, 182–190 Wairau Road, Auckland 10, New Zealand
Penguin Books Ltd, Registered Offices: Harmondsworth, Middlesex, England

First published in Great Britain 1988 by
Hamish Hamilton Ltd

Copyright © 1988 by Edward Blishen

British Library Cataloguing in Publication Data
Blishen, Edward, *1920–*
The disturbance fee.
1. English literature. Blishen, Edward –
Biographies
I. Title
828'.91409
ISBN 0–241–12525–1

Typeset in 11/13pt Plantin and
printed and bound in Great Britain by
Butler & Tanner Ltd, Frome and London

To Nance
We've been together now . . .

PROLOGUE

Kate said she didn't think a picture of my feet in the water would amount to much. Going round the world with a camera had made me trigger-happy. Well, what was the name for the thing you ... pressed to take the photo? Shutter-release button, I said. What she meant was that I was shutter-release-button-happy. It didn't matter, said Kate, except that we already had so many books, and slides, and tapes, and there were all my diaries: and sometimes she thought if we died now our sons would need to mount a great research operation; they'd have to take time off from work and bring in secretaries and assistants to look through all that debris. And somewhere along the line they'd find that part of the haul from this expense of time and money amounted to a picture of my feet in the water of Minnow Lake.

Or, of course, they could have a great bonfire.

We grinned, thinking it was an old argument but this was the first time we'd conducted it in Ontario. Anyway, I knew when it was developed Kate would like the picture of my feet. That wasn't because they were *my* feet. It was because of the character of that whole moment. I'd known when I took the photo during our walk that afternoon in Petroglyph Park that it was the one I'd remember of all those I'd taken on this trip round the world.

We'd been led, in hot sunshine and hot shade, by my cousin Bobby. It was an area partly tamed for taking circular walks in, but it still had much that was unmastered about it. The autumn leaves had formed a roof of gleaming brass: and generally it felt a world of raw metal – metal

3

dissolved into trees and rock: gold, silver, copper. The petroglyphs, incised centuries ago on a tilting table of rock and, for all the walking there'd been around here, only observed lately by a passer-by with unusual eyes when the sun was at the right angle (now they'd darkened the lines of the drawings to make them visible), had affected my view of the woods, the water, the miniature escarpments topped with tall trees: the sudden patches where the world appeared simply to have decayed, the trees were stripped sticks, there were dead reeds and dying grass, and the water itself was black and looked corrupt, like some extreme form of corrosion. A few yards away there'd be a great healthiness of silver birches. It had all belonged once to the incisers of these petroglyphs, who'd depicted themselves as stick-men riding stick-horses, their spears and bows and arrows bigger than themselves. They still didn't seem very far away.

Kate had curled up against a head rest of rock and Bobby and I had made our way down to the lake. We'd taken off our sandals and lowered our feet gratefully into the water. There they'd been haloed by little shoals of minnows. It was sixty years since the last time Bobby and I were so memorably together in the presence of water. That was on the beach at Southsea, c. 1926, when my father and I had gone to holiday with Uncle George and the seven children he'd had on his way to accumulating, by his first marriage, eleven. Marrying again, he'd impatiently shaken most of the eleven off his hands: some had come to earth in Australia, a couple in the Caribbean, and Bobby in Canada, where in the course of time he'd been transformed from a small chunky boy into a small chunky academic. He tended to side with Kate in the matter of one not having too many books, papers and records in general: but I thought, looking round his house and especially his study, which would have comfortably accommodated half a dozen professors, that his children would have to make the same decision as mine: burdensome sifting of documents, or bonfire.

I looked down at my feet and they had bright veins running through them, as in marble, the shivering mesh made in water by sunlight: and there was a fruitlike quality about the water itself; it was a shaking blue on the edge of being silver like the bloom on a plum. After two months away I was beginning to think of home, which was and all my life had been in Barton, on the edge of London, and Bobby was asking what had changed in Britain since his last visit. It was between us a joke with a dark edge that the country was on its way downhill, and that I had failed to act to prevent this or that phenomenon of decline. So I hadn't stepped in to forbid the arrival of the fast food chains, and I'd not exercised my veto in respect of London turning into a sort of non-London. 'How did you let this happen?' Bobby had asked, last time we walked through Leicester Square, transformed into a funfair remotely related to the capital city. He'd not been impressed when I said I'd thought of launching a Campaign for Real London. Now I told him what had happened to the Red Lion in Barton. The town, first pause for coaches going north, had always been rich in taverns: among them, the Red Lion, on the way in, which had favoured the Tories, and the Green Man, on the way out, which had favoured the Whigs. Both were still there, rebuilt. At the Red Lion a lion, suitably red, strode on a bracket above the pavement. It had done so, that is, until the year before, when centuries of history were cancelled: the Red Lion was renamed the Dandy Lion: the red lion itself was painted yellow: and the old inn was reopened as 'a fun pub for the 18–30 age group'. Recently there had been a stockings-and-suspenders contest, close on the heels of a macho man contest. In prospect was an occasion when customers were invited to turn up wearing babies' napkins and bibs.

He didn't believe it, said Bobby. He didn't believe that even I would allow such a thing to happen. It was vandal-

5

ism. Well, I said: did he realise that, in a Pacific island described by earlier inhabitants as 'the land of the long white cloud', you could eat faster than fast at a Gobble 'n Go. The name of the island? Bobby asked, taking his feet out of the water for the pleasure of plunging them in again. South Island, New Zealand, I said.

Being invited to New Zealand was what had made this trip round the world possible. Well ... trip round the world! I was a little ashamed of using the phrase. If we'd been Francis Drake, that would have been one thing: but as we were not Francis Drake, and achieved our circumnavigation at the cost only of the modern anxiety of users of airports and occupants of aerial sardine tins circulating seven miles above the earth, the phrase seemed pretentious. I remembered when the letter arrived, saying the New Zealand Library Association would like me to be the main speaker at their annual conference: and I'd taken her morning tea up to Kate, who over thirty-five years of marriage had never ceased to appear interestingly astonished that it was I who was around to wake her: and said, as I left the bedroom, 'Oh, by the way, we're invited to New Zealand.' I'd said after making the last long journey of the kind that I'd not go without her again. This was partly because it was so unsatisfactory, returning from some far-flung adventure and failing to give an adequate account of it. I'd often thought how far short of the occasion the heroes of *Coral Island* would have felt they'd fallen, back home after their startling experiences, making blundering references to cannibals: or how feeble, since he wasn't Robert Louis Stevenson, might have been Jim Hawkins's attempt to give his friends and relations some notion of what it was like to sail to Treasure Island and, so surprisingly, back again. I wanted Kate to be, not the polite audience of a stammering tale, but a participant. I also wanted her company, frankly, as the best packer of suitcases I'd known, after my father, whose oppressive excellence in this field had ensured that I was the worst.

6

And I wanted her as a friend. Thousands of miles from home, among strangers who were not carrying their heads under their arms but were quite as exotic in their strangeness as if they were, I'd longed to have the familiar companion with whom to exchange a wink, a cryptic comment, or simply a pressure of hand in hand. If I was going to the other end of the earth, it was with Kate, or not at all.

'To *New Zealand*!' Kate had cried that morning, and had instantly made the case for our regarding that country as merely a place to pause, a sort of immense Red Lion, on a journey round the world. We were old, she pointed out. Our inward sensation of being nineteen coming up to twenty was at odds with, for example, newspaper reports that plainly referred to *elderly* persons in their sixties. Persistent common use of such terms suggested that elderliness was our condition. To have been on the planet without encircling it in some single sequence of journeys (given half a chance, and this appeared to be more than that) seemed to her despicable. The possibility that we'd be able to do it was what I'd always described as *wistful* thinking: and now it had come. I agreed with her that we should avoid being despicable. 'Let's go via India and Malaysia and . . . what's that other place? – and Australia and – what's halfway between New Zealand and South America . . .?' Kate cried. She looked out through the bedroom window at Dead Man's Bottom, the patch of fields across which in 1471 the hunchback Duke of Gloucester had marched his men on his way to provide me, five and a half centuries later, with one of the first historical facts I was able to commit to memory: the death of Warwick the Kingmaker (as he was familiarly known to the children of Barley Road Elementary School) somewhere among those trees Kate was regarding absently, her mind on the later and blanker pages of the atlas. 'There surely is somewhere halfway between New Zealand and South America?' she murmured.

We'd flirted with half a dozen geographical fantasies

7

before settling on a much more ordinary sequence of stops. Calling on Bobby was the last of these before we went home to Barley Wood, our corner of Barton, to see if we'd been burgled, or if the neighbourhood watch had worked. A tree in the lane in which we lived bore a message addressed, I suppose, to literate robbers, as our grandson Tim preferred to call them, which warned them haughtily that we were all on the *qui vive*, faultlessly vigilant night and day, and they might as well go and conduct their depredations elsewhere. I liked my neighbours, but thought they were not, as watchmen, in the league this message suggested. Kate had nervously applied a recommended poison to the path leading to the front door, on the grounds that two months' weeds would beckon burglars in. I'd thought a more likely result was that we'd find the path deep in dead postmen. We felt altogether ashamed of making such a fuss about the protection of our possessions; and I wondered why Kate didn't perceive that a thorough burglary might save our children from that *post mortem* sorting out of books, papers, records, photographs and the rest.

Oh, I thought now, for the final setting of a journey such as ours, what better place than Minnow Lake? We'd been in a sensational spot or two, and among arboreal and geological amazements of several kinds: this was modest, as modest as the little fish it was named after, and the light was perfect: and, above all, the colours, as I'd noted of natural colours since I'd worked on the land during the Second World War, were often what you'd not expect. A patch of water was apricot: a patch of rock opposite was one of those stark greens Van Gogh used, and you thought were present in paintings but never in nature. Bobby himself, musing, his feet making cooling movements in the water, had been designed by Jackson Pollock in collusion with Seurat: there'd been a struggle between bold blobs and dots. Well, they were reflections of the little splashings in the water, minnows and smaller, and their effect on the light dancing on Bobby's face.

8

He looked – I thought, and told him – unlike George Straker, though both were short and solid. He remembered George? Bobby had met my old schoolfellow once at a party in Barley Wood, when George had told him about Canada: inaccurately and at deadly length about its history, on which Bobby was an authority, and inaccurately and at even greater length about its current condition. Bobby said he'd not interrupted – partly because George, piecing sentences together like someone dipping for words into a series of miscellaneous receptacles, some of them difficult to open and some empty, was technically very difficult to interrupt: but largely because he was fascinated by George's assumption that a Canadian knew nothing about Canada, while he, George, on the basis of a handful of visits and his reading of *The Times*, knew everything about it. But then, I said, my one-time schoolfellow was unable to conceive of himself as imperfectly informed on any matter whatever. There'd been general talk once about Yugoslavia, and I'd said to George (and should, after all those years, have known better): 'I can't remember if you know Yugoslavia?' 'I know every inch of it,' said George. Knowing every inch of everything was essential to George's well-being, and over the years I'd become less and less tolerant of this trait of his.

Well, I'd become generally less tolerant of George in the last six or seven years. He now stood in my mind for the flight from social generosity that had occurred during that time, and for the takeover by persons who supposed themselves to know every inch of the business of government. It was a takeover, in a way, by my father, who, like George, like our current governors, had had nothing of that gift for being tentative, for not being absolutely certain, on which human hopes seemed to me to rest. As a small example, George had been adamantly in favour of butchery at Bush House. That is, when the size of the grant to the BBC's External Services was under threat, he'd known at once the actuarial as well as the political and philosophical grounds on which savagery should commence. 'I know the arguments rather well,' he told me. The fact that I worked in a corner of the External Services added, I think, to his natural taste for the knife, the pleasure of knowing that I might be a little gashed, too. The programme I presented was about books. 'You will not think,' said George, looking round his living room at the glass occasional tables and their burden of volumes – they were volumes rather than books, not one of them much smaller than eighteen inches by a foot – 'that I speak as ... ah ... someone opposed to literature. But first things first. If this room were on fire, and I had to rescue what I could, do you imagine that the books would head the list?' It didn't seem to me that, in the national sense, such a choice had to be made, or that it was sensible to jettison a programme that made countries throughout the world aware of what was being currently published in Britain, on the grounds that John Bull had time only to snatch the carriage clock off the national mantelpiece and bear it off together, perhaps, with his wife. Actually it struck me, but I did not say, that George's wife, Barbara, might be left to burn, judged less worthy of salvation than some framed prints of which George was very proud, and which exhibited mid-nineteenth-century scenes from the Home Counties, of which he knew every inch. Barbara was a compulsive talker who, in the circumstances George was asking me to imagine, would have given the fact that the room was now a raging inferno only the corner of her concern. 'George, I think something needs attention,' she'd have called, before continuing with her current monologue.

One of those threats to the BBC department I worked in ended with its being cut in half. I thought it was as if Saint George had rescued half the maiden. The saint's namesake said the image was amusing, but then it was levity that had brought the nation low. From the way he looked at me I could see he thought I'd been among the destructive jesters.

Bobby now asked why I continued to have anything to do with George, and I said that, with a miserably small gift for cutting people out of my life, I felt I wasn't far from some perhaps spectacular end to the relationship. Spectacular? Well, I said, nothing in the nature of fisti-cuffs, nothing calling for the intervention of the police force; but I might shout at him. Bobby grinned: like me, he'd reacted against the ready belligerence of the Blishens. Our fathers and their brothers had spent much of their lives sending people to Coventry, giving them last warn-ings, refusing to acknowledge them in the street, returning their Christmas cards and, in the case of my Uncle Will, writing letters to them on toilet paper. (In the lavatory at Uncle Will's home during my childhood you'd make use of scraps of newspaper, found hanging on a nail: he pur-chased toilet paper only as stationery). I said I'd certainly bring my fifty years of uncomfortable acquaintance with George to an end when, as I felt he would do at any moment, he blamed the decline of the nation (before that recent uplift George and his friends had imparted to it) not simply on my being given to laughter, but also on my years as a teacher. I'd observed, when education was mentioned at one of George's dinner parties, how he'd stiffen and make thinner his already very thin lips. He'd then glance at me. There'd been a time, which he would have forgotten, when he had smiled with a rather frosty benignity on my account of experiences in the classroom, and my hopes for the battered boys I taught in North London, and my belief that the secondary modern school was a device for cutting them off from the more ambitious reaches of practically everything. But George's ideas about education were now uttered with a swish, as of canes. His latest attitude was that we were on the brink of a sort of educational conscription, a great calling up, a process in which teachers would assent to being sergeant-majors or be dismissed. His eyes lit up at any tale of the dismissal

11

of teachers. Teachers were soft, careless, idle, given to growing beards, greatly in need of a course in business management, which George argued should be at the centre of any system of humane studies. He used the word 'humane', I thought, because it was what was traditionally used in this context: given half a chance, he'd have replaced such courses with inhumane studies.

Goodness, said Bobby, I *did* dislike him: and I had to agree that, after years of the struggle to remain friendly, I did. It wasn't only that we differed so radically on the character of the political climate: George treating it as a long stretch of carefully controlled and perhaps not always recognisable good weather, I miserably wrapped in oil-skins and sou'wester. It was also, I thought, an effect of ageing. Well, that's what we were doing – ageing! Here we were, Bobby and I, sixty years on since our first remembered encounter, almost as old as Great Aunt Ada had been then: that gritty lady who had not taken well to being of advanced years. I thought our fathers' dominant aunt (out of a spiky half dozen of them) had never been of anything else than advanced years, inwardly, but the actual destruction of the packaging, her being visited by sensational forms of varicosity, her long spine most painfully running out of elastic, her legs aching for years on end – these marks of decline, which formed the main subject of any conversation with her, even if you were only a five-year-old ('I've been telling Dick's boy about my sciatica'), caused a deepening of her view that the great graph of morality was fast heading downwards. It was a family in which males had an easier time than females: which I imagined was why Great Aunt Ada had trained her body to resemble a flagpole. That was precisely what she might have had in mind, coming from a family of soldiers, the odd sergeant but mostly privates and corporals (my father had been a bombardier: or, as he pronounced it with an effect of demotic pedantry, *bumbardier*), and during the Second World War sleeping night after night in a tenement

12

in South Kensington under a Union Jack. It was to the women in the family that Great Aunt Ada looked for the roots of moral decline: very simply, they led the men astray. Among those her nephews had married, my mother escaped her censure by dint of being so plainly devoted to her husband that even Great Aunt Ada's sourness had nothing to work on. But on my aunts she pounced: hussies, all. Given to boldness, Gladys, Muriel, Beryl, Dorothy, Rose. Given to sapping their husbands' strength by processes confusingly hinted at, so that for a long time I believed my uncles were nightly used by their wives as, in some fashion, vaulting horses. A sort of (in Great Aunt Ada's view, unwise) domestic PE occurred, in which the need of the men to be in good physical trim for the next day's work was recklessly overlooked. If much of my childhood could have been defined as a long process of sex miseducation, then Great Aunt Ada was one of the tutors most responsible. ('Dick's boy listens to everything I say. A serious little fellow. I think Dick worries that he's too serious.' After I'd gone to the grammar school, her comment underwent a small change. 'Dick says that boy of his is *much* too *serious*!' Her verdicts on us all hung in the air of my childhood, dowdy banners: none of us, even my mother, came out of it with much credit.)

Bobby and I had both been in trouble, all those years ago, for stepping on Great Aunt Ada's toes: which, since she had feet of phenomenal length, could hardly be avoided. 'Ageing, you see, Bobby,' I said, wondering if Kate was still asleep, her head against rock in the scrubland above Minnow Lake, 'ageing seems to shorten one's temper. Even tempers as disastrously good as yours or mine.' It was at this point that I noticed how my feet in the water, treated by minnows as an interesting new coastline round which to perform their mesmeric slow manoeuvres, would, photographed, sum up the whole occasion: and took the photo that, for Kate – and until she actually saw it – summed up, instead, the recklessness with which I added thousands of photos to thousands of books and thousands of gramophone records and thousands of documents ... and thousands of written words.

'Did you ever expect to be in your sixties?' asked Bobby. 'Did anyone?' I asked in return. I remembered George Straker's sister, encountered a few weeks ago in New Zealand. She was one of the little multitude of people I'd met there who were related, or were friends of friends, or had known a cousin of mine in circumstances left indistinct. New Zealand was full of the outermost twigs of almost everybody's family tree. George had never mentioned his sister. I understood the reason when I saw that she was accompanied by a woman friend, with whom she'd plainly fled from Barton c. 1950, in search of some domicile where her love for her friend did not cause hostile whispers to run the length of the High Street. Well, not far from where I lived in Barley Wood was a house occupied once by Radclyffe Hall, author of the banned *Well of Loneliness*, and her lover: they'd lived there for a year or so, and then fled, claiming that the house was too far from the station. The station was within a minute's downhill walk. George's sister had clearly been happy in New Zealand: a country not conspicuously friendly to homosexuals – when we were there they were making the most tentative approaches to legislation designed to reduce the national frown to a national half-frown – but not as ready as Barley Wood in that other case to point the finger at the enormity of two ladies who loved each other and had elected to live together. Though it did strike me that New Zealanders might simply have been slower than Barley Woodians in perceiving that here was a reprehensible happiness.

But it wasn't this quality of George's sister I remembered from that moment when, at the end of one of my talks in the North Island, she'd come up and introduced herself. It was what she'd said when I'd wondered aloud how long I'd known George ... since 1931, I'd supposed. 'I am slightly older than George,' said his sister. 'He was

14

nine in 1931. Work it out for yourself!' She'd said that quite sharply, so I felt I had a distinct duty to respond ... I *must* work it out: but I was tired after my talk and a long day's journeying, and a demand that I come to a certain conclusion on an arithmetical basis defeated me. 'It means,' said George's sister, 'that I am well on into my sixties.' She sounded as if she thought I was responsible for this situation, and I was ready to apologise. But Kate, invaluable Kate, stepped in. 'You don't look it,' she said, though George's sister seemed at least ten years older than she was. 'It must be a special pleasure to have your wife with you on this visit,' said George's sister.

Bobby thought we should make sure that Kate hadn't been scalped by some phantom inciser of petroglyphs. ('Stone pictures, Bobby!' I'd protested. 'Damn it, why don't they call them stone pictures?' Bobby had frowned slightly. He was a social scientist, and we'd had many arguments about certain features of sociological language, which I thought made the common inaccessible by resort to uncommon nomenclature: Bobby's argument being that the straightforward everyday word carried with it over-tones and undertones with their roots in emotionally charged daily usage. So to call the petroglyphs stone pictures might open the door to appallingly loose and unscientific accounts of those improbably discovered works of art. 'The end of that road is Gobble 'n Go,' said Bobby. I wasn't convinced – but for the umpteenth time each of us rested his case.) We slipped our wet feet into our sandals and began to climb back to where Kate was sleeping. I remembered suddenly the apologetic consultant surgeon who, shortly before we'd come on this journey, had discovered in me a condition that could turn, he said, very nasty. It was, somehow, a phrase out of childhood. 'Put that down,' I could imagine my father saying. 'It's very nasty!' I must check with the surgeon, so embarrassed by the lethal aspects of his occupation, two or three times a year. It seemed at the time like being condemned to walk

15

around with your own firing squad in tow, and I'd wondered how it could be borne. One answer seemed to be that in nearly two months I'd thought of it no more than half a dozen times. Well, that was because a dormant condition was dormant. Long live dormancy! I had thought lately, though, that when it was all over, I'd approach the supernal authorities and demand a disturbance fee. It was what the BBC paid when it wanted to acknowledge, but minimally, that it had taken an interviewee's time. I'd found the disturbance of being alive very interesting, *very* interesting: but they needn't think (and the voice inside me spoke in the tones of one or two belligerent interviewees I'd worked with) that I was going to endure it for nothing.

We found Kate happily asleep against a stone that (I noticed) had unpredictable patches of Prussian blue in it: and when we made gentle coughing sounds she stretched a hand for the usual Barley Wood morning cup of tea. 'We've been talking,' said Bobby, 'about being older than we were, Kate.'

'When,' asked Kate, 'did you ever talk about anything else?'

PART ONE

1

'I was thinking when I was on my way here,' I said, 'that growing old is like being vandalised. You wake up in the morning and there's another window smashed, another piece of graffiti's appeared. Part of you has obviously gone, and the trouble is you can't remember what it was . . .'

My producer laughed, but I thought I'd chosen as unsuitable an audience as I could. She was pure breathlessness, and existed in tumbles and billows of cloth. When we'd recorded last week's programme she'd appeared as a sort of black tulip. She made me think how being very young was to be constantly astonished. She was a great self-amazing bird. Whatever dress she wore, it came close to making her winged. The programme was being blown about in the gale of her excitements, and that was good for it. Soon she'd go on to other scenes more receptive to storms, and we'd be staid again.

'You're not growing old,' she said briskly. That was a proposition I'd not wanted to argue, one way or the other. I'd wanted only to pass on this sudden comic perception I'd had of the process. Milly dipped into her enormous handbag, which always lay on the floor by her desk, and brought out a rainbow heap of tissues. She turned even blowing her nose, I thought, into a carnival. That done, she laughed hugely, for no good reason: but then, she needed none. Finding herself for a second or so at a loose end, Milly either surrendered to laughter, or gave way to the greatest gloom. But her gloom was colourful, too: this, you felt, was the season's novel and exciting shade of black. 'You're no older than Maudie,' she said.

19

That was a bit much. Maudie, a secretary from elsewhere in the building, famous for being simply a set of splendid roundnesses, was in the room at the moment, come to chat with colleagues. She was lightly dressed, as if the damp day were tropical. A striped shift was in fashion, and she wore that. Or rather, it insecurely enclosed a portion of her that seemed to have been chosen at random. It wasn't possible, I thought, to imagine a more tempting footballer. My attention having been drawn, I said: 'My goodness!' It would have been dishonest to say nothing. The secretaries who, if they did not speak in chorus, seemed to do so, now appeared to cry together: 'He doesn't know where to look!'

'That's not the problem,' I said. 'The problem is that I *do* know where to look.'

The young and the old, I thought with some sadness, were different races. In that office there was the quick chattering stream of secretaries: the deeper water of producers, most – and Milly aside – in early middle age: and the drowned depths that I represented. I thought the lightfooted young in their everlastingly experimental dress were amused by the exchanges between most of my producers and me. It was twenty amused by forty amused by sixty.

Perhaps falling in love with the young was one of the diseases of growing old. I clearly shouldn't offer that idea to Milly, who was now tunnelling through the hill of books that, while she was producing the programme, accumulated around her. 'There's something I want to ask you about,' she cried, before disappearing in a froth of some sort of amazing near-purple. Well, in Barton High Street, I'd been moved at the weekend by the sight of a girl with a foolish face, wearing jeans monstrously with high-heeled shoes. Her feet wincingly stabbed the pavement. Her boyfriend had no brow. From the beginning the world had been filled with persons of no importance, whose enormous importance lay in their being alive: and my heart ached for this young couple, because they were walking so carelessly (but she was tottering) across the floor of the terrifying laboratory in which the chain reaction of human affairs occurred. In circumstances of appalling danger they felt themselves to be ... immortals, she sorefooted. He was so tightly clad that I couldn't believe he hadn't some soreness, too.

In the Friar's Holt, our favourite pub, the girls had lately gone into such garb as might have suited a newly invented species of monkey. They wore sweaters for which the adjective hardly existed – to call them hugely floppy would have been to suggest a skimpiness they did not have – and long johns ringed in black-and-white, blue-and-white, red-and-white. They were absurd: they would have exhausted even Great Aunt Ada's capacity for horror. I remembered her in the thirties measuring the approaching end of the world in the quarter-inches by which skirts grew shorter.

They made me, those girls, want to laugh aloud with a sort of melancholy rapture.

And on the train this morning – how sometimes everything chimed together! – I'd observed old men eyeing censoriously a sad boy with a tic, whose temples were naked, and who had a purple prow of hair. I wondered how these contemporaries of mine would look, if they dressed according to their fantasies. And at that moment I heard the most cheerful of chuckles and traced it to a girl whose face was chalk-white, her hair an upstreaming bush of jet black. Her long coat was black, and she wore high boots, with straps. She was thin and wiry, in a particular London fashion: and looked for all the world like a minor messenger of death. But when it came to her suitability for that morbid role, a problem sprang from her possession of another London quality: she was most perkily buoyant. Faced with Death himself, dressed much as she was, she'd have made a hearty joke about bones. She was talking – a matter largely of grinning and chort-

21

ling – with a friend who was in some quite different style, based on a wish to resemble a burning bush or the last moments of Joan of Arc.

We got out at the same stop, and I was behind her as she made her macabre way along the platform. Extraordinary! There went a living *memento mori* on two black-leather legs: and every step she took spoke of the most tremendous high spirits.

Milly emerged from the mountain of books, empty-handed. 'I forgot what I was looking for,' she said. The phone rang. She listened, and then: 'Nell Shilling's at reception,' she said.

2

With Nell Shilling, whom I was to interview about her latest book, I'd recently been on an Arts Council tour in the north-west. Nell had come originally from that part of the world. Jim Hunter, a novelist from the Midlands, had completed the party.

Nell was a woman bowled over by life, sent spinning by it, boxed on the ears by it, who had complete comic mastery of her own misadventures. If life had ever treated her well she'd have been sunk: but one suspected that calamity had been built into her existence in advance, as the appropriate material for her gift to work on. The characters in her novels were displayed in a state of constantly transitional disgrace. They were always in trouble on the way to being in trouble. Occasionally one of them, driven by a sequence of domestic desperations, each in itself manageable, found that he or she was engaged in some act of murder. This often involved an unlikely weapon, some tool or gadget whose primary purpose was quite another one.

In Nell's presence I always felt a creature of fiction myself, and had a sense of being faintly disobliging in that

I didn't regard myself as qualified to be drawn into her brisk network of mishaps. I hadn't the stamina for it. Submit to the spell she cast, and there you'd be, walking carelessly towards the end of the plank walked by all her creations, in fiction or life. Among other things, she was a woman of the most practical tenderness. When I arrived for the tour I had a cold, and was under instant if faintly scornful medication at the hands of the most enjoyably sinister novelist I knew. I confessed I'd been moved on arrival by the silhouette of one of the city's abandoned churches, a brown spike in the air: if that local artist L. S. Lowry's figures were pin-men, this was a pin-church. Nell sent me to bed – 'Sleep that off!' – with a further admonition: 'And no more of this blubbing over churches!' It was as if one of the witches in *Macbeth* had cautioned you against walking home after a battle. I imagined how Nell would have scolded Macbeth himself, whom she'd have recognised at once as a creature heading for the sort of denouement typical of her own novels. 'And no more of this hanging about and soliloquising, or whatever it's called!'

Jim Hunter, a self-made writer of the most remarkable kind, had had a stunning success with his very first novel, written in, he calculated, some fifty-seven cheap exercise books. He'd submitted it in this form to a publisher who'd had the sense to look beyond the breach of the convention that a novel should be submitted in typescript. I'd wondered, being with Jim and Nell together, at the freakish nature of the literary gift. At the back of my mind, when I tried to account for it, were those stalls at the annual Barton Fair where a light, set moving, flickered from number to number until, slowing, slowing, it settled on one ... only to give a startled last leap ... and perhaps another ... and you compared the number where finally it halted with the number of the ticket you'd bought. So, among the millions, it was Nell, and Jim, with whom the literary light had stopped. Jim had done as well by the chance as Nell. Only once or twice had he come close to the quality of his first book, which was the right book at the right time and place: but the gift persisted, he did nothing badly, and in his twentieth novel there were still traces of the force that the greatly famous first book had displayed. Jim was like a lighted thing himself, there was an intense glow under the shyness that people immediately noted in him. Some thought him naive, but it was a most subtle naivety. Born out of view of every kind of literary establishment, he had become a one-man literary establishment of his own. He had a mild, wary, determined face, and for some reason always reminded me of the White Rabbit. There was a tendency to waistcoats, and to producing, out of their pockets, spectacles and watches: but it wasn't entirely this. He looked as though, like Lewis Carroll's creature, he was always botheredly in the middle of mysterious errands: but you knew that was because this almost entirely literary man was perpetually scuttling from book to book, story to story.

A tour of the kind we were embarked on makes, of the writers concerned, a kind of Vincent Crummles and Company. Nell was the Infant Phenomenon: Jim the staple member of the company, ready at any shy amused moment to offer an expected reading from his triumphant first novel, or an unexpected one from some literary-philosophical essay of the kind he wrote, I thought, to demonstrate that a novelist whose formal education had stopped at fourteen could be as abstract as the next man. Like strolling players, we were hurried from one hall to another. We came to awkward compacts as to the time each of us would take with a reading: feigned to be tolerant about this, but found ourselves edgy if there was much of a departure, however accidental, from the agreement. At question time we felt often enough like Aunt Sallies: being pelted with questions from aggressive admirers or from men or women who had literary aspirations themselves and held us, on the whole, in incompletely polite disdain.

24

There were those for whom every novel written by Nell had been snatched from them at the very moment when they were about to sit down and write it. And Jim was bullied as to his most famous book in the spirit in which Tolstoy might have been required to say why he'd only once written *War and Peace*.

Between performances we wandered through the city. Nell, having decided her next novel would be based on an actual nineteenth-century murder with theological overtones, bought a prodigious number of books on Victorian religious controversies. Directions were given to pack them and send them to her home, and I imagined carter after carter appearing with crate after crate of mildewed disputation. Some of these books, I thought, were wide of her mark; but clearly if you were writing this sort of novel, security came from saturating the target. How much, if he'd had the nervous modern appetite for research, would Shakespeare have made himself know about the cities of northern Italy in order to write a play set almost entirely in Verona?

Nell also added to a collection she'd made of stuffed animals. The involuntary and grimacing presence of the extinct seemed important to her: and her purchase on this occasion was of the head of a large antelope shot (said a plaque attached to it) in Tanganyika in 1926, and having an expression distinctly accusatory. I made a note not to visit Nell without taking a precaution or two. Given the general trend of her fiction, one should perhaps beware of a tendency to take short cuts in bringing about, what Nell seemed to favour, a predominance of the stuffed over the living.

When it was all over, Jim made for the Midlands: I rashly returned to London with Nell. She contrived that we caught the wrong train, and were obliged to rely on being picked up by a normally non-stopping train at a very small halt. Somehow, I was entirely in charge of the stuffed antelope. I had it in my arms as the train, warned to rescue

25

us, approached. I thought it stopped reluctantly. And what engine-driver, peacefully at work on a slumbering stretch of line, would wish to pick up a startling novelist and her friend, in his arms the horned sorrow of a beast distinctly not indigenous?

When we boarded this train, Nell commanded me to place the antelope's head in the luggage rack outside our carriage. I did this, and parts of the melancholy trophy detached themselves in a rain of desiccated skin and ... a kind of dark grey dust which was what the stuffing had turned into. All of this fell on to the brand-new luggage of (as we discovered) a honeymoon couple. It was an incident from one of Nell's novels, and Nell deplored it: leaving the carriage again and again to attempt, with handkerchief and spittle, to limit the damage. Doing that made her extraordinarily grubby. I sat throughout the journey at the side of a distinguished novelist whom Great Aunt Ada would have identified at once: *'Gutter urchin!'* It reminded me, I said, of what might have been called the first review I'd ever received. I'd written boldly, on 10.5.27, of Bonnie Prince Charlie, who, as my seven-year-old self asserted, 'was asked by the English to come back. He was very glad to do so, although he had to be very careful as Cromwell's men did not like him.' For this early feat of understatement I earned a tick, but an overloading of my pen with the soot and water that at Barley Road passed for ink had led to a blot; and so, as always followed, to a melancholy scatter of sub-blots. Which, in its turn, led to this laconic review, in blue pencil: *Dirty*.

It was the word for Nell Shilling, sitting beside me on that train.

She was anxious to be home. As I understood her, the house was ringed by police, for a reason connected with television licences. I found myself hoping that she would go to prison. A novel she wrote about that must be a marvel: and she would be made, anyway, quite comfortably, an Arts Council sponsored Prisoner-in-Residence.

As we assembled this morning in the studio, Milly said: 'He's worried about being old.' 'Oh, not worried,' I said, alarmed at being handed over to Nell's ironies. 'Just interested, and amused!' Nell took Milly by the arm and spoke in a theatrically confidential fashion. 'He is a man who at the mere sight of a church has been known to boo-hoo,' she began.

It was going to be one of those interviews from which Milly would have to cut my utterly unsuitable shrieks of laughter, which would merely puzzle our more earnest listeners in New South Wales.

3

'Still . . . what is it you do? . . . Chatting up writers?' asked George Straker that evening. 'Asked' is perhaps not the right word, though I am not sure what the right word is. There was in the delivery of many a question of George's a strong hint of his lack of enthusiasm for an answer. And the term 'chatting up' was chosen after hesitation, in the manner of someone, personally fastidious, who wished to make a rough-and-ready interlocutor at home by using one of his own coarse phrases.

'Still *interviewing* them,' I said.

'Who,' asked George, plainly driving himself further along a distasteful road, 'did you . . . *do* today?'

'I talked to Nell Shilling,' I said.

'I'm afraid,' said George, 'you'll have to do better than that. The lady is unknown to me. Tell me something about her.'

When George spoke like this, it wasn't to make a relaxed confession of ignorance. It was to cause you to feel that the knowledge you had was such as no intelligent man of the world would wish to have. I was declared guilty at once of knowing who Nell Shilling was, and of believing a person unknown to George was worth interviewing.

I really would knock him down. Then I would walk all over him. I would tip up his occasional tables, spilling out the large and lavishly illustrated books they contained. No, Kate and I would simply, icily leave. On the doorstep I would pause and speak at length. 'George,' I would say. 'One aspect of ageing appears to be that people grow weary of the contradictory bundle of characteristics they carried around when younger. The friend who'd attempted to express at once the conservative and progressive traits in himself elects to be, quite simply, conservative. Another, who'd been jolly when he wasn't being grim, comes down heavily on the side of grimness. You belong to both these types: together with a further type, who tires of being alternately rather pleasant and extremely unpleasant, and decides in the end to be, almost unremittingly, nasty.'

It wouldn't do for the doorstep. There was never the occasion for the sumptuous expression of what one felt. If I lost my temper finally with George, I'd be reduced, almost certainly, to the usual intemperate exclamations. If only I had that lack of squeamishness that had enabled Uncle Will to set out on toilet paper in full, and eloquently, the nature of his disenchantment with mother, brothers, cousins, old and dear friends.

I found it difficult to remember the complex George I'd known at the grammar school, fifty years earlier. He was then sharply bisected as to character: one half of him was a sort of friend, but from the other half I shrank. The friendly George was in favour of open spaces, long walks, music, and a host of the forward-looking tendernesses of the 1930s: I think, somehow, of Underground stations circular in shape, and *sans serif* lettering.

When it came to such things, some of us glowed, and George glowed as radiantly as the rest. But alongside this eagerness, he had qualities curiously stern. In this aspect, he reminded me of Sergeant Clinker, the Boer War veteran who in our early years at school took us for what was shamelessly described as 'drill'. The sergeant's view of

28

humanity was simple: it needed constant reminders to pick its feet up, stand straight, keep its hands out of its pockets, and avoid playing with its private parts and those of others. About this latter requirement he was terrifying, and in the periods of rest granted during a drill session – involving our standing intensely at ease, they were more exhausting than the periods of activity – he would bark out a scenario, related to our irreversible possession of genitals, that made us blanch. I see across the years that Sergeant Clinker was having the time of his life, using these quasi-military occasions to justify roaring references to our sexual organs as a sort of forbidden weaponry. He wanted, he'd say, to turn out lads who didn't spend their lives thinking about what was below their navels. It was a phrase of my father's, who had a sergeant in him, too. BELOW YOUR NAVELS! The echoes of the bellowed words would hang about in the drill shed, forming part of the sexually dismaying atmosphere of the place. We'd come away from drill feeling like apprentice satyrs, shaggy and helplessly ithyphallic below the moral frontier so ineffectively guarded by our belly buttons.

The Sergeant was also famous for hitting upon unpleasant forms of a boy's name. A fat boy called Butler was known to him as Buttocks: one called Dodgson, as Dogdirt: and George himself was always Stinker. As we pounded round the playground, raising yellow dust, these terrible names would be barked at us: addressed to individuals, but adding up to a general scornful statement about us all. We stank, and the best that any of us could hope for was that we'd be scraped off someone's boots: almost certainly the Sergeant's. He shone with polished leather, and we were so baggy, so dishevelled, so dusty. The Sergeant made much of the dirtiness of the handkerchiefs that from time to time were shaken out of our pockets by that endless pounding, pounding, round and round and round. I detested him for his need to add to the humiliations of being a crumpled schoolboy.

29

Like the Sergeant, George as a boy barked. He was stern if you'd borrowed his football shirt – 'I don't regard that as clean! I want it back properly washed!' He was stern about jokes: 'I don't think that's funny, and anyway you got it out of last week's *Wizard*!' In that dreadful playground, hunted by bullies from the Upper Fifth whose intentions were invariable – they simply wished to stuff your head into a lavatory basin and pull the chain – you'd think of possible allies: and decide against appealing to George, though he was so usefully chunky and aggressive. He'd say: 'I have better things to do.' Or he'd ask, bleakly sarcastic: 'Who do you think I am? The United States cavalry?'

It sprang, perhaps, this sternness, from a terror of being soft. But it meant that the boy given to theoretical gentlenesses was also given to practical ferocities. At times I was happy in his company: at times he made me angrily miserable.

He'd drifted back into my life during the 1960s. After school he'd gone away, to the war, to the world of business. He'd been fearfully stern, I gathered, in a number of industrial situations, and had then achieved some sort of super-sternness in an executive role. It was his phrase: 'My role today is entirely executive.' I'd met him again at a party, where as well as speaking in his old glowing style of the world of school we'd shared thirty years earlier, he'd spoken in the fashion of a managerial Sergeant Clinker about the ardours of being a man of business. The trouble was that his memories seemed to have been extensively edited. I spoke disrespectfully, not seeing how one could do otherwise, of our old headmaster, Percy Chew, who had added to the curriculum an invisible subject, more powerfully promoted than the rest: Snobbery. 'A fine man,' said George. He was now also much moved by his memories of the Sergeant, who had been so systematically disobliging to George through so many dusty hours. 'A man of character. Old-fashioned, but I'm not inclined to think the worse of him for that. I recommend that you call to mind those quite entertaining little talks he used to give us when he stood us at ease.' I'd remembered lately an addition to the use the Sergeant would make of those occasions, his dusty victims tensely relaxed: he'd discuss the moral geography of the town, naming precise streets where no decent boy, if such a character were imaginable, would be seen. There were boys present, as the Sergeant well knew, whose homes were in the streets named. 'Oh, come on, George,' I said. 'Entertaining?' 'He always made us laugh,' said George. I remembered our invariable dismal silence. On an occasion when we were not enjoying ourselves officially, subject to parade-ground sarcasms and the near-certainty of having to do it all again after school in a drill detention, it was not amusing to be warned against enjoying ourselves unofficially, too.

... We'd come to dinner this evening with the promise that a fellow-guest would be a journalist we very much liked, who'd continued to endure George as we had done: out of some sense of what was owed to long acquaintance, and because now and then, never for an entire evening, but it might be for an hour or more, George was transformed into his younger self: or the warmer side of that self. It was usually talk of some surprising domesticity that did it: he was a great jam-maker, and his bread was famous. When I had the desire to beat George with an extremely large instrument, not particularly blunt, I'd think of him at his best, in a kitchen, or opening an oven with a look of the brightest surmise.

But alas, the journalist had been unable to come, and here was Billing instead, understood to be an important business colleague of George's. Billing was a man entirely compounded of discontent. Kate and I waited breathlessly at every encounter for him to express some very small mild satisfaction. It never happened. He had been to the theatre four or five times during recent weeks, to plays widely admired, and had been bitterly disappointed. He had attempted to read a number of well-reviewed recent novels and biographies, and found it impossible to finish any of them. He had been on holiday, following advice and going to a particular resort in France, a disaster. He'd taken his wife to a certain restaurant for her birthday, the *Good Food Guide* was ecstatic – unspeakable! It was a curious aspect of Billing's need of dissatisfaction, that it always used as its springboard other people's sensations of satisfaction. His wife was his echo, but left the talking to him: mostly at the crises of his dismal tales she rolled her eyes to heaven, shrugged her shoulders, or otherwise mimed the view that such was life, and all were fools who entered into the conspiracy to suggest that it was anything but a flop.

As soon as possible, we bobbed our goodnights under the absurd canopy at George's front door. The Strakers lived in a house that had all the air of a faintly reduced palace. There was about the façade an impression of everything that lent itself to such treatment, and some things that didn't, being supported by pillars: those at the front door being extremely large and taking the weight of this curiously trivial canopy. It was as if a strong man was triumphantly lifting a wafer above his head. The front door itself offered a confusing number of means of attracting attention – a knocker shaped like a fist, another like an owl's head, and several bell pulls. Although she sympathised, Kate would never, when we arrived on a visit, allow me to ring (and bang) the changes that these made possible.

Now, as we made our way out, I felt almost sorry for George. It looked as if he had another hour or so of the Billings to endure. He was always affable at departures: if he were never anywhere but in the kitchen or on the doorstep, he'd be an excellent companion.

'Oh God, what an evening!' said Kate, as we drove out through George's wrought-iron gates. 'How *insufferable* George is!' We fell exhaustedly silent. Then Kate said:

'Poor old George!'

It summed up everything.

4

'Shall we do,' said Stella, who'd replaced Milly, 'a book called *Family Relationships*? It seems to say a great deal about . . . grandparents. I expect you of all people would like to know what a . . .' – she glanced at the dust jacket – '. . . distinguished psychologist and toxophilist has to say about the role.'

'Toxophilist?'

'No, toxicologist. Sorry. It seems a curious combination . . . Oh, sorry again. It's his wife who's the toxicologist.' A slip of paper fell out of the book. 'Oh, sorry yet again. The book, which came in yesterday, was published the month before last.'

'Let's not do it.'

It was easy, in fact, not to do enormous numbers of books, there being at any particular moment . . . enormous numbers of books. We could manage exactly six a week. It was sometimes a relief when a publisher failed to send us a book in time. I had occasionally a blasphemous vision of the Bible arriving, unfamiliar to any of us, a cause of excitement round the office – though we'd strongly suspect that the author had already come and gone and that we'd not be able to interview him over the line because he'd turn out not to live within easy – or even difficult – reach of a BBC studio. Then the slip of paper would fall out and we'd discover that though there'd been a recent translation – well, 1611, but that wasn't too bad as some publishers went – the original date of publication was round about the fourth century.

'Let's not do it,' I'd say.

But I was particularly glad, as a grandfather, not to do this one. Odd relationship, grandparent and grandchild.

33

I'd have felt reluctant to discuss it in academic terms with a psychologist married, or not, to a toxicologist.

The middle of the stage is occupied by others, and they, the older creature and the younger, have, to begin with, this affinity in being off-centre. They are both engaged in piecing things together. The old are trying to give a shape to the story of their lives – like people who've read a novel without paying real attention to it, so that only now, looking back, do they begin to make out the narrative line, the beginnings and ends of chapters, the division into parts. The young are simply attempting to make a map, any sort of map, out of the fragments of coastline they've bumped into. They fill the empty spaces with spouting leviathans, giants carrying their heads under their arms.

Sitting outside a hall in which, for some local cause, my neighbours were selling to each other the products of their knitting, cooking and painting, I waited for my grandson Tim to appear and shame me. I had a great certainty of shame. He came, with a friend, neither able to contain his scandalised delight. 'We're going in again,' shouted Tim across the polite heads of neighbours, 'to see the picture of the bare lady who's showing her bum.'

'It's sexy,' he said, on another occasion. 'What do you mean by sexy?' someone asked. 'Taking your clothes off,' said Tim. He asked me if I liked sleeping with Kate. Yes, indeed, I did. Why? Because she was my wife and lover. 'If she's your wife,' said Tim, 'she can't be your lover.' Earlier he had urged that we couldn't be married, being too old. He observed that at playschool you were not allowed to kiss. Where was kissing allowed, then? In houses, said Tim.

He was filled at times with unbearable excitement. His first teacher said she found it necessary to start the day by calming him. 'I sedate him with hugs,' said this excellent woman.

On the basis of something or other half-heard, he reproached a young woman visitor, who was pregnant, for

34

her language. 'If you swear,' he said, 'the baby will come out swearing.' He was a creature of squalls and storms, gravities and sweetnesses. Early one morning he played the piano while I was listening to music on the radio. I asked him not to play, and became the most unpopular grandfather in history. My disgrace took a ceremonial form: as if to the rhythm of some great funeral march, he removed his breakfast things, and himself, from my end of the table to Kate's. If grandfatherhood had involved the wearing of epaulettes, they would have been ritually torn off. At another breakfast, on my birthday, he held that the occasion was not being fitly celebrated if I did not eat cake. He sang innumerable versions of 'Happy birthday to you'. 'We went to the Zoo,' he sang, leaning enthusiastically against my shoulder, 'and saw an ugly monkey, who looked just like you.'

The summer lawn was packed with people – friends, relatives, all accidentally visiting together. Every chair in the house had to be brought out. One end of the garden guffawed: at the other, a hum of talk. In some small matter Tim's patience had snapped, he'd shouted and stamped, he'd broken something, he'd been flung – actually, had flung himself – out of Eden. It was Kate who kept him in her memory – she rarely failed to see the world as a small child saw it – and noticed the setting he'd contrived for his exile. He'd pulled the curtains over the french windows and was sitting in the darkling living room that resulted: but he had left a gap of six inches, so that his wretchedness might be observed by any guilty eye, looking across from those laughing chairs. It was Kate who drew him out and made a gap for him in the terrible circle of adults. 'May you tell me a story?' he asked a visiting uncle then, using his curious permissive tense. 'May you give me a biscuit?' he'd inquire. 'May you mend this for me?'

He began a day well, considerate, quiet, sensible, and then fell to pieces as if ruined by the mere operation of the machinery, the breathing, the going here and there. He

35

was often angel, often devil: I thought a simple change of colour, perhaps from white to red, might have helped. 'I'm not talking', he'd announce, at the first sign of difficulty: 'I'm not listening.' He was curiously and sometimes embarrassingly perceptive: on an occasion when the presence of an unlikeable person was causing general strain, which we thought we were politely controlling, Tim said: 'You lot are all worn out': and to me, 'You're breathing much!' I'd wonder what he'd say if he ever accompanied us to a dinner date with George Straker.

Kate said being a grandmother was like having a second chance to be a mother, but slowly. A grandmother was a slowed-down mother. 'I like you,' said Tim, in one of those simple statements of praise or dispraise that reveal the child at work, mapmaking. 'You tell me what I ask you.' A grandmother has time to give answers. Possessed by the anxiety of being old, she responds to the anxiety of being young. 'Do you know everything?' Tim asked me, and was clearly relieved when I said no, I didn't: carefully not confessing to the actual extent of my ignorance – Tim didn't want a dunce for a grandparent – but indicating that I didn't feel it necessary to have an answer to every question. To the very young: a world composed of questions and answers. Life, an unremitting questionnaire. Perhaps the natural industry of the adult was the production of answers? You could sense his relief at being assured that he didn't have to have omniscience as one of his goals. On the same occasion, he disposed of another troublesome notion. 'You don't have to tell everybody everything?' No, I said. It wasn't even possible to do that. 'Oh, good,' said Tim.

I'd never had grandparents in any useful sense. My paternal grandfather had dropped dead at forty, on his way to the double work he did: by day driving a van for a department store, by night being a market porter. Of my mother's father I knew only what my mother had told me once or twice but had clearly not wanted to go on saying:

36

that as far as she knew he'd died in prison. Her mother had spent the last quarter of a century of her life in an asylum suffering from what was defined as melancholia. My father's mother, the only one of my grandparents with whom I'd had an everyday relationship, was a woman without a grandmotherly bone in her body. As a child I'd thought, given the quarrelsomeness of the Blishens, that a family was an organism created so that ruptures and rows could take place. At the heart of all that ill humour was my grandmother. 'Whenever I come,' she said once, on a visit, 'that boy sits there with a long face.' It was because, whenever she came, the sequel was a quarrel. Between members of the family, she stirred it up.

So I had no pattern, when it came to this relationship, and was delighted by its taking place so interestingly at the edge of the stage, between someone newly entered and someone on his way out.

I talked on my programme to a young writer who'd published a striking novel about old age. I said I wondered how she knew so much, so accurately, about being old. She probably didn't, she said. She'd been drawing largely on a fascination with age she'd felt as an adolescent – not able to understand why, so near the end, the old were not running around in total panic. I said this was something that mystified the old, too.

But, of course, every relationship was changing. My son Dan, for example, seemed to me now more uncle than son. He was gently large, and regarded me with interested amusement. His work was in electronics, and part of the amusement flowed from my failure to understand the merest basis of this science. Years ago my other son Tom had wandered into a workroom in London in which Dan was practising his trade. He said Dan was testing electronic items with what Tom thought was a screwdriver: most of them produced a shock for Dan, and when that happened he uttered an oath and threw the item into a cavernous sack. Inside the sack, said Tom, a rat lived. The rat was a friend of Dan's, the good feeling between them seeming to survive the rain of discarded electronic material. I understood none of this, and had made heavy weather of understanding Dan's subsequent career. When he left home he removed most of the tools in the house, later saying he'd thought they would be of little use to me. The point seemed to be made by my failing to notice the loss for six months or more. Now when he left after a visit I would not have been surprised if he'd pressed a 50p piece into my hand. It was a deeply comfortable relationship, and though we were undoubtedly and pleasantly father and son, there seemed an element of exotic exaggeration in saying so.

Dan had always made jokes suddenly, unprepared one-liners. The sea of life would be smooth and humourless, not a wave, not a ripple, and then Dan would make a joke, and there'd be a brief and often beautiful spout of water. So Kate worried once because someone vaguely known had vaguely said: 'Is your husband a writer?' She was certain, said Kate, that this fact had been mentioned or fairly plainly alluded to on a number of their encounters. 'Perhaps,' said Dan, 'she thought you said: "My husband is a write-off."'

Tom had become a teacher. He'd passed through such an apprenticeship of slapstick anguish as I'd known myself, and was rewarded, as I felt I'd been, by the exhausting daily entanglement with children largely embattled, funny, wry, fierce, impossible, sometimes dangerous. When I'd written years before about the boys I'd taught at Stonehill Street, a reviewer had said I'd turned them into angels with dropped aitches. Actually I thought I'd turned them into what life itself had turned them into, angels and devils who spoke, because they were Cockneys, in a Cockney fashion. Tom's teaching stories confirmed this view of schoolchildren as inclining to extremes of personality – sometimes extreme fusions, so that to the obvious categories were joined the army of angelic devils, devilish angels. This was perhaps true of them everywhere (they'd been much the same in the high-flying prep school where I'd taught before going to Stonehill Street): it was certainly true in the backstreets of London and the northern city where Tom worked. (I sometimes thought it was true of human beings of any age: I didn't imagine that in either Hell or Heaven we'd find ourselves in unfamiliar company.) Tom had to take his children through the dreadful eighties, when education was at the mercy of those without natural or cultivated care for the fate of any who had hands on none of the profitable social levers. About this Tom raged as the HMI did who said, at a school where I'd given away the prizes, that of all the cuts he thought the most despicable were those inflicted on education, since their effect would be most obviously felt when those who'd inflicted them had gone to their distinguished graves.

Tom was moved as I had been by the conviction that for thousands of despised children, the hope that they'd grow into adults who didn't despise themselves lay in the simple offer of encouragement and support. A witty and sympathetic colleague said of him that he'd not be surprised to see a piece of child's writing at the foot of which Tom would have commented: 'This is appalling work. Well done.'

'It must be strange,' Tom had said after the birth of his first child, 'for a father to see his son becoming a father.' It was strange also, and moving, for a father to see his son becoming a colleague in that enterprise of education that, in one way or other, deepens the nature of everyone who engages in it: teaching making even the worst teacher aware of the dramatic and often breathtaking mysteries of a child's transformation into a near-adult.

5

And relationships with the dead changed, too.

Nowadays I think often of the tender things I knew about my father. Our association had been a disaster. Afraid, like my son Tom, of being ungenerous in judgement of others, since being human seemed amazingly difficult, I not only infuriated my father, but must have deeply bored him. Much of the pleasure he had in life came from being unjust. If ever he'd listed his hobbies, injustice might well have come first, or neck and neck with gardening. He did, in fact, combine these two favourite activities: he was furiously unjust to other gardeners. Walking with him down a street was to pass from snort to snort: one directed at a man's roses ('Doesn't he *know* how to prune?'), another at a lawn ('Good God, look at those daisies!'), and so on until the last garden left him speechless. ('There's nothing to say about those ... are they supposed to be *marigolds*, or are they *buttercups*? Will you tell me?' The question addressed to my mother, who would sniff with despair. It was becoming clear after fifty years that she wasn't going to persuade him to be kind about other people's gardens – or anything else, much.)

Yet, drawing closer to the age at which he'd died, I'd think of him bored, wanting so much to be his own coarse man, away from all fastidiousness of opinion. I'd think how as a little boy I'd loved the vigour and intemperance of his displeasures, addressed at the passing world. I'd remember how he'd always brightened up on encountering some cheerfully unpleasant man, with raw prejudices to express. And how, though there must have been much darkness in his affairs, he'd have nothing to do with sadness, as a proposition: my mother's idea, perhaps, of the proper response to a situation. 'I feel sad for Mrs Bo'sun' – actually, Mrs Baston, whose husband had just died. 'What's the good of feeling sad? Will it help Baston,

40

the poor bugger? *I* don't feel sad.' And so on. All that was from fear, I now see. He hated it when I listened to some tragic drama on the wireless: and I hated him for his hate: thinking myself luckless to be the son of a man who thought Shakespeare, for writing *Hamlet*, was morbid, and a cause of morbidity in me. If he could have taken out an injunction against Shakespeare, for encouraging gloom in his son, he'd have done so. It was fear, and now I worry that I responded in the only way I knew how: with anger, and scorn. Though I guess there was no effective way I could have responded to the fact of his being fearful. ('I'm not afraid!' he'd have said. 'I haven't got *time* to be afraid! *You*'re the one who reads books and listens to bloody plays to make himself afraid!')

He knew Shakespeare's type. Someone incapable of satisfaction until he'd brought every skeleton out of every cupboard. It was what my father, who'd never seen *Hamlet*, believed all artists did: out of unhealthy fascination, or a desire to feed the unhealthy fascinations of others, they were drawn to those things it was best to think about as little as possible.

Yet I'd find myself thinking tenderly of the truth, discovered late, that his general bile masked very exact and sometimes intelligent distastes. He did not like gush. He did not like idle talk, for its own sake. He did not like pretension. He would not, it struck me, like the latest version of George Straker: for though George had a systematic unpleasantness of disposition that should have pleased my father, he had also a pomposity that my father would have despised. He would not have admired the trivial canopy at George's front door, or the architecturally dubious columns that feigned to support it. (He would, with no difficulty, have scorned George's garden, for being the creation of an underling. A man who did not do his own gardening was my father's idea of the totally effete human being. The fact that I was a dreadful gardener, inept with weeds, illiterate in matters of pruning, never made me as low in my father's sight as George would have been: I did at any rate labour to create my own horticultural fiasco.)

So I'd find myself thinking of my father at particular moments, and adding my snort to his. For example, when at Christmas friends sent euphoric synopses of the year past, in the form of duplicated letters. Nothing had happened that had not deepened the smile on their faces. Kate and I found ourselves curiously enraged by these communiqués: and I'd imagine my father's rage alongside ours. How could anyone's life be so continuously bright? How could people wish to present themselves to their acquaintances in this unconvincing fashion? Such assertions of unalloyed contentment made us imagine, instantly, the miseries that had been excluded. 'Nothing,' I'd growl, 'about William being charged with exposing himself with intent to insult a female.' 'Or Jenny's shoplifting.' 'Or the terrible rows between the elder son and his wife.' Our friends had probably been free of such dramatic miseries: but their claim to intolerable happiness ('The best holiday ever', 'William is kept blissfully busy as secretary of half a dozen societies') made us think of them, for the moment, balefully.

We'd imagine (and even my father might have admitted Shakespeare to the argument at this point) the duplicated letters sent out from Elsinore. 'Claudius has been the second husband my dear first husband would have wished me to have.' 'Hamlet is back from Wittenberg for the hols and is enjoying himself enormously, dear boy. The other night we had one of the most delightful evenings at the theatre I ever remember!' I'd hear my father's bark of a laugh. He might have feared tragedy and sadness, but he'd not have been in favour of such a pretence of well-being . . .

But I'd think that at that point I'd better halt my father's acquaintance with *Hamlet*. He'd need to know little more to perceive that Claudius was a typical Blishen, operating a scheme in respect of brothers that left Uncle Will, with

42

his mere ultimatums on toilet paper, far behind. A lep'rous distilment in the porches of the other chap's ears! An interesting improvement on the throwing of chairs which (Uncle Will's ploy aside) had been the main means by which Blishens of my father's generation had expressed their fraternal emotions! My father would have warmly identified himself with Hamlet's uncle. Gertrude, in his estimation, would have been any woman, at any time – tricky, dangerous, at once worth having and definitely not worth having. All my aunts were Gertrudes, and I think my father simultaneously desired and despised them all. My mother must have been a great irritation to him in respect of this general view he had of women. Her wiles, if they existed at all, were barely to be counted. At most she was capable of concealing the expense involved in providing my father with a favourite dinner. But, though by the accident of being swept off her feet by him (for the second time, in her early twenties) she might once have broken the heart of a railway clerk called Strickland (except that she was quite clear that Strickland had nothing much by way of a heart), she was a woman dreadfully honest. From beginning to end of the seventy years of their acquaintance this honesty bedevilled all my father's calculations. He might, I suppose, have caught an exotic echo of her nature in Ophelia, honest enough to have died for love. My mother would have thought *that*, in terms of Ophelia's self-imposed fate, to have been absurdly not in her style. When I was adolescent I'd have loved to think my mother might have been pulled from her melodious lay to muddy death: but she'd have had no doubt that that was an end for which she was not fitted. Given the possibility of some denouement more down-to-earth, however, and less likely to cause comment by the apparently unwashed condition of one's dress, she'd certainly (provided the necessity of it had been made plain) have died for love.

But oh dear! When my father came to the prince, he'd

have recognised the type at once. Rashly encouraged to take a scholarship to the grammar school: fallen into the hands of pretentious schoolmasters: everlastingly reading: given ideas beyond his station (my father would have thought that even a prince did not *need* to go to university): encouraged in morbidity by education and an interest in the theatre! My father would have known him! Jokes about cyclostyled Christmas letters, momentarily amusing, would not have concealed from him the real issue. Which was that *Hamlet* was a play about educational conceit in an offspring – and my father knew where *that* led!

6

Being in your sixties was to have lived a life with a cast of thousands: but it was increasingly clear that, in that supporting swarm, many who appeared to resemble one another were in practice light years apart.

So my good friend Rufus, an astonishing writer for (they said) children, was, in the matter of being rather given to injustice, much like my father. In essence, I insisted on being fair-minded, while Rufus insisted on *not* being fair-minded. It was not a matter of a virtue or a vice, either way. We were doomed to be as we were, and greatly enjoyed the difference. I had what Rufus must sometimes have thought was a cringing fear of being less than fair – in the matter, especially, of what was written by our colleagues. If to be unjust relieved his feelings, Rufus would have said, that was reason enough for it.

He was one of those friends who provided the worst of my experiences as a broadcaster. I found it difficult to shift from the coded fashion in which you converse with an old acquaintance into the plain manner that, if it is to be useful, a five-minute interview demands. So, talking on the air to the novelist, Finsbury, I allowed his natural inclination to be elusive, as well as allusive, to triumph.

He'd written a thrilling story, a metaphysical drama, based on the idea of some congruence or affinity of shapes that had, as I understood it, a background of fairly raw scientific inquiry. Finsbury could have written a novel that sprang from his detailed response to the theory of relativity, and it would still have been an excitement, even to mathematical dunces like myself. If he'd been around when I was a boy, to make geometry and trigonometry joke about themselves, I might have been less of a dunce. Face to face in the studio with his spectacles, which were of glass so thick that I'd imagine I was staring into the lenses of two astronomical telescopes at once, I allowed him to be mysteriously scientific ... as well as scientifically mysterious. Oh, with Finsbury mystery *was* a science! The result was unusable. A meeting of the Royal Society would have scratched its head over it. If we'd not had a private relationship which made me one of Finsbury's favourite persons to bewilder, and him one of my favourite persons to be bewildered by, I'd not have let it happen.

It was worse when I interviewed Rufus. That didn't arise from the comparable situation in our case, that I enjoyed being outraged by his more arbitrary opinions, and he enjoyed outraging me. And in truth, every judgement Rufus made, in every department, was related to his needs as a writer. He was deeply a creature of those needs: sometimes consumed by them. He worked well only in the interests of working better. His opinions were not to be taken seriously: they were rockets fired to speed or slow his own industry. His wastepaper basket was always crammed with excellence, scorned. Lately he'd written, in his usual turmoil of doing it and redoing it and feeling contempt for what he'd redone and redoing it again, two stories for children taken from the Bible. 'Oh Rufus,' I'd felt bound to say, reading one of them in manuscript. 'I wish *you* had written the Bible!' Of course I *didn't* – but all the same, the exclamation wasn't wholly dishonest. I could imagine the alternative Bible Rufus would have written (and rewritten in preparation for again rewriting it), full of startling comedy and laced with the macabre. Rufus could make you laugh at the same time as he froze the life out of you. Given the length of the Bible, it would have been too much to leave it all to him: but there are a number of passages that, in Rufus's version, I believe, would have filled churches for the laughter they'd have caused, and emptied them for the dread.

He found being interrupted whilst writing quite unacceptable. He'd once said he thought of Christmas Day as Interruption Day. And he was still telling a stunned story of an occasion when Nell Shilling, who didn't drive, had rung to say she was in desperate need of fish and chips, and that Rufus should pick her up at once in his car and take her in search of them. 'I was in the middle of a sentence,' Rufus would say, tragically. He had obeyed Nell, of course, some terror of taxidermy at the back of his mind. When the story was told in her presence Nell would listen with interest. 'But,' she'd say, 'I wasn't at that moment thinking of Rufus as a writer, but as a mere instrument for getting hold of fish and chips.' I suggested to Rufus this might make a refreshing addition to the quotes on the dustjackets of his books. 'Not so much a writer as a mere instrument for getting hold of fish and chips' – Nell Shilling.

The problem in interviewing Rufus was that one of our favourite pubs, the Marquis of Abergavenny, was not far from Bush House. On the whole, Rufus thought of pubs as places where we could sit while I read his current manuscript under his frantically anxious eye. If my expression became for a second less than happy, he'd leap with dismay. 'What's that? What's *that*?' he'd cry. Meanwhile, we drank. On the occasion of our first interview, we then crossed to Bush House, our minds perfectly clear, but with that hazy edging that a shot in a film used to have when it was intended to suggest a flashback. Great clarity in the centre, a pleasant mist at all the edges. As we stepped out of the lift at the seventh floor, Rufus said: 'This is where you change into your uniform, I suppose.' He had often alleged that inside a BBC building I became unrecognisable. 'A businesslike quality. Perfectly pleasant, but it's not what your friends know you by.'

And so we sat at the microphone, and I asked Rufus a question. He began an answer in his usual grand and natural manner: being, in speech as in writing, always the creator of sentences boldly modelled. It was, I'd think, like watching a fine ship set out from harbour, under full sail, bright bunting from stem to stern. But on this occasion, a short distance from the quay, the vessel, without ceremony, suddenly, sank. Rufus stared at me. His face was cheerfully blank. We started again. The great ship set sail, and sank.

On the occasion of our second interview, we took the precaution of not going to the Marquis. Stella picked Rufus up at reception. In the lift she said: 'You remember the convention – because it's heard at various times in various places, we do the programme as if it came from nowhere and was fairly timeless. Best to imagine it's coming from the moon.'

'The last time we did it,' said Rufus, 'it sounded as if it was coming from the Marquis of Abergavenny.'

7

Of course, even when you were coming up to your 24,000th day of existence, there was at any time a great deal of presentness around. Each new day, woken up to, was a fresh island in the ocean of time: much like all the previous islands you'd found yourself marooned on, but always with this unique addition: that it was now, and not time gone or time yet to come. But into this transient novelty the past constantly intruded. You were walking about in this spanking new environment and suddenly ... It was like being converted from second to second into an archaeologist: here you were in Holborn, very much of this moment, and now here you were in the depths of a dig, blowing the dust off old bones.

It was Marylebone, not Holborn. At a school's morning assembly I was to announce the winners of a short-story competition and to talk about the writing of fiction. About that I had only one thing to say: that you didn't have to scratch around for stories, or groaningly construct them out of exotic material. Infallibly, every day, you found yourself in the midst of them. They fell into your lap.

And I walked out of the Tube station and was at once inside a story. At first I couldn't place it. Here was Cabbell Street: here was Lisson Street: here was Chapel Street. The names belonged, undoubtedly, and in just such a sequence, to a tale I'd once heard. Then, suddenly, here was Bell Street, and I knew where I was. I could hear my mother talking about her childhood in – of course! – this corner of London. These were the names she had recited, as those of roads followed on her way to and from home: though I suspected it was a series of homes, rented rooms briefly occupied. It was round here, anyway, in the late 1890s, that you might have seen Lizzie Pye taking what she hoped would be an unnoticeable swig from a jug she'd been sent to have filled with vinegar. My mother's passion for *that* I shared. And round here, she'd gone to school. 'Where was that?' I'd ask. 'Oh, terrible big place!' I believe she felt that an assertion of its sheer size would balance my knowledge of the limited nature of her attendance there: she'd barely gone to school before she'd left it again to go into service. 'Amazing big place! Bell Street, Paddington!'

And there, seventy years later, I stood for a moment, halted by astonishment. Walking on, I found that halfway along Bell Street I had to turn into another road to reach the main entrance of the school I was visiting. When I met the headmaster I was still dizzy with the strangeness of it.

48

I told him what had happened. 'So afterwards, you see, I shall go back and search along the rest of Bell Street for that terrible big place.' 'No need to do that,' he said. 'You're in it.'

I wasn't strictly inside my mother's school, but I was inside the space it had occupied. It had been pulled down to make way for the school I was actually standing in. The headmaster took me into the playground: there you could see part of the ground plan of Lizzie's school, the smoothed-out lines of its foundations. Into the new school wall they'd cemented a stone from the old building that said: BELL STREET SCHOOLS MARYLEBONE.

And so a quarter of an hour later, instead of claiming as an abstract principle that stories occurred all the time, I could give an instant example: told in the tones of a narrator who, like all lucky storytellers, is astonished by his own tale. And afterwards I visited a class that was working on a history of the district. They'd got hold of the architect's copy of the elevations of that amazing big place of my mother's. If only she had lasted a year or two longer, I said, I'd have brought her along as a visual aid. And I imagined how delighted she'd have been. Being a visual aid was among the multitude of ambitions she'd never entertained. When she talked of her time at Bell Street, it was another goal to which she laid claim: especially when I was at the grammar school, and perhaps George Straker, being a near neighbour, had called to check on the evening's homework. She'd have listened to our talk of French, or Latin, or mathematics, subjects that filled her with awe but also with helpless amusement because of their pompous names. 'What I loved,' she'd say, 'was mapping.' Only the cruel need to go into service as soon as the law would allow (which, then, was very soon) had stood between my mother and the certainty that she'd have been one of the great mappers of our time.

'With a special nib,' she was always careful to say:

knowing it was a detail that enforced belief – in herself, as in us.

And curiously the past would strike again in the form of uncertainties of pronunciation.

The tendency of literature to be written by Russians, Spaniards, Japanese and Czechs, to name only some of those who caused me problems, meant that I was sometimes given to spectacularly floundering in the middle of a script. I'd long for a week when only the Smiths had put pen to paper. But it wasn't simply a problem of out-of-the-way foreign pronunciations. It was worse than that – and as I got older, the embarrassment it caused seemed to spring from more and more remote sources in my history. It was, I'd think, a scarlet-faced schoolboy who was trying to contain his fury and shame as his tongue betrayed him yet again.

'... poet and novelist,' I'd read, 'who lives in Mee-army...'

'My-ammy,' my producer's voice would come. 'Or so it was when I was last there.'

Well, damn it, I knew how to pronounce Miami, so why did my tongue play this trick on me? It was what it would do when I least expected it. There'd be some famous mispronunciation of a word, an error amusedly avoided by infants, and I'd opt for it. Over a recent lunch a senior producer in the department, a charming man whose reluctance to hurt flies extended to freelances, said: 'What I don't like, you know, is the way you pronounce "illu-strate", "ill-you-strate".' He smiled with perfect kindness and bought me a coffee. And I had to say how difficult I found it, being unable in my sixties easily to smile at such comments, or at the discovery that I'd said 'repeat' with the stress on the first instead of the second syllable. It was a cause of fury to me, partly because I loved the sound of words and hated to be untrue to them: and partly, I supposed, because I was still the boy who'd had to be taught how to sound his aitches and to replace the Cockney diphthongs of home with the vowels favoured by the grammar school. He was still growlingly alive at the roots of my tongue.

But then, of course, we all carried our younger selves with us. The annoyance lay, I thought, in having supposed that at sixty one would turn out to be mature, even wise, certainly proficient, and discovering it wasn't so.

Well, for nearly forty years you'd been heavily engaged: the Battle of Life, you might sighingly accept that it must be called – a seabattle, perhaps: smoke, thunder, blood, the tremendous smell of cordite. And in the midst of it, as you desperately fed the guns in preparation for another broadside, you thought that at least you were ripening. You had this subliminal and energising conviction that it would all have been worth it, because out of it you'd step at last, transformed into some sort of sage. Life itself would raise its hat to you.

And then the sounds of battle died. Your children had left home: such achievement as you were ever going to be able to lay claim to was largely visible, almost completed, not to be much improved upon. You waited for the sensation of wisdom. Instead, you had such a sensation of folly as you'd not known since your twentieth birthday. It dawned on you, then: you had not really been maturing, you'd merely been extraordinarily busy. The uncertainties, inadequacies, plain daftnesses of late adolescence slouched out of the shadows and took up their gauche positions if not centre stage, then very close to it.

Once you'd been a young ass. Now, suddenly, you discovered yourself to be an elderly ass. And if at the age of fourteen or so your tongue had learned a great distrust of itself, you might at sixty be saying Mee-army instead of My-ammy, or pronouncing the names of great Russians in a manner you'd anxiously invented for yourself fifty years earlier, to cover the general probability that the sound of such names must have some dash of oddity about it.

Having kept a diary since 1934, I could check on the origins – and simple persistence – of some of these forms of latterday folly. For example, of the paranoia that surfaced at times, to my horror, and lay in the feeling that I was regarded as the least amusing or most unimportant person present in some gathering. Worse, I would be secretly disturbed because all were united in praising some other member of the circle. He'd sit there smiling modestly while they expressed their appreciation of his sense of humour, or the wit of his phrasing, or his bone structure, or anything at all, and I'd smile too: but under the smile I'd be frowning. Their admiration for him, this was the disgusting gist of it, was a demonstration of their lack of admiration for me. I would on these occasions deliver astounding silent lectures to myself: I would even take myself off in the hope that, in sudden exile, this unacceptable self would come to its senses. There were times when all was laughter and delight and amity; but if my true posture had been revealed, half of myself would have been seen standing sulkily, stormily in the corner, while the other half prowled up and down, uttering teacher-like growls.

Well, in that old diary of mine, there was Founder's Day, 1935: several thousand words in the tiniest handwriting. I was suddenly infatuated with the school. Taught since 1932 in a new building, we'd returned for the occasion to the dilapidations of the original foundation, Elizabethan and Victorian, where I'd spent two years in a sort of social shredder. Almost everything I had been until the age of ten was found unsuitable and, in a fairly public manner and amid the sarcastic cries of gowned schoolmasters, was forcibly dismantled. My vowels, which were those of my father and mother, were mocked: together with most of our social habits. I would have remembered that this had

52

produced a healthy hostility on my part, if the diary didn't prove otherwise. On June 15th, I was simply alarmed that I and my schoolmates might have failed to do justice to what I called 'the beauty of the occasion'. 'By all the laws of poetry we should not have been our usual lackadaisical, unimaginative, unimpressed and unimpressive selves.' That is what we were, it seems, disgracefully usual, as we 'slowly and sadly revisited and re-encountered our past': including 'the quaint Gothic entrances' of the old school and the mulberry tree in the middle of the playground, 'still verdant, and still surrounded by the splintered palings through which we had clambered and wherein we had often lain hid'. At fifteen I was already sixty-five, looking back on remote glories. And already words were letting me down. I noted my memories of Sergeant Clinker, in intervals in sessions of drill 'spinning charmingly ambiguous anecdotes of his own daring and entirely fictitious exploitations'. It must have been with recollections of an occasion or two like this – the Sergeant telling us how he'd made catapults as a boy and thought they were well-named, cats being his major target – that George Straker had blotted out his memory of the man as he mostly was. The piety of my thoughts during the service in the parish church, which stood opposite the old school, made blushing seem, fifty years later, quite inadequate. 'The loves fostered at school,' I reflected, in an outstanding instance of prophecy gone astray, 'will blossom forth in ecstasies in the unknown world outside.' School, I thought, was 'something greater than a house of learning: maths and languages mere camouflage, mere footstools, mere rungs, mere ascendencies'. (This child drunk with words clearly believed ascendencies to be a superior sort of rung). Having lately become an atheist (damped down, on the advice of our English master, Williams, to agnostic) I battled with 'the Christian emotionalism' of the service, remaining 'stolid and with my mind as inexpressive and unimpressible as possible' throughout 'the long prayers, the longer anthem, and the quavering Last Post'.

But amid these seizures of admiration for a shabby grammar school, never repeated, I discover the record of sensations that are still familiar. Parrott, a school governor who used to take me out in his MG with the double aim of restoring my faith and stroking my bottom (not one of the sensations I'm concerned with), 'looked at me fiercely as I left the Church. Presumably in the sacred portals it is neither gentlemanly nor religious to recognise a friend.' Paranoia was at work. I had already avoided the eye of one of my favourite masters, who'd provided Alan Bolton and me with tickets to the first concert of classical music we'd attended (the experience had given Alan such sensations of maturity that within a week he'd added atheism and socialism to his new-found passion for Tchaikovsky). 'I carefully did not look at him, though I knew that, on this morning of mornings, he would have no time to pursue finicky acquaintances.' (I seem to have thought that 'finicky' meant, or could be made to mean, 'minor' or 'negligible'). And later, after an overwrought account of the reading of the School Chronicle (a piece of pastiche by the headmaster, Percy Chew, read by himself and concluding: 'And in 1929 Percy Chew was appointed Headmaster, and the school did mightily flourish'), there we were on the school playing field, for the Past v Present cricket match: and I was occupied not only with the 'sunny serenity' and 'ancient dignity' of the scene, but also with the sensations of someone being cut dead. So here came 'Snowy' Brown, who in the first two years at school had been, alternately and in fairly undramatic fashion, friend and enemy, and had since left. 'I had due right by old acquaintance to greet him and be greeted by him: yet at me he but grinned weakly, and walking to several others, shook them frenziedly by the hand.' I remember Snowy, a quiet boy, and cannot believe that frenzy entered into it. He was persuaded once to bite the art master in the ankle, but that was as the result of a bet, on one of those Friday afternoons when a small boy easily lost touch with his own essential character. It seems I thought on that astonishingly passionate day in 1935 that he should have paid me more attention than he did, and that his failing to do so pointed to a grave absence of attractiveness in myself.

'Why dilate unnecessarily?' I cried somewhere in those fervent pages. I think I mean that I had written enough about *that*. But though I wasn't lucky enough to interview Tolstoy, and unlucky enough to have to get his name right when recording my script (my tongue would turn the 's' into 'sh', out of that old conviction that a Russian name couldn't be pronounced as it was spelt), I thought of the fifteen-year-old paranoias that had become the sixty-five-year-old paranoia inside me whenever I interviewed, and so later had correctly to name, Mario Vargas Llosa, Jorge Amado, or Buchi Emecheta. And, of course, any scribbler from Miami.

8

My tongue, again. When I ran into George these days I tried to remember not to make a lighthearted remark. Such a remark made him frown, and then subject what you'd said to massive hostile examination. There'd always been a touch of that in him at school. 'When is a door not a door? When it's ajar,' you'd venture, only to have George at once prising the joke up, as it were, probing underneath it: shaking it furiously in case there might be some sinister fallout.

We'd been to Stamford, and I'd thought of Lord Burghley lying on his tomb in St Martin's that it had been a mistake to represent him with his staff of office in his hand. It looked as if he'd died poking the fire. Before I could stop myself, I mentioned this to George, unexpectedly encountered in Barton High Street, and he at once became chilly. A great man. Could do with him today. Conventions of figures on tombs not always understood by modern observers. Touch of philistinism. Growing readiness to sell the country down the river by deriding its heroes: statesmen and businessmen in particular. 'George, I didn't know you felt like this about Lord Burghley,' I said helplessly. Appalling tendency, I gathered, of George's friends to underestimate the range of his interests and the catholic nature of his admirations. 'You knew every inch of Lord Burghley?' I suggested foolishly, but George had turned to talk to Kate: who profited from my errors, and was carefully humourless.

There were times when I saw that George's refusal of ready laughter saved a good deal of wear and tear. Receiving a letter from our friend Sally Roberts he'd have thrown it aside as unreadable. 'If she can't take more care, she can't expect to be read.' It was another effect of ageing: Sally's handwriting, never absolutely legible, decayed. 'You should see my loins,' she would seem to have written. 'Such a good year for bums! Last wink Molly came down and fished out my ashes. Did you get the kangaroo I sent you? If the waiter stays as timorous as this you should have a lousy bellyache. Do sleep and twitch. Blast fishes. Silly.'

We'd guess, at the outset of the feat of decoding that followed the arrival of this letter, that 'loins' was either 'lawns' or 'boils'. Probably lawns. Even Sally, we thought, wouldn't write ecstatically about her boils.

Ecstasy was Sally's normal style. Even when she was in the dumps she was ecstatically in the dumps. She was overwhelmingly one of those people who point things out: exclamatory about aspects of the scene one had grown accustomed to taking in one's stride. 'Oh the sky!' 'Oh how green!' 'The birds!' In the middle of a heatwave she'd be newly alert to the existence of the sun. She would cry 'Your hair!' and then dash on to some other statement of rapture: so that you'd never know if horror or admiration lay behind that cry.

Our son Tom, aged about nineteen, at his philosophically fiercest, had once excoriated us for milder symptoms of the same disease. We were reifying, he said. It was mentally to convert things . . . into things. I thought he might require us to write, a thousand times: 'I must not indulge in reification.' Sally might have invented it. At home, she lived in a whirlwind of things misplaced. 'Where is my soap powder/book/television set/walking stick?' she'd cry. 'Oh the muddle!' The scene in her kitchen might have been used for one of those lessons in a foreign language in which a multitude of miscellaneous objects are illustrated as being present, for naming, in a single setting. It was in the kitchen that you could expect to find Sally's missing novel, the one she believed she was currently reading: it was in the living room that you'd have looked for the soap powder. Her energy was enormous, and was almost totally devoted to making life difficult, and exclamation inevitable. Living alone in a cottage in Shropshire, she had lost real touch with the world, but had invented a conversancy with its latest ways. This involved her in crying, long after the term had ceased to be generally used: 'Oh smashing!' Later she replaced this with 'Oh super!', also outmoded, but so pronounced that I suspected she thought the cry was 'Oh souper!' The question of what a souper was would not have troubled Sally, so given to regarding the world as an extraordinary place.

Holidaying in Shropshire once, we'd met her at a friend's house, and she'd clung to us ever since. She was ecstatic about friendship. 'Oh Kate, having friends . . .!' She'd lost a husband along the way, but had never thought much of him. 'Oh that William . . .!' He'd been universally known as Bill, but Sally, who'd never quite abandoned the attempt to get herself known as Sarah, was not in favour of abbreviated names. All that was part of a coarse world, lacking in reasons for ecstasy, that she had put behind her. She was anxious to float in a fine atmosphere of grand names, grand and largely exclamatory talk. It was, I thought, more evidence of a common enough condition. There were people with an appetite for glory, seen as a state of protracted refinement. If you were denied the education proper to your ambitious energy, as Sally had been, the appetite became breathlessly foolish, mistaking its needs, creating for itself absurd kinds of hauteur. Privately, we thought of her as the Duchess: and had Lewis Caroll in mind. Grandeur in a disordered kitchen: that was Sally. Our pleasure was to tempt her into being the lively woman she was, under the pretensions so touchingly necessary to her. Under the lofty Sally was the low Sally, with a gravelly chuckle to match. Suddenly, when we'd succeeded in bringing this other self of hers to life, the fine gown of her manner would be hitched above the knees, the shoes would be sent flying, and with a happy coarse cry Sally would begin to dance. She had a fund of stories from her London childhood that revolved round dropped aitches, wild Saturday nights, cockles and winkles: with a wonderful tale or two in which the private parts of men and boys were thought of in terms of such tiny proletarian shellfish. Then superior Sally would resume her sway, with a cry of 'Oh what fun!' 'Kate, such laughter!' 'It does you good!' she'd add, needing to justify this emergence of original Sally from the billowing robes of Sally near seventy.

I knew a great deal about her: but when I was oppressed by the difficulty of knowing anything much about anybody at all, would think of Sally. What in truth, and in detail, lay behind the chaotic nature of our friend? When in the 1930s she was enjoying herself earthily in some rough street in London, as she'd now call it, where was the haughty Sally – where in that whirl of handsome young energy were the seeds of the older woman, keeping every-dayness at bay with endless expressions of amazement?

9

'"The character which a man exhibits in the latter half of
his life,"' Kate read aloud, '"is not always, though it often
is, his original character developed or withered, attenuated
or enlarged: it is sometimes the exact reverse, like a
garment that has been turned."'

'Like Sally Roberts?' I wondered. 'And George Straker,
I suppose, simply has forgotten which is the outside of his
coat and which is the lining.'

We were sitting in a little garden in Provence, and
Kate was reading Proust in order, she said, to keep all
Englishness at bay. But it turned out that Proust knew
everyone we knew, though in socially superior embodi-
ments. Here he was, acquainted with Sally, who'd have
been gratified by the connection.

We'd borrowed a friend's house in a village near Orange.
The journey had begun uncomfortably a few days earlier,
our local trains being subject to delay. And cacelation – so
one of British Rail's blackboards had proclaimed, turned
by years of use into a greyboard. In wandering capitals it
asserted that 'some trains will be subject to delay and
cacelation this due to staff reaction to the introduction
of training on modified surben trains BR regret's any
inconvince this may cause love Bob'. There *was* incon-
viction, and we nearly missed our boat: but it was all made
easier by Bob's affection. If I didn't teach him, I had
taught many like him, who'd always come to those particular blunt and sensible compromises of spelling: and
had always shattered ceremony with some off-duty cheer-
fulness or other.

There were similar difficulties in Lyons: but here Bob's
homespun English and half-ironical amiability had given
way to someone else's silky French, and fine balance of
deference and disdain: 'Following an arrest of work by a
certain category of personnel,' the notice murmured, 'we

inform our clientele that some perturbations may occur on the line St Etienne-Lyons.'

Through delays, cacelations and perturbations we made our way to St Mathilde, and to a small house that smelled of cherries. It looked out on the street, and morning after morning, opening the shutters with a shade too much energy, I all but tumbled into the roadway. It was a bruising house, for the lintels of the doors were low and a fortnight was not long enough for me to learn infallibly to duck. My failure to do this made Kate angry. It was what always happened, we'd observed, some such anger, once or twice on any holiday: which, whilst renewing our affection, also reminded us of our never quite unexasperating differences. Kate had said once: 'Holidays together remind me that you are not practical, and remind you that I'm not an intellectual.' Well, I wasn't an intellectual myself, but it was a word for the distance that reading took me from home while Kate was busy making herself useful in her immediate setting, something like that. So I'd huff and puff at some point in a holiday because Kate had become impatient with some over-fine discussion, and she would be angered by my incapacity, as she saw it, to avoid hitting my head on doors. Oddly, in this matter she seemed to think that an intellectual approach on my part might help. 'All you have to do is to tell yourself: "I will not hit my head on a door!" It just requires a little thought!' 'I cannot,' I said, 'go around with such an idea perpetually in the forefront of my mind. It would not be natural to be in such a pleasant house as this in Provence thinking: "I must not hit my head on a door!"' Kate went away and made a brusque omelette. I went away and gazed through our neighbour Madame Brie's window. Then we reconvened for laughter.

The pomposity that built up in you!

To enter our house without the grand fuss of coming through the front door, which was like a miniaturised door to a dungeon and required the use of a giant key, we came through a path at the side that brought us past Madame Brie's windows. She liked us to stop and exchange a few formal remarks. In my case they were appallingly formal, for I'd always found that in France I tended to prepare speeches for the most everyday encounters in what I faintly remembered as the manner of Molière or Racine. Madame Brie was a widow, whose husband was said to have worked in the local *cave* and drunk himself quite rapidly to death. She liked us at least to smile as we passed her window. Often our smile was wasted, for she was to be seen watching television whilst bolt upright in a hard chair in the furthest corner of the room from the set. No part of her gaze was to spare. I had never seen anyone watching television with such dutiful intensity. It might be some cowboy film, some shrieking situation comedy from Paris, but she'd be grave, absolutely attentive, not even faintly at ease.

Chien méchant et perspicace said the little plate screwed to her front door. The dog was very old, extremely subdued in manner and probably an imbecile. But of course a statement to this effect would not have kept burglars at bay.

You turned a corner, and there were patches of garden, surrounded and divided by bits of walls, walls broken or never completed. And so to the back of our little house, with its stable door, and the low dusk of its interior, and the cellars they called *remises*, and the table in the yard where we mostly ate: and the little neighbouring house, not cut off by wall or fence, occupied by Moroccans. The woman was quite wonderfully beautiful, but shut away in her shyness, never seeming to leave house or yard, always to be seen in a tumble of children, themselves beautiful. The friend we'd borrowed the house from said she felt terrible, being obliged to think she ought to keep at a distance from her neighbours: but encourage the children, she said, and they'd be everywhere, they'd never go away, you'd find them beautiful and inconvenient in every room in your house, even in your beds. Please, for her sake, we should be pleasant but remote.

We slept in a great upper room, the biggest space in the house, that had once been a store: its distant great peak of a ceiling was no ceiling at all, but beams and the underside of the pantiles, and there was an everlasting rain of spiders. There was a window that went down to the floor, where a hoist had once stood, and its white muslin curtains were forever a brilliance of captured sunlight. It was marvellous to wake in the morning among such lofty shadows and such floating patches of sunshine. There was a mistral one night, that turned the rain of spiders into a downpour, and brought about an unsurpassed banging and creaking of doors: but during the day that followed the wind died as if it were obeying a conductor's baton, a perfect *decrescendo* that was followed, for the rest of our stay, by faultless good weather.

Well, how say it was anything but beautiful, beautiful, beautiful? Here was one of the best walks we'd ever known, to the next village. There was a junction of lanes smelling of broom. There was a field of barley like a pelt, bleached bronze and gold, and as the wind danced on it, it gaped momentarily to reveal poppies: and also, as if the field had been sowed with dazzling white stones, marguerites. Another field of wheat was turquoise-coloured, the wind blew pale ripples and dark ripples across it, and again seemed to be painting in and painting out hundreds of dabs of red, poppies revealed and hidden. Turn the corner, and there was a bank of poppies, this time orange. In the distance, it was as if mountains had turned liquid, a wash of them. And everywhere the bright green health of the vine, and more dabs of red where the farmers had followed their habit of tipping a row with a rose bush.

Within a day we were profoundly intimate with St Mathilde, couldn't remember ever being anywhere else or talking to our neighbours in anything but patchwork French. One neighbour approached us like Birnam Wood, bringing cherries *en branche*. We lay in the little crumb of a walled garden reading, and falling asleep, and waking to read again. Everywhere, swallows, appearing to be entirely devoted to the pleasures of flight. Everywhere, the brightness of the vine leaf, increasing with the evening light. Everywhere, except in Madame Brie's yard, the passionate dogs. My head ached from being struck on low doors. The Moroccans kept up a babble till very late, seamless chatter and laughter, in which the children were joined by their mother and father. They seemed enchanted with one another, and to live in a world in which such exchanges of private pleasures were more important than sleep. It was sad to be so near it, and so distant.

And reading. I thought as I'd often done that, if you were what one of my neighbours at Barley Wood called 'a reading fellow', you led a divided life: your own, and that of the world of the book you were in at that moment. In St Mathilde it was, part of the time, *Pride and Prejudice*. Perhaps it was being away from England, reading it against the French background, but I had never been so aware of it as a chronicle full of the horror Jane Austen felt for stupidity and moral emptiness. Partly it was Proust. 'Caught,' Kate would chant suddenly from her desk chair, 'in the treadmill of their own maladies and eccentricities . . .'

'Who do you have in mind?' I'd ask.

'. . . their futile attempts to escape serve only to activate its mechanism,' Kate would continue, 'to keep in motion the clockwork of their strange, ineluctable and baneful dietetics.'

'Ah, yes.'

We reminded each other of the good poet we knew who held that Proust's language, especially when it came to natural description, did not stand up to being inspected. It was novelettish, he said. Sometimes great admirers of Proust would ask him to remind them of this view of his, for the beautiful astonishment of it.

We'd swop books, and it would be my turn to read a passage of Proust aloud from a deckchair. '... the heart changes. And it is our worst sorrow: but we know it only through reading, through our imagination: in reality its alteration, like that of certain natural phenomena, is so gradual that, even if we are able to distinguish, success-ively, each of its different states, we are still spared the actual sensation of change ...'

I'd think of my fifty years of diary, on a shelf at home, and how, though the chronicler had not known he was doing it, it recorded the stages of many such changes. It was true, though, I thought, that if you did keep a diary, and if you did read any fairly long stretch of it again, you became aware of patterns you'd never otherwise have been aware of. A diarist, I found myself thinking, was like the man who came every few months and read our gas meter. Over the years, the record he made told a story.

I tried to imagine this cross reference to gas-meter readers being made by Proust, in the marvellous maze of one of his sentences. Even in French, a gas-meter reader couldn't sound particularly splendid. But the idea was on the right lines, surely. What I greatly loved about Proust was the way he constantly related the highest matters, deep questions of our mortality, to matters of the lowest and most everyday kind.

In the Papal Palace in Avignon we were guided by a girl with ivory shoulders, from which her blouse was always about to slip. She talked of the Darning Hull, the pal-arse, the Gobblings that hung on the walls. She asked us to immer-gin that this fireplace had been used to kip the ditches warm when they ate, as well as to hit the room. KEEP OFF THE COFFERS, said a sign. I tried to imagine a Pope, any Pope, lying in the Papal bedroom, all birds, squirrels, leaves and birdcages.

In the theatre at Orange a teacher murmuringly sum-moned his party of children to gather – they were scattered all over the great arena. I heard him say to himself that it was an uncommon pleasure for a teacher to be able to rely on such sonority, and I thought, his ordinary sentence having such an extraordinary sound, that perhaps my own approach to the speaking of French, the belief that it ought to be grand, might not be so absurd after all. After a good French sentence there was such an effect of perfectly lubricated syntax.

When I failed to return from a walk within a reasonable period (I had simply followed several miles of enchanting smells), Kate formed a satisfactory sentence of her own. She imagined what she'd long thought of as the type of my end: having taken a photograph, I had stepped back and fallen under some passing vehicle. In this case, she said, which she was able exactly to visualise, it was a bicycle, ridden by a rather small old man. She had imagined going to Madame Brie with the surely perfectly expressed cry: '*Mon mari est mort!*' Her pleasure at my return was laced with some regret at having done so much homework for nothing.

We started the journey home at 200 mph in the great TGV. A party of children on their swift way to Paris ate their entire provisions, plainly meant to last a day or two, within half an hour of leaving Lyons. I was struck by the marvellous sound of the expostulations with which their teachers attempted to prevent this, and astonished, translating them in my head, to realise that most were international teacherly banalities of the order of: 'If this conduct continues, someone is going to be very severely punished.' The prettiest of the teachers seemed to address this threat to me, and I had to confess to Kate that I was thrilled. *Ah, la concupiscence des vieillards*, said Kate, who seemed likely never to speak English again. Throughout the journey members of a party of Japanese were brought through the carriage two or three at a time, going in the direction of the locomotive. The great train was clearly being shown off to them, though my memories of Tokyo suggested they might have been familiar with trains even greater. (Rufus, I recalled, was in Tokyo at the moment, receiving some award or other, and when I last spoke to him had prepared his grateful speech as far as the opening: Ladies, gentlemen and samurai.) The children rose to their feet and clapped as each party went through. Their teachers seemed to be experiencing perturbations that grew worse as the children replaced clapping with wild cheering. The odd thing was that none of the Japanese returned. Could there be an alternative route through the train? Were they all, thirty or so of them, packed into the driver's cab?

On the line to Barley Wood, where the admiration of foreign visitors was not being sought, there was delay – perhaps the same delay we had been part of a fortnight earlier. There was also cacelation. The latter, said a voice over the sordid public address system, was due to unit failure. *Manquement de module?* Kate hazarded. But at home we found it probably should have been *Défaut de bloc moteur*.

10

Shaving my father's face in the morning, for he seemed increasingly to be inhabiting mine, I'd hear him being scathing about our French holiday. Only the Great War had ever taken him out of England. 'Edward and Katherine,' he'd say to some neighbour encountered on one of our visits, 'never have a meal without ... wine, you know ...' 'Dad, that's not so.' 'And they never take a holiday in their own country, of course. They all go abroad now, have you noticed? So they can come back and say they've been abroad, I think.' 'Now, *Dad* ...!' The neighbour reeling under my father's pungencies. 'Well, I'm sure, Mr Blishen, it's very nice to get away and have a complete ...' My father's briskly scornful laugh. 'Well, won't hang about. Sea breezes aren't always good for you.' The neighbour turning pale, wondering if he'd suggested sea breezes

66

always *were* good for you, and had forgotten doing so. My father could give the lightest comment a deadly edge of accusation.

He'd certainly not have approved of my not intending to retire – as well as being in no position to do so.

I can't have been more than twelve when he first sat me down ('Stop hopping about, sit down and listen to me!') and required me to give thought to retirement. It was closer than I imagined, he said. It depressed him to see so many young men who supposed they were going to live forever and had no regard for such questions. In no time at all they would be sixty-five and in despair. He didn't want this to happen to me. In my thinking about the future, the need to get a job that offered a decent position was paramount. 'Don't just pick up that damned comic and start reading it again! Think over what I've said!'

Now, in the shaving mirror, he pointed out that his warning had been ignored, and that he had been right – in no time at all, I *had* become sixty-five. 'You're not wearing particularly well, if I may say so. Must be thirty years ago I suggested you do something to bring those damned eyebrows under control. Too late now. But then you never knew how to prune.' I would make the electric razor roar noisily up his cheek, and then remember it was also mine. 'No good trying to shout me down!' It was an attempt he'd often accused my mother of, addressing at him some murmured protest. 'You won't be able to go on working forever, you know. I shouldn't think the BBC's keen on a lot of old men tottering about the place.' He laughed at the image. He'd always offered a vision of the BBC as an institution hopping from foot to foot as it attempted to formulate a reason for getting rid of me. I remember that the matter of my eyebrows, showing signs of meaning to climb vertically upwards, was raised in respect of what my father saw as the precarious relationship between me and the BBC. They'd catch sight of my eyebrows and that would be it. They weren't keen on a lot of men walking about the building with strange eyebrows.

I menaced the end of his nose, but he was in full flight. 'I've noticed how stiff you are, going downstairs in the morning. By the way, why can't Katherine get a cup of tea for herself now and then? I don't want to put ideas into your head but . . .' There wasn't a head he'd ever had anything to do with in which he'd not wanted to put ideas, if possible to the total exclusion of any ideas the head might be inclined to think up for itself. And especially ideas about retirement.

Well, some people seemed to retire happily. For some it seemed like the removal of the skeleton, the system of bones that had held them up. It was so with an old friend of an old friend, Jerry Smee, who'd never been a man of high spirits, but when he came after nearly fifty years to the end of his office life, and of the daily requirement that he travel from Barton to town and back again, he was made catastrophically miserable. Having for so long risen in the morning for the purpose of going to work, and gone to bed at night to be ready to go to work again the next day, he could make nothing of the terrible blankness into which the week had been converted. He rose, but desolately: he went to bed, bewildered: between, there was nothing that held his attention. He was an extreme case, and there must have been dejection in him from the beginning, made tolerable only by that fierce corset of a timetable: but everywhere I saw the dismay that followed from the removal, from one day to the next, of accustomed routine. In happier natures than Jerry's, it was still like the summer holidays at school, so intensely looked forward to, and discovered to be so difficult to endure to the end.

I was glad not to have to stop work, in this sudden fashion. I felt lucky, to have a form of work that didn't have to stop like that, and could, if you were fortunate, be co-terminous with life. But I was ready to give a point or two to the angry face in the shaving mirror. 'Of course, Dad, there *is* anxiety . . . I don't deny it. There *is* an ebbing of energy. Though in my trade there ought to be much that's not conditioned by one's age, still ... there's a sensation of getting out of touch. Unfamiliar names increasingly fill the newspapers. And of course I might become ill or go mad ...' 'I don't know about going mad!' He *did* know about going mad. There was a strong inclination for members of both my father's and my mother's families to succumb towards the end of life to some spreading melancholy. I'd been aware of the edges of that, waking some nights, thinking that the end was a sightless unhearing unstirring blackness, and that the living soul cannot bear the idea of it. But into some souls before they die may flood such a strong premonition of that state, of that absence of everything, of that nothingness which the living creature cannot think of as the effect of a single moment of death, but must fear as if it were like enduring strangulation throughout eternity ... such a powerful forewarning of this may fill their imaginations that they are unable to remain sane. '*I don't know about going mad!*' Any story of madness had always made my father particularly angry. 'But you *might* become ill ...'

I remembered one of those paradoxically tender things I knew about him – how he'd been such a good nurse when, as children, we were sick. There'd been a desperate gentleness in him, then. Well, visiting him in hospital during one of his last illnesses, when he was near to death, I'd had the sensation of his being the child, I being the father. Perhaps in the end, and despite the bitter failure of our relationship, he would ... had he been alive ... have reversed that experience of mine. The sick son would have become a child again.

I shrugged at the face in the mirror. He'd given up on the question of retirement, anyway. Years before, he'd known it was one of the matters in which I hadn't a shred of common sense. At the moment he was busy with that proposal that I visit New Zealand. Did I know there were Blishens there? A boy of Will's, he thought. Perhaps another of my Uncle George's. 'Well, *they're* likely to be anywhere!' His advice from the shaving mirror was curt. 'Have nothing to do with them. Keep away. As time went on I had as little to do with my family as possible. Keep yourself to yourself. That's my advice.'

It always had been. Every man a hermit. I had touches of the feeling myself – a sense of human sociability as a form of suffocation. In him it became a ruling principle – a way of life – the avoidance and exclusion of others.

But I knew that he'd not have been able to apply the principle to his great-grandson Tim, who would for moments on end have enchanted my disenchanted father out of that other suffocation than that of death, his misanthropy.

They'd decided to improve on the old storyline. So the opening tableau of the nativity play at Tim's school was composed of a representative selection of living creatures: peasants, of course, small boys in their mothers' summer hats, picking their noses: and the wives of peasants, dressed mostly in leotards and legwarmers, with here and there a careful length of straw, to indicate the brutal nature of their occupation. There was the odd king or queen, a miscellany of rabbits, and one little girl who had clearly refused to become part of any group, and whose legwarmers left areas of thigh more thrillingly revealed than those of Marlene Dietrich in *The Blue Angel*. From the beginning her act consisted of pulling her leotard away from her chest and peering down it appreciatively. Later she blew down it. The boy next to her, monarch of a country given to kitting out its kings in cardboard crowns to which something dreadful had happened, involving their being flattened and trodden on by muddy boots, could not believe his luck in being next to this little girl; and turning squarely towards her, he set himself, from the play's beginning to its end, all of ten minutes, to observe her performance open-mouthed.

Tim entered as the leader of a team of three spacemen.

This did not come as a surprise, Tim having, on Kate's estimate, spelled out the plot to us in detail close on a thousand times. He wore traditional spaceman's dress, a cardboard doublet with baseball player's shoulders: so capacious that all three astronauts were able like tortoises to retract their heads and make them vanish – a temptation they did not bother to resist. Before he became headless, however, Tim uttered a line with which we'd become numbly familiar. 'People of Earth, what are you doing? Why are there all these bright lights?' The answer was a little late in coming, the boy who was to deliver it having suffered almost terminal aphasia, as well as having got himself into a part of the crowd remote from these extra-terrestrial visitors. 'We are celebrating Christmas,' he at last brought himself to announce, while the entire cast stirred uneasily, many yawning. An astonishing amount of picking of noses now went on. Tim, uttering the sentiment any space traveller at this point would be moved to utter, said: 'We would like to know about Christmas.' Another long wavering silence was followed by the line: 'Then we will tell you all about it.' The spacemen gratefully abandoned the attempt at theatrical alertness and explored again the pleasure of withdrawing their heads inside their great silver shirts. There was a relentless silence as the cast languidly reminded itself of the need to switch from this prologue to the main body of the drama. By now most were in a state of giggling uncertainty that remained until the end. It was obvious that they had difficulty in bridging the two contrary emotions of the actor: pride in being on the stage, and bottomless embarrassment at being there. As each scene in the drama was completed by actors amazed by their own memories, there were general exchanges of little tittering tremors. There were surges and saggings: the whole cast would suddenly achieve something not a thousand miles from animation, but almost at once this would fade. When it came to singing, the vigour with which they hit the first notes was the prelude to almost complete musical collapse.

Audience and cast alike were amazed to find themselves at the play's end. They stared at one another, some of the actors vaguely moved by the idea that they might join their parents or simply take to their heels, their parents by the idea that it might be the moment for applause: which, when it came, led on stage to universal astonishment, from which the children were rescued by the headmistress with a brisk cry of: 'That's it, then! Well done, all of you! *Stay where you are!*' Soon after that the actors went off to knock to the ground and trample on a number of spacesuits, crowns, rabbits' heads and the infant Jesus. Tim threw his arms round my knees and asked a question any actor might ask after his first and last performance in a leading role: 'What's for tea?'

11

My mother had dreaded madness, too. Well, her own mother had gone gently out of her mind, and had stayed out of it for the last quarter of a century of her life. My mother's resolute and even comical insistence on her sanity, which caused her at the end to define madness as what had overtaken everyone else of her age – she'd indicate the old ladies round her and whisper, but she'd never had a gift for really whispering, 'They're all *bonkers*, you know!' – sprang from her knowledge of the ease and suddenness with which your wits could vanish.

I was glad she never knew what happened to Nat, who'd come into our life as a friend of the son of old friends, and whom she'd liked for a courteous way he had with him. He'd bow to my mother, who'd never been bowed to by anyone before. Even my father came close to liking him. 'Polite lad. Ought to watch it, though. Could be *too* polite!'

That wasn't the danger for Nat.

He'd taken years before to our piano, which he played well, but with a stutter. His fingers, though I suppose it was his mind, had an affliction, a stammer. He worked over a year or more of visits on the opening movement of Beethoven's Pathetic sonata: and it was when the runs were really flowing that the helpless repetitions began. It was as if the music was an inner tube which had suddenly developed a weak patch, and was ballooning. Heard again and again these elated splutters were deeply irritating, but we felt unable to protest. And that was because of something deeply, dismayingly sweet in Nat himself, of which his elaborate courtesy was part. I'd look at him across the lid of the piano and he'd bite at his lip and smile, though it was really a huge rictus, the grimace of a man putting as good a face as possible on the fact that he was clinging to a cliff edge.

It was like that in his conversation, too. There was always a desperation in it, whatever he was saying: but there were also pockets of plain craziness. He was at the mercy of wild theories of every sort: and had a deep love of the untenable. 'You see, Teddy' – he had picked up Kate's name for me – 'the conjunction of the stars is against it. I shall stay put. I shall not be tempted to stir from the house until a planetary analysis provides the all clear. You follow me?' And there'd be that excessive smile. He spoke always as from a position intellectually unassailable: crisp, professorial. These other kinds of stammer would appear without warning in the course of his fairly ordinary talk. And there were reports of expeditions he'd made, to visit necromancers largely in seaside resorts: astrologers, fortune tellers. On other occasions he'd touch me on the brow with courteous fingers. 'Can you feel that little bump, Teddy? That's the origin of your verbalism.' Huge smile for Kate. 'The female cranium, of course, exhibits interesting differences. I haven't got round to that, yet.'

For a long time it seemed to us that a clever mind had been undercultivated, and was taking a bewildered revenge. His parents were elderly, and had had little sympathy for his awkward bunch of passions: music,

73

language, bits and pieces of several sciences. They'd quarrelled with him throughout his adolescence, dissatisfied with this odd creature, most belated of several sons: and he'd fled more than once from home, taking refuge for some months, when he was twenty or so, with a young woman in Notting Hill, West Indian, with a small daughter. Of that relationship we caught only glimpses, in Nat's reference to the little girl, whom he adored, and who was subject to his mania for teaching. He taught her bits of music and language and science, and we could imagine how the stutter of it, from one topic to another, must have bemused the child, whilst she'd have been fascinated by that mysterious sweetness that was as plain in Nat as if it had been the most ordinary quality in the world. Of the woman he spoke less, and usually distractedly, in terms of suffocating claims made upon him, or of his agonised rebellion against his need of her. He'd leave on his way to visit her as someone might set out on a dangerous mission.

But then, as we increasingly understood, there was as time went on a smaller and smaller area of life that did not represent danger to Nat. I look back and see that the charming boy we knew, who became the attractive odd young man, was moment by moment having the security bled out of him. It became clear that he was playing a desperate game in the matter of where he might live. There was Notting Hill, there were other places with other women, there were the homes of a little network of friends and the friends of friends. Like a revolutionary or terrorist, anxious for the safety of his cell, he kept the existence of most of these a secret from the others. Real quarrels and abrasions must have made some of these homes impossible for him, for a while: but so, I now know, must have imagined sequences of prohibitions and taboos. Voices within him would forbid him to visit the Cotswolds: he would pick up, out of the air, warnings of the conversion of old steady allies into new steady enemies. In the midst of one such desperation he appeared with all his music, Beethoven, Bach, Mozart, Brahms, and deposited it with us. 'Convenience! Convenience, Teddy! A sort of convenience, a sort of ... It will make things easier *all round* if for a month or two ... You follow me?' The smile, now not much like a smile. On another occasion he housed an unexplained suitcase with us, secured with straps and rope, monstrously heavy: but this was withdrawn from our care almost at once. 'It seems ... not quite the right place for it, not quite! You understand me, Teddy? An astrologer I know in Shanklin ...'

Then he vanished, became a rumour, ceased to be that. He was added to the growing list of friends or acquaintances we felt guilty about, those we somehow didn't get round to seeing, or to making effective inquiries about. Life was this drama with a cast of thousands, and thousands of the thousands disappeared in what for us, with our illusion of being centre stage, were the wings. I was struck by a variation of this image once when I'd spent an evening with my oldest friend Ben Fletcher, and thought we might well have been characters out of two startlingly different plays: *Seven Against Thebes*, say, and *Rookery Nook*.

I was at Bush House when Kate phoned, saying there was something she must prepare me for. There'd been a ring at the door and she'd found a derelict man standing there. Encrusted with dirt, he had a sunken face and broken teeth. He stank. Out of mere alarm she'd almost closed the door again, but then something, perhaps the faintest element of an exaggerated smile, told her it was Nat. And he was in the living room now, and not smiling. 'I keep smiling,' said Kate. 'Well, it's all I can think of doing. But he glares at me. Sometimes there's a little bit of a smile – a surprised smile – he seems surprised, from some great distance. But then he glares again. I would be glad to have you here.'

So I went home, at once. He was worse than Kate's description had prepared me for: as if someone had taken

75

the Nat we'd known and thrown him against a wall, battered him with bricks, rolled him in garbage, and starved him. The alternation of the little smile and the hard blank glare was horrible: the smile seeming to belong in its minimal way to a Nat who most faintly remembered there had been other times, another way of being alive. It was like the very last glimmerings of a torch bulb.

He was on police bail, he said. He'd incautiously bought a pair of second-hand trousers, and these had behaved as trained by their previous owner, so that cheeses from a supermarket, unpaid for, had found their way into the pockets. At the same time he was being hunted down by two men from his local psychiatric hospital, who had the gift of being everywhere. They had vowed that if ever there was a Catholic in the hospital they would blow it up. Did Nat need to point out to us the connection with the IRA? Did he need to remind us that he was a Catholic? There followed a crazy rattle of words about astrology, uttered in a flat echo of his old crispness. We tried to talk about the past, and friends we had in common: there were great holes in his memory, so that he remembered some, but of others had no memory at all. He recalled our son Dan, but not our son Tom. He smoked endlessly, sitting on a couch, rolling his own cigarettes. He'd been accused, he said, of being an arsonist, a fire-raiser: he laughed in a fashion from which all amusement was absent, and drops of burning tobacco fell everywhere about him. He asked for paper and, dividing each sheet into squares, began sketching out his forward plans. Tomorrow, at the ripest time, which he made out to be 11.45 a.m., he would call on Denis Healey at the House of Commons and expound the conspiracy by which he, Nat, was surrounded. 'What do you advise me to do, Teddy, about those men from the hospital? I have reason to know they're not five minutes' walk from this house, at this moment.' His glaring smile, amid sparks of falling tobacco.

We reminded him of his music. He stared at it, unre-

76

cognisingly. Then he turned to the Pathetic and attempted the first page. That was terrifying: for the music swept forward, and swept back again, he turned his doubts into shrieking ornament: plain mistakes did not make him pause, but were repeated, over and over, turned into traps of sound.

Friends were coming to stay, next day. Kate had made the house tidy for the occasion. Nat's boots had weeks of mud on them, and wretchedly Kate went round laying down newspaper. 'It's terrible to have to do this, I hate myself,' she said, 'but I can't do all that work again.' It was a busy time, and there in the middle of things was this wreckage. He rang friends who lived ten miles to the north of us, ignoring his own view that the stars required that he do this at 7.22: but they could not take him.

In despair, and fearing there might be violence in him, I rang his mother. 'Oh God! Oh my God!' she cried. 'How is Kate? Is she bearing up?' *Of course* he could be violent. She had heard that he'd refused the injections prescribed for him. He certainly had been a cause of fires. 'You must call the police!' I returned to the living room. 'I don't need to sleep, you know,' said Nat. 'Take a look at this.' He held out a hand. 'This bump between finger and thumb? Thanks to that, I haven't had to sleep for nearly three years.'

I rang a friend, a psychologist. 'You *must* call the police,' he said. 'If he has not taken his injections ... You *can't* pass the night with him in the house. Believe me, the police will know what to do. Ask them to bring a doctor. You can always go and see him tomorrow and explain why you had to do it.' I felt a traitor, but did not see how it was possible to spend the night thinking of those flying sparks, and of the flat wildness in Nat's eye. So I rang the police, and they said if he'd never been committed into care there was nothing they could do: they'd come if he behaved dangerously. Nat said: 'Do you think Healey is the man to go to, Teddy? Or should I see the Prime Minister?' He looked with hatred round the room, with hatred at Kate, with hatred at me. Perhaps that wasn't what it was, but it was an expression you'd have difficulty in distinguishing from hatred. I tried to imagine how he really felt, into what habit of tinder-dry animosity his terrors had driven him. I felt that with that ever-falling burning ash it might be himself he'd set alight, the stuff inside him so ready for the fire. He might attack Kate simply because he could not sustain the effort to distinguish the dangerous from the safe. He must be close, anyway, to not knowing the difference between them.

We persuaded him into a bedroom, and then, with this continuing sense of shame, locked ourselves into our own. We heard him up and down the stairs: we imagined fire: somehow, we fell asleep. And in the morning, he was in bed, like someone who'd been bundled up in bedclothes by someone else, a dead bundle: I was glad to find him breathing. Kate and I had both to be out that day – the visitors weren't coming till the late afternoon: it was not possible to leave Nat in the house. I found him, at his request, a razor: he appeared with his face, the collar of his shirt, lavishly bloodied. And so we drove him to the station in Barton, and left him to make his way to the House of Commons, to Denis Healey or Margaret Thatcher.

It was like abandoning a lost, bewildered child. He stared at me as I said goodbye, the trace of an old smile on his face, not knowing what to do with itself. Nothing in him knew what to do with itself. If we had put aside every plan we had ... If we had attempted suddenly to acquire impossible nursing skills...

I found myself patting his cheek, helplessly. But he wasn't, officially, a child, he wasn't officially defined at all in terms of care: and there was nothing to be done.

He'd had with him two soft bags and some papers. Kate said he'd suddenly cried, before we left the house: 'I don't know how I shall carry all this!' And she knew he was talking of the bags and papers, but that what he was really talking of was the intolerable jumble of things in his tormented mind.

12

Everyone was under stress, I was sure: and George Straker as much as the rest. All the same, I was made angry by his reported response to the story of Nat's visit. He too had known Nat as a boy, and was cool about him. To George this was a simple story of someone who did not pursue his studies with diligence. 'Music,' George would say. 'Science. Thought a lot of himself when it came to French ...' 'He was *very good* at French!' 'Neither here nor there. A lack of system.' Told of Nat's terrifying decay, George restated his case that it was all fundamentally due to inattention in class, and to allowing his head to become a free house for ideas. 'One must decide where the main thrust will be.' Nat could have been saved from schizophrenia by a course of ... management studies.

The main thrust in local affairs, George thought, should be in the direction of permitting the erection of a vast Do It Yourself emporium on Barton's last green hill. The hill had remained green because for decades it had been supposed that a great ring road would pass through it. But ideas for great ring roads had been supplanted by ideas for greater ring roads, which lately had given way to the idea for, and then the realisation of, the greatest ring road of all: and Barton's accidental grassy summit was now at risk. Some of us wanted to preserve it as a green stud in the Green Belt. George, who in his youth had hoped Le Corbusier might be persuaded to reconstruct Barton, replacing my father's house and many like it with white towers, and turning the spaces between the towers into greennesses, now wanted greenness to go, in the interests of national revival. If Britain were to cease to be the home of permissiveness and strikes, then it must grit its late-

79

twentieth-century teeth and build DIY emporia in every remaining meadow. George said he didn't expect to have me on his side. After all, I was the helplessly (and unhelp-fully) nostalgic person who'd objected so strongly to that cheerful modernisation that had permitted the Red Lion to stride towards the twenty-first century. And so on.

He stared at me when I asked him if he remembered the sportsdays Tom Foster had held year after year, in the twenties and into the thirties, on that last of Barton's green hills. George had difficulty in remembering Tom Foster himself, that king of greengrocers whose shop in Barton High Street had been a work of sculpture in fruit. 'Now-adays, George,' I said, rashly, 'you could put Tom Foster's shop as it was on a Saturday night straight into the Tate Gallery and it would be recognised as a typical and great twentieth-century work of art.' 'If you want me to think admiringly of this ... shop,' said George, with unusual verve, 'you're going the wrong way about it.' 'Oh George,' I said. 'I despair of you. How could any Bartonian of our years forget Tom Foster?'

The fact is that Tom didn't think himself responsible only for Barton's vegetables and fruit: he was also mindful of its general entertainment, and on a Saturday in August would invite us all to that green brow of the town to take part in and witness his Great Sportsday. Anyone could compete, on the delirious basis of his having filled in a form, or forms, in Foster's shop at any time during a month or so before the Day itself. The shop was not really made for the orderly reception and filing of such forms, and it was obvious that some were hurriedly snatched up to wrap celery or rhubarb: so that a feature of the Sports, of which Tom Foster might well have made a popular official item, was the absolutely continuous argument about who was taking part and who wasn't. (Having begun life as a member of Fred Karno's troupe of vaudeville actors, alongside the young Charlie Chaplin, Tom Foster called everything in his Sportsday, as he called everything

80

in his shop, Grand, Splendid, Sensational. To the Amazing Three-Legged Race he could well have added the World-Beating Entry-Form Shindig.) In the end, and on the whole, everyone ran, or jumped, or hopped, who wanted to do so. This sometimes meant that very large children made a clean, or shady, sweep of prizes intended for very small ones, and fathers were to be seen squaring up to fathers. Not all of those who took part in the Grandparents' Race (or Grand Grandparents' Race, as I think it was called) had a plausible appearance of being a grandparent. In the Flappers' Furlong, which was obviously Tom's own favourite race as it was mine – it was designed to lead frankly to the bouncing of breasts and the damnably brief baring of thighs, and produced a great giggling hush throughout the field – not every competitor was under twenty-five, as it was vaguely held that the rules required. I remember the not entirely credulous excitement I felt when this race was run: it was linked in my mind with moments at Christmas, when my aunts made much, among my uncles, of the festive shortcomings of their dresses, and there was an enormous undercurrent of feeling about knees. I guess what was registered by the small boy I was, there on the top of Barton's last green hill, was a final flicker of a deeply innocent form of public entertainment, hand-made, naive, able to exist alongside the silent cinema but with not much longer to go.

Well, a few years before, and indeed five days before my parents were married, it was a Bank Holiday: and the copy of the *Barton Press* in which the wedding was reported ('The bride was attired in pale grey crêpe-de-chine, with veil and wreath of orange blossom, and carried a bouquet of white and pink carnations'), contained an account of that other occasion, Whit Monday. It was written in a prose that, for its successful attempt to be enjoyable, would cause modern local journalism to blush with embarrassment.

'Glorious weather,' it read, in a single solid paragraph,

'prevailed throughout the Whitsuntide. Barton was never more full of visitors than on Monday. If thousands left London for the seaside, thousands left London also for the Northern Heights. There was a continuous and ever-swelling influx throughout the morning and afternoon. Barton Fair never drew a larger crowd than was seen in the town on Monday. Incoming trams, which ran every two or three minutes, from Moorgate, Holborn, Euston Road and Cricklewood, were packed. Frequently there was a line of cars stretching from the top of the hill to the terminus, each car waiting to reach its destination to unload. Buses were laden, while the local railway traffic was the heaviest in years past. Not a few of the visitors, chiefly young people, came on foot. The latter included a number of Boy Scouts and Girl Guides, who spent the day on the outskirts of the town. All day also there was a constant stream of motor traffic through the town. Between eleven and twelve in the morning over three hundred cars and motor bicycles passed the Parish Church. Most of the visitors, who numbered many thousands, made for Barley Woods, which were crowded. Local tradesmen who were open for the day did a roaring business, and had a harvest. People paid without a murmur anything they were charged. They were only too glad to get their wants supplied. Caterers were bombarded, and although they made special provision they sold out, many of them, long before the evening arrived. Quite a number of private residents shared in the prosperity. They provided teas and were well rewarded for their enterprise. Towards evening the town became somewhat lively. There was very little actual drunkenness, but many were near the border line. Women were as conspicuous as men. The hilarious were chiefly of the 'Arry and 'Arriet type. They were not quarrelsome, and gave little or no trouble. The rush for the trams and trains in the evening was unprecedented. For hours there was a long queue of people at the tram terminus. Such a sight was never before witnessed in Barton. It was eleven o'clock before the town assumed its normal quietness.'

I think, reading that, how much longer ago it was than seventy years. In the same way, Tom Foster's Great Sportsdays, as I knew them, were centuries ago, ultimate saturnalia: providing one of the two or three occasions during the year when the town broke out of the shell of that normal quietness, and came close to a sort of civic bawdry. I certainly had the feeling that, given only a little more licence, I might have retired to some green corner with my love, Jean Rawlins, and joined with her in exceeding all the bounds of propriety: which I thought of as being permitted to place an apologetic hand on one or other, but not both, of her knees. (My experience with my aunts and uncle had convinced me that what all the lowering of voices and the flushing and blushing was about was knees.)

The crowning event of Tom Foster's Great Sportsday followed from his having, when he left Fred Karno, been a Covent Garden porter. At a snap of the Great Greengrocer's fingers, as I admiringly saw it, porters arrived from all over, complete with their plaited baskets, and ran the Great Covent Garden Porters' Basket Race. With towers on their heads they triumphantly tottered rather than ran, wonderful plaited giants, from one end of the heaven of that green field to the other, and all those private residents of Barton, turned for the day into blatantly public residents, shouted with excitement. They did not really know, among so many unfamiliar figures, whom to support: but a general passion soon developed for one tower rather than others, and, carefully hurrah-ed along the track, the favourite tower always won.

Or perhaps I imagine it did; thinking back to a day so intrinsically distant that I can't believe it has anything to do with me, and that seemed to offer what I'm sure Tom Foster knew he was offering: every event, itself ideal, being ideally consummated.

Bluntly, and even faced by the dominant Britain of the eighties in the form of George Straker, I did not believe that the site of such old felicities should be taken over by a building, the fifth or sixth of the kind in the district (for all George's claims to business soundness, I wondered how any neighbourhood could support so many giant providers of the means of doing it oneself), that in the grudgingly exhibited plans had all the appearance of a vastly magnified pudding basin in fashionable liverish brick, with a roof like a hat enormously too large for the head it covered.

13

'You're beginning to look like a hamster,' said my father in the shaving mirror. It seemed an extreme comment on this ... slight new pouchiness. 'Pity about your mouth. It's all ... closing in, you see. Makes you look very grim.' His unfriendly laugh. 'Wouldn't care to meet you in a dark alley.'

I'd thought recently sitting in a crowded Tube train how the weight of what one was came down on the mouth. It was a hole that took a strain bearing down from all parts of a man's or woman's features. Sometimes it was forced wholly downwards by the pressure and became part of a mask not so much of tragedy as of a fixed absence of amusement. When we'd had our house underpinned, after the hot summer of 1976, I'd thought how like houses our faces were. 'Once you build a house,' a jovial architect had informed us (he'd just built us one), 'it begins to fall down.' Create a face, and it began to cave in. The mouth constituted a grave weakness in the structure. I was fascinated by the loose, easy, full mouths of the young.

Teeth were, on the whole, a fault in the design. They – or the absence of my original teeth – were responsible for my mouth closing in. For many, not strong enough: for most, not long-lasting enough. It was taken for granted

84

that the teeth in my family were doomed. My mother's
had barely lasted until my birth. Her misadventures with
her false teeth were features of my childhood. She had hit
upon a quite spectacular use of them to punctuate her
thoughts: she'd cause the top plate to shoot out of her
mouth and remain there for several seconds before being
reclaimed. I still think of it as if it were one of the natural,
and not necessarily undignified, ways of saying: I'm
worried. Almost continuously worried throughout the
1920s and 1930s, she shot her teeth out frequently. On
one occasion, being sick, she lost them down the lavatory.
After that, whenever she was sick (and that seemed rather
often: perhaps it was another consequence of worry), my
father would shout up the stairs: *'Mind your teeth!'* My
own teeth showed an early inclination not to accompany
me far along the way. About 1930 I was taken after a
weekend of agony to have a tooth out: it was my mother,
who, at the door of the surgery, fainted. I didn't like my
mother fainting, but she did it in a manner that caused
discussion – in a split second she was transformed from
a small anxious woman holding my hand into a small
unconscious woman lying with her usual neatness flat on
the floor – and the mere interest and mild fame of it helped
me when it came to the after-effects of ulceration. My
youth was full of teeth splintering. I dream even now of
having a mouthful of decrepit daggers. Well, my parents
could not afford preventive dentistry. Much of the larger
labour of demolition was carried out by a dentist famous
among his resigned clientele for being, mostly, drunk.
This had led to poor circulation, so that in the middle of
an extraction he would leave you and stump from his
surgery down a flight of stairs and, after a pause, back
again. It was believed that the pause was for yet another
intake of whisky. Once when I was under gas the device
inserted between your jaws to keep your mouth open had
been allowed to slip, and it had dug a deep hole for itself.
Mortality was at work so early in my mouth that when I

faced some of my first practice lessons in merciless London schools it was with a handicap for which my education tutor had no answer: I had only one tooth in my lower jaw, the plate not yet being ready, and as I set out to impress difficult classes with my serious worth as a teacher, the attempt was brought methodically to nothing by the solo antics of this tooth. It was no good: on the stage of my lower jaw, there was this clown, capering.

'Saw Fred Astaire on television last night,' I'd remark to my father in the mirror. 'He looks more like a hamster than I do.' I knew my father wouldn't believe that. He'd not quite survived into the age when television began to look back on the heroes and heroines of films made in his prime, moving, from one shot to the next, from yesterday's smooth beauty or handsomeness to today's crumpled collapse. It was, I thought, more shocking than the skull on desk or table with which earlier ages had attempted to remind themselves of mortality. Watching such retrospectives, I thought of the graphics in films about the development of the planet that showed the continents detaching themselves from a single great squash of land. Except that the history of the human figure seemed to reverse that movement: the clearly articulated continents of the body fell together, vast planetary rheumatisms made the head sink, the arms shrink, and, where there'd been spritely separations, brought about dismal mergers.

I remembered, when it came to my father's comments on the effects of age, how, nearly sixty years ago, he'd said of Lady Gobstopper that she was worse than a hamster: 'A shrivelled old rat,' he said. Her name wasn't really Gobstopper: that had been conferred upon her by the children of the town, she being the widow of one of two knighted confectioners who happened to live locally. She was certainly the last Bartonian to go shopping in horse and carriage. She wore black: the horses were black: the carriage was black. Some of the children, myself included, who'd contributed to her fortune by committing part of

86

theirs to the purchase of sherbet dabs and miles of ribbon-like, vile-tasting and much-loved toffee, would escort her carriage up and down the High Street, making disrespectful remarks and keeping out of touch of the tip of the coachman's whip. I see her still, in her black wrappings, someone who'd accepted mummification whilst still alive: having a choice of joints brought out to her from Friday's, the butchers: or, for me more excitingly, being offered by the manager of Sainsbury's a review of cheeses: he'd be on the pavement, lifting a tray for Lady Gobstopper's inspection, and I'd know that behind him, in the shop, my aunt Barbara was busy at the butter counter, working wonders with her butter pats. I have a memory of being forbidden the shop at one point, having invited too many of my schoolfriends to enter simply to stand and observe my aunt at her lightning work. She could, at her best, cut you off a quarter of a pound of butter with one exact blow of her wooden pats, bright with the water into which she dipped them between one operation and the next, and she never needed more than a flake or two to make up the amount.

Now Aunt Barbara herself – who in the 1920s I'd thought of as a queen of butter – was older than Lady Gobstopper had been then: and, poor woman, had not only false teeth, but false hips and false knees. My father would not have believed that, either – that so much of his original sister would have vanished.

But there, in the studio at Bush House, was one of the country's best lexicographers, not a wrinkle, not a pouch, her teeth surely her own. She looked so like Mary Queen of Scots that whenever she arrived after the birth of a new edition or a reduction or expansion of her dictionary, I felt I should not so much interview as execute her. And that was in the week when I'd made the acquaintance of an even less wrinkled arrival: my second grandson. Again I'd forgotten that babies were so small. Well, they were infinitesimal. I'd not remembered how tiny weathers

87

flickered across their faces, satisfactions and sorrows each no more than a split second long. I'd forgotten how rigid they became when filled with milk, their arms stiff at their sides, not so much asleep as in a petrified trance: you could pick them up and wave them round your head and they'd remain as stiff as frozen banners.

Becoming a grandfather for the second time reminded me in an odd way of going into paperback: or receiving a repeat fee for a broadcast recorded long ago. Something about having a deeply pleasant reward that was related to some extremely distant original labour.

It must be difficult, I thought, to be such an apologetic practitioner of medicine. Mr Baynes, the consultant surgeon, had completed his examination. Gently he had recommended the removal of the cyst by a small instant operation. It would be sucked away by his syringe, but might well return. Almost certainly benign, but they'd know about that in a day or two. I thought he looked almost certainly benign, too, but called myself to order: you didn't practise in this field without severity entering in. And indeed he was sternly mild. The syringe appeared to be summoning reluctant fluids from various parts of my body: it was like being pierced by half a dozen drills from inside, outwards. I followed an almost lifelong practice when having to fortify myself against pain by shouting at him as if he were Brian Green, who nearly sixty years ago had brought his gang, really a juvenile army, into action against me in the Barley Road playground for being a rival for the love (worthless, as it turned out) of Jean Rawlins. 'Oh my God! – Brian Green, you swine! – I'm sorry, Mr Baynes! It makes it easier! Brian Green was a – Ow! That will do, you rotter!' Even if I had called him by his own name, said Mr Baynes, he would not have minded. Cysts did not always submit philosophically to being dispersed.

And that *was* the cyst, he said. The literary life, now –

88

that must be very interesting! Well, I said, yes: but at the moment I was possessed by a notion of how interesting it must be to be a consultant surgeon. You came into a patient's life suddenly, reassuring or the reverse, and –

Literary occasions, he said, had often, from the outside, struck him as ... Well, interesting was a dull word, but it *was* the word. He'd seen on television a moment or two of a recent prizegiving. I'd been there, I said, and remembered it as a haze of dinner jackets. I was sitting at a table with seven Chinese writers and one English writer of science fiction. The Chinese were deeply dismayed. Much had been done to make them feel at home, but I had rarely seen people who looked more terribly abroad. They detested the food: abhorred the wine: and were horrified by the announcement of the prizewinner, made by the chairman of the judges, a novelist who swallowed his words, ducked and bowed and gobbled, and laughed at jokes only he, but perhaps not even he, had heard. I'd remembered the story told on the Greek island of Lesbos of villagers who, after centuries of isolation, spoke a baffling form of Greek, laced with a baffling form of Turkish. Two of them, it was said, once went to China. They were overheard on arrival by an astonished local citizen, who cried: 'It didn't take *them* long to learn Chinese!' But the delegation at the prizewinning dinner seemed to feel that, though he was not speaking recognisable English, the novelist was not speaking Chinese, either. Oppressed by their dejection, the writer of science fiction and I helped to drink their untouched wine. As the hearts of the Chinese grew heavier, we had grown more light-hearted.

Well, you see, said Mr Baynes, that was not the sort of thing that ever happened to a consultant surgeon. I wasn't sure if he meant that a consultant surgeon could never expect to find himself in the midst of disconsolate Chinese, or that he could never hope to have his ration of wine augmented in such a manner. Anyway, he said, this did

89

bring him to the other matter arising from the consultation. *That* perturbed him, rather. It could become ... *very nasty*. It was, alas, an irreversible condition. It was vital that I had it seen by my doctor every three or four months – or I could come to him, at rather more expense. I opted for him, not out of disrespect for my excellent Dr Smith, but because this was absolutely his field. It would be like having trouble with one's aitches, and going for treatment to a speech therapist who in his professional life had had no truck with any other letter of the alphabet.

In fact, I'd gone only reluctantly to Dr Smith, who'd sent me on to Mr Baynes. I'd always been slow to go to doctors: doing merely that, let alone being investigated and treated, was time-consuming: and much that might drive one to the surgery was of a nature that defied definition. How to begin to describe some of the causes of one's unease? And many disorders were perfectly ludicrous, as was one that a year or so before had made me visit Dr Smith. Standing for any length of time, especially at parties, I was aware of a complete absence of sensation between my right thigh and my knee. It was as if this stretch of myself had been cancelled. I had not known till then how painful and disturbing such a mere blankness might be. I began to be woken in the night by this missing upper leg.

Dr Smith confirmed what I'd already confirmed for myself, that this section of my body was still in place. 'You know,' I said, 'that I wouldn't trouble you if it weren't that, too often, I very uncomfortably lack that bit of leg.' She said: 'Well, of course, something must be done about it if it goes on. But if I sent you to the hospital, it would be the beginning of a long process of inquiry. I know you're busy. You may find this an odd thing for a doctor to say, but I have concluded that, in our journey to the grave, many things happen to us, very odd things, sometimes very alarming things, and most of them come to nothing.' I looked back over the alarms of a lifetime and saw the sense of that. 'I like it as an idea,' I said. 'Though I don't suppose it would cheer anyone standing on the scaffold.' She wrote out an agreeable prescription, and I went away reflecting that simply to have seen the doctor was a kind of cure.

At our next party, I had no upper right leg, but found myself resting fairly comfortably on Dr Smith's philosophy, if that's what it was.

Mr Baynes said now that since I'd asked what they'd do if things went wrong, he had to say they'd begin by performing a biopsy. That was biopsy, not autopsy. It was, of course, surgically, a difficult site. Sorry about that. You'd have thought, so personal was his regret, that he had the guilty knowledge of having invented this disorder of mine, which had a name like a Greek island.

It seemed, I thought, an extraordinary thing to be talking about on a Tuesday afternoon: though when I put it like that, I had to say I didn't know what day of the week would be better for it.

I sank into frightened gloom. It seemed that for the rest of my life I was to stand in the place of execution, knowing that the warrant might be acted on at any moment. I would have to say, wherever I went: 'Sorry about these chaps hanging about ... they're the firing squad...' I was doomed to feel permanently unsafe. Of course, this was merely a case of a specific absence of safety, as compared with the general absence of safety with which all men and women are familiar. But this situation made it clear to me that the fact that we never cease to be in peril is always endurable if a precise cause of peril has not appeared. Mr Baynes had made my peril apologetically plain.

And there was the threat to Kate – to her happiness. In the midst of our pleasant days, what a dismal note to introduce! I'd always thought of disaster and bad news in these terms: as obliging one to be a spoilsport.

It was all right to go to New Zealand? I asked absurdly. Oh, of course, said Mr Baynes. There you were! Another demonstration of the superiority of the literary life over the medical. While I amused myself – and others, of course – halfway round the globe, he would be continuing to ply his mundane syringe on the outskirts of Barton.

Oh such an absurdity of phrases I found in my mind, at this time! For example: 'I came in writing, and I will go out writing!' This was not even based on a truth: I'd not begun to write until Miss Stout proposed the outlines of a method at Mabel Street School, in 1925. I mentioned the phrase to a friend, saying that if the condition were fatally to develop, I'd at least use the process as copy. 'Been done,' said my friend. 'You couldn't write about it as well as James Cameron.' And I was wryly amused to observe that, much though I admired the valiant and terminally amused piece that vivid man had written for publication after his death, I felt the irritation any writer must feel at any time, being informed that a topic has been triumphantly disposed of by someone else.

Rufus was, as always, one of my best advisers. 'Play loud music,' he urged. 'Wagner! Or the end of the Seventh!' I played Richard Strauss. It helped because there is a defiance about loud music. Accompanied by trumpets and drums, any of us might be emboldened to go anywhere, however perilous.

On the brink of our journey to New Zealand, we had a summons from George Straker. 'Come and put me in the picture', he said. And I felt for a moment as if, actually commissioned to paint some great group portrait of our acquaintances, I'd furtively allowed George to drop off the canvas. 'We hear you have plans and would like to know something about them,' he said.

I was always aware of George's view, only just submerged, that being a writer laid me heavily under suspicion. He'd have been happier, I think, if I'd been required every other day to report at the local police station. The offence was one that a series even of Tory Home Secretaries had failed in their duty of defining. If the definition had been sought from George, he'd have started with the close resemblance of writing to vagabondage. 'You've been drifting in and out of Broadcasting House, I suppose,' he'd say, as if to hint that I shouldn't think I'd always get away with that: and with a strong stress on the word 'drifting'. 'You're writing a book?' he once asked. 'I imagine you will be glad when that is in your publisher's hands.' It clearly was not the sort of thing that should remain in the writer's hands longer than absolutely necessary. 'How long will it take him to knock it into shape?' I replied, smiling with difficulty, that knocking it into shape was my function, not his. 'An odd task, making sense of other people's manuscripts,' said George: and began, with no implication of *non sequitur*, to bemoan the low level of literacy among secretaries employed by his firm. 'But I won't, like some, grin and bear it. The girls are paid quite enough for us to expect decent performance. A couple of major errors, at most, and she's out, as far as I'm concerned.' We were clearly still talking about the quality of my manuscripts. 'I suppose you drift about the house wondering how to fill that blank piece of paper in the typewriter?' The word 'drift', again. 'I don't go in for blank pieces of paper, George,' I said. 'Something must be written, from the moment you sit down: once you've got words on the page, you're in business.' 'From the moment you sit down,' George murmured. It was clearly a significant confession on my part, probably inadvertent: that I sat down. I couldn't see how even George could suppose writers commonly worked at their trade whilst standing, but I suppose he saw some kind of slipshodness in it.

And then, as my fists were clenching, the other George would slip into his skin. 'Don't let me forget to show you

93

my latest toy in the kitchen. Oh look, come and taste some of the bread I've made, to quite a new recipe. Will you?' He'd be bright, suddenly, and funny. And it would strike me that it all had its roots in school, long ago. George suspected me then, as he suspected me now, of enjoying myself. It was why we had a respite from the uneasiness between us whenever he could show me some kitchen triumph: for in the kitchen it was George who enjoyed himself.

But this evening he was at his sternest. New Zealand? 'It is not,' he said, laughing briefly, 'high on my list of priorities.' Patently never having visited it, he could not claim to know every inch of it. But if he could not adopt the strong position of knowing everything about a place, George was still able to adopt the strong position of not thinking it worthwhile to know anything about it at all. 'It's not a place they can tempt me to visit,' he said, suggesting a considerable campaign to bring about that end.

And then, as though we'd showed signs of expecting to be thrilled as never before: 'It's not the most exciting country in the world, you know!'

PART TWO

1

What we were really up to, I thought, was flying twelve thousand miles to attend a Thistle Do in Dunedin. The Mayor's invitation had arrived in a small parcel of such proposals, most of which required us to make choices. On this or that evening, on one or other of those islands fallen so recently into the hands of the organisers of Thistle Dos, would we prefer to eat in an authentically Italian fashion, or an indisputably Chinese one, or in some other mode described as Traditional? What would our decision be as between simultaneous receptions, demonstrations of library machinery, parties lit by candle or by moonlight or, it might be, not lit at all? It was a long way, as Kate observed in the flying garbage dump in which we were hissing across the world, from the journeys of Captain Cook. *He* could never have imagined that his temerities would end with Kate and me hopping over from one day to the next in order to be present at an oyster supper.

Well, garbage dump. I was impressed again by the thought that eating in an aeroplane was much like eating inside a dustbin. There was all that unpackaging of meals, in a crazily limited space: so that before a first mouthful could be taken, I'd be trying to make sense of little heaps of cellophane, plastic lids, small envelopes ripped open in the expectation of salt but yielding pepper, or sugar. Plastic knives and spoons would fall to the floor. Beginning to .eat, I would also begin the work of imposing plane stains upon myself. Whatever I did with the tiny paper napkin, huge areas of my clothing were left as targets for coffee, mayonnaise, gravy, amazing sprays of milk or cream. The debris would be collected in time to allow for a new meal, as cunningly packaged, to be served. Once again I would become my own inept dustman. Where Captain Cook had been becalmed for days, and scurvy had taken its toll, we made the effortless transition from breakfast to supper, and thought nothing at all of the Indian Ocean by reason of being at lunch as we passed over it.

An absurd and perhaps psychologically dangerous way of spending twenty-four hours, flying from London to Sydney in a single gulp. Actually, a gulp with three acts to it. Twice on our everlasting way we had new crews, and thought we should have been replaced ourselves. There was a touch of the Flying Dutchman about it. How many skippers and bosuns were there on *that* eternal voyage?

With seats near a galley, we became enormously accustomed to each cabin crew. We noted the growth of flirtatiousness as between stewards and passengers: the stewards becoming more and more skittish, and growing numbers of young women being observed in the galleys, fingering their dresses, hitching shoulder straps, giggling late into what might, or might not, have been the night. Lights were lowered, and restored; films were shown, flickering fantasies added to the general fantasy of our being seven miles above the earth, a large number of people accidentally brought together, with an accidental servants' hall thrown in. I thought Chekhov might have made something of it, this three-act experience, with domestics deferentially insolent, relationships so deep and shallow at once.

There was the enormous longing to take a bath: to walk vigorously, a mile or so: to stretch out, spreadeagled. I became aware again of the need I had, a growing need, to vary my situation, my posture, simply in order to redistribute the furious contents of my head. As we age, I thought, the mind becomes an increasingly irritable trapped insect: at times it is barely endurable that we contain this huge buzz of consciousness, all these memories and half-memories, thoughts and half-thoughts, this tumult of connections fitfully made, or half-made. On that aeroplane, on so long a journey, in the midst of the paradox of travelling so far without appearing to travel at all, tormented by meals, swollen of feet, uncertain of time and place, we were close to agony . . .

And this great stillness was Sydney, old friends, a bed, a day slept away, convalescent talking under a night sky in which all the stars were in disarray.

2

Well, it wasn't home: but I did have this curious feeling of having travelled twelve thousand miles in order to step round the corner. 'Our national dish is fush and chuts,' said our first morning's host. He sat in his office in the university in Auckland: outside the window, bumping decorously over the sleeping policemen, British motorcars went past. It was as if, on some cricket field in the 1980s, one should see Hobbs and Sutcliffe going out to open an innings, closely followed by Wally Hammond. Here were cars from the days when the British made cars recognisably British, most gleamingly preserved. There were half-forgotten Sunbeams, even a totally forgotten Trojan. 'Fush and chuts,' he said, 'is of course, fish and chips.' He'd been pleased to be mistaken for an Englishman. Actually, I'd thought he might be Irish: he had something of the style of my old teacher, Logan – a habit of amusement. He was instructing me now in the mysteries of local pronunciation. The statement 'Ear sick horse' should be understood as 'Yes, of course'. 'I hut hum' was 'I hit him'. As to road signs, GIVE WAY TO PEDS was found ambiguous by newcomers: especially when the sign appeared on the university campus, where PEDS was widely and sometimes seriously taken to mean PEDANTS. And if we ran into local talk about the Nippon-clippon, that was a Japanese-made extension to a bridge over the harbour, built too narrow. Auckland was ill-fated in that sort of respect, he said, things being invariably either too small or too huge. The city itself simply covered an area ridiculously too large. Indifferent to space, it had spread in every direction, to find itself one of the world's most diffuse cities, in which you could drive for days – well, he exaggerated, but not much – to spend an evening with a friend.

We'd been talking all morning, developing what I thought was the sort of closeness that occurs between schoolboys: we were near to giggling, and at any moment might begin throwing things. I remembered the lessons our headmaster, Percy Chew, was always late for: and how hilarity would build up in us, fatally, so that his arrival always coincided with Reg Wheatfill doing his dance, with a display of sock suspenders. Percy Chew would be astounded and appalled, and we would be astounded and appalled, and there would be condign punishments, and grief: and it happened week after week. I could feel the same dangerous amusement growing in this office now. On the shelves were bound copies of university theses, and I tried to keep my eyes off their titles, which invited jokes. It was difficult. THE OPINIONS OF SELECTED SIXTH FORMERS ON GOD, I couldn't help noting. We thought of the counter-thesis, THE OPINIONS OF GOD ON SELECTED SIXTH FORMERS. My host gave way just in time to a journalist, who wanted to know how such a well-known and busy figure, whose name at various moments in the interview he had difficulty in recalling, had been able to spare time to visit New Zealand. The idea that to do this amounted to an act of selfless generosity had not occurred to me, and I had difficulty in producing a sensible answer. Well, I'd come because I'd come because I'd come. It was wonderful to be given an opportunity to go almost anywhere. I'd always wanted to be at this end of the atlas. There'd been that business, in my earliest brushes with geography, of Great Britain being on page 1 and New Zealand being on page 56 – very beautiful, I always thought it, two bone-shapes floating in the sea. Great Britain was clearly huge and accounted for much of the earth's surface, and New Zealand wasn't and didn't. The world was divided into pages. When you came to New Zealand, you could go no further except into the index. It struck me, and I said now, that for small children the atlas may be a most misleading introduction to the character of the earth. I'd always, anyway, longed to make my way some time to the end of the book. As a small child besotted with adventurous fiction, I'd thought of New Zealand as a sort of coral island – better still, two coral islands-ripe for being marooned on. And here I was, oh long answer, sorry, here I was happily marooned, jammed contentedly against the back cover of the atlas. It was nice to know one was leaning one's elbow against the index.

He seemed still to think it was a strange thing to do, almost as if he'd been George Straker. Was New Zealand defensive about being New Zealand?

Kate was elsewhere, being taken round the campus. Neither of us had the slightest gift for being important, in the sense in which our roles as visiting speaker and wife made it necessary to regard us as important. My own most serious passion was for apology. As evidence accumulated that this was not the most serviceable posture, I'd attempted to resist it: but with no great success. And here I was again in circumstances that called for people to acclaim me as if I was the cat's whiskers: which precipitated in me what, that first evening, facing my first audience, I found myself describing as a crisis of modesty. Forgive me, I said, I would get round to behaving importantly, but at the moment I was struck by how simple and obvious everything I had to say must seem. In fact, I was experiencing, at its worst, the sense of absurdity that often crept over me, seeing that several hundred people had given up their evening to listen to me, talking.

Kate said it picked up after that, but really I had to play along with the idea that I was worth listening to. She made new arrangements of the flowers we'd found in our hotel bedroom, meant for her, and the fruit, addressed to both, and the welcoming cards, and the little bottles of this and that, gifts from well-wishers. Though she was modest, too, Kate was determined to enjoy all this. 'All I want,' she said, 'is for you to promise that you won't actually tell them they must have better things to do.'

3

Sometimes it was a hotel, sometimes a private house. Sometimes we took a bus, sometimes we flew. Usually, before the meeting I was to address, there'd be the dinner: that kindly event in which the speaker was overfed and talked into the ground. Sometimes, on the topic to which he was to address himself, someone held forth with what seemed to him pre-emptive brilliance.

And once there was a British cultural occasion, essentially formal, polite, pleasant: great views of the harbour from high windows: delicious canapés, pressed upon us by handsome servitors, man and woman: and the most marvellous oysters. As to Britishness, there were the familiar extremes: severity, shyness: in the case of an important wife, tragic frost. *She* was an ice matron: he, by some wild marital quirk, was a steamy man, plump, a chuckler. It was a marriage of lemon sorbet with rum baba. When they entered, the evening's inclination to enjoy itself was crossed by the evening's wish to throw itself out of one of those splendid windows. I drank too much of the good white wine, and looked across at Kate, who had the gift of enjoying herself without a touch of inebriation. With my sons I wondered sometimes at such a skill as that: we were all ready to give excitement, in its efforts to surface, some assistance. Kate worried about us, having the sober person's conviction that the less sober might fall prey to any passing bus.

I talked to the warm husband, who had begun life in England, in the original Cambridge or Lichfield or Richmond ... names I'd found on the map of this far Pacific land: familiar tags for wildly unfamiliar places ... and had since made himself as much at home as he could in the world's enormous back yard. For him, New Zealand was the latest form of a variety of exile to which his family, as I gathered, had long been accustomed. They had been born in Britain only to be scattered widely, in diplomatic or mercantile roles. It seemed odd to be someone who had on the whole known Barton, and only Barton, talking to someone who had a Barton at the back of his mind (it was the Yorkshire Richmond, in fact, where he'd grown up, and to which his imagination clung), but was essentially a citizen of the world: except that what the world offered seemed to be a variety of estrangements. He was at home with estrangement, as we already felt we were becoming at home with being abroad.

There was a young Maori novelist present, with whom I talked happily about writing. Happily, that is, until I said that anything was grist to the writer's mill: he was always observant, note-taking: in John Mortimer's phrase, he was a caterpillar that devoured the leaf it was sitting on. I recalled Arnold Bennett, writing of his father's deathbed: he'd sat there, truly grieved, and also aware that, making inward notes, he would somewhere in his writing use this experience. Kate said later that at this point she looked across at us and saw a deeply attractive young man resisting something; something I'd offered that was totally unacceptable. I was aware of his sudden anger. This, he seemed to be saying, was European detachment of an appalling kind. I seemed to be replying that there could be no regional difference in the behaviour of writers. We were all, in the most intimate circumstances, makers of notes.

He flared, then was appeased. I didn't understand the change in his mood, but easily assumed that I'd offended against some deep Maori view of death. Or perhaps it was a Maori view of what was due to a father. If there were such a view, I'd certainly in my writing offended against it. On this evening in Auckland, aware only that as a writer I wished to contribute to some universal reservoir of attempted human truth, I was distressed to think that I was taken, instead, to be a cynical opportunist, ready to turn any misery to literary advantage. It was like having written a jubilantly confident essay for our English master, Williams, at the grammar school fifty years earlier, only to be confronted with some damning reason why it could not be accepted. Amid those wonderful oysters, and offered that superb view across one of the Pacific edges, an earlier enchanting blue becoming a curiously colourful black, I felt disgraced. And then, out of his pockets, he produced copies of books of mine, which he wanted me to autograph.

I made no sense, then or later, of the occasion. Maori friends said there was no intrinsic reason why he should have rebelled against my quotation of Arnold Bennett. I thought, if that was so, there could only be a fury that had no obvious roots: the true origin of the young writer's anger being perhaps in my Europeanness – and my having, on that polite official evening, claimed for us as writers a general drift that an understandably angry part of him was not willing to accept.

If it was that, I'd known it, and been hurt by it, and struggled to understand it, in Africa, in the company of African writers. It was the anger of the dispossessed, not even in the universal community of writers wishing to make common cause with a representative of the dispossessors.

4

Foolish, how long it took to adjust to slight unfamiliarities of vowel. We'd called him Jim, methodically, and he was Geoff, having asked us (we now perceived) to call him Giff. My joke about calling them Keats and Gloucester, because they seemed to have introduced themselves as Shelley and Leicester, looked inane now that we gathered their names were Shirley and Lister.

Aircraft were fine, buses that happened to take to the air, but landbound buses were better. We'd leave the No Frills Food Barn on our left, the meatworks on our right (perhaps the blander 'abattoir' was to be preferred), and head for yet another improbable landscape. It was a European eye, of course, that was struck by the idea that all landscapes here were invented: with, I thought, adhesive sheep or sloping cows, for there were sudden tiltings, not so much hills as little mishaps of land. Yes, an accidental landscape: you'd not recovered from the sensation that someone was holding a hill carelessly askew before you were in the presence, on an endless level, of more tussocks than you'd ever expected to see, knowing the tussock only as an occasional phenomenon. In New Zealand there must be a ratio of, at least, ten tussocks to one sheep: astonishing in a land drowned in sheep. WANDERING STOCK, said wayside notices. It seemed odd to be experiencing in a conveyance as ordinary as a bus these dreamlike transitions from one topographical oddity to another. The rate at which a bus travelled was closely related to the requirement that, on boarding, each passenger should answer a questionnaire covering the main details of his or her history to date. A good-natured endlessness was the character of every halt. Kate and I sat as often as possible immediately behind the driver, for the fascination of watching what he did with newspapers. These, wrapped in bundles or individually, would lie along the shelf in

105

front of him, and at points along the journey, thrilling to attempt to anticipate (and a hundred miles or more might be involved), he'd slide back a window and, with no apparent effort of reference, take a single newspaper or a bundle and hurl it out. Accustomed to *The Guardian* sliding dry and punctual through our letterbox, we were entranced by the notion of receiving the day's news by a hazardous sort of visitation. In bad weather, of the kind that in New Zealand would within seconds reduce the stoutest newspaper to pulp, did you wait for the bus, a sort of wicketkeeper? It was dry during the journeys we took, so we saw no sign of an anxiety that seemed unavoidable, if this newsdrop – or newsthrow – were not to be turned into a pulpy farce . . .

So many little towns called Public Toilets! And such a sensation of being adrift in some British gazetteer gone mad! Oxford was next door to Cambridge (or had been, until they replaced Oxford with a local Maori name). In Scotland now, you were a moment later in Wales. Blenheim was (given the prevailing wind) within spitting distance of Wakefield. It was geographical pandemonium. And under the comedy of *that*, such a sense of the worldwide absurdity of trying to tame extraordinary landscape by giving its features gently familiar names.

There'd been an attempt to backpedal on all this, offered as a gesture of reconciliation with the Maoris: but, some said and I suspected, springing in fact from an assessment of the tourist's passion for the obviously exotic. So, some Bicesters and Cirencesters and Baths had been displaced to make way for Maori names. This among liberal New Zealanders had produced, a friend told us, such an anxiety about getting the pronunciation right that she'd been bothered by the difficulty of a name glimpsed in a department store: WIREWARE, it said, and she'd struggled to do justice to the stresses (or rather, to get the Maori effect of no stresses at all) before discerning that it wasn't a Maori name, after all.

Most days were corker days as I talked my way south. The phrase was dying out, they said, but librarians seemed intent on keeping it in circulation. I ran into the ghost of Bernard Shaw, quoted as urging the New Zealanders to forget about butter: they should make or grow something no one else made or grew. They fêted him, and disregarded his advice. In his globetrotting straw hat he leaned on an umbrella and gazed at geysers, mildly challenging, as if they need not try their tricks on him. As we neared Christchurch, I thought of Samuel Butler, who in 1859 (fifty years before he was given a public dinner in London arranged by Shaw) lived three days' journey on horseback from the city, and so from any bookshop, but somehow read, and enthusiastically admired, *The Origin of the Species*, fresh from the press. He claimed once to have seen one of his bullocks on that farm near Christchurch take an eyelash out of its eye with its hindfoot: I wondered how he, strictest of notemakers, and of course rough on fathers, would have got on with the young Maori novelist in Auckland. I thought of Butler a lot, and how he'd had to do the washing-up after each meal (being, however surprisingly, a pioneer), and would do the knives first, because it might please God to take him before he came to the forks, 'and then what a sell it would have been to have done the forks rather than the knives!' We ourselves must have been the cause of a huge amount of washing-up. Kate said uneasily that they seemed to be fattening us for something. The demand that any meal should be accompanied by a speech from me was sometimes more irrational than usual. A restaurant in Palmerston North, or it might have been Wellington, was constructed to recall the earliest sort of settlers' accommodation, and was an open-plan space with raucous half-floors reached by logwood ladders. Six or seven other parties were enjoying themselves at the tops of their voices as, at the top of mine, I tried, as requested by the programme, to make a subtle point or two about the educational use of libraries.

Someone told me about J. B. Priestley's visit, and how he'd been conducted into one great public meal, eagerly expected to entertain his fellow diners for an hour or two: but on the way in he'd murmured to a neighbour, 'How long should I go on for?' and the other had said, 'We like things kept short here.' So Priestley spoke for three minutes only. No one was precise about the fate of his misinformant, but I had the general impression that he was hanged.

In Wellington I went to see a cousin – 'One of my brother Will's boys,' as my father commented gloomily from the shaving mirror.

5

Uncle Will was the earthiest of the brothers – and I think, for something warm in him, though he had the family gift of sarcasm and stinging irony, he was my favourite. He was the one who most despised my father for electing to work in an office. 'What's it like sitting on your little stool then, Dick?' It had led to a throwing of chairs – one of ours: the repair was pointed out from time to time as reference might be made to a feature of some old battle-field. A problem for my mother, when it came in such circumstances to cheering on one or the other: for it was clear that, for all her helpless loyalty to my father, and respect for the figure he cut as he left for the office, newspaper perfectly folded under his arm, something less respectable in her longed for Uncle Will. Delirious during one of her last illnesses, it was Will she called for. Officially, he appalled her by his habits. He kept pigs, and spoke of them companionably: he not only read *The News of the World* but made (she thought, deliberately) meagre squares of it and hung them on a nail in the lavatory. He'd once made fun of my father's bowler hat, saying if he'd not seen it on my father's head he'd have thought it was for pissing in. He had the earliest gramophone I ever had the pleasure of listening to: I'd sit in the lee of its great green horn and vibrate to the enormous marches, mostly those of Sousa, that he favoured. Aunt Bea was made for him, sharing not only his contempt for over-refinement but his belief that my father represented an outstandingly despicable attempt to achieve it. As a child, aware of the dual strain among the brothers – Harry and Will and Arthur aggressively earthy: Jack a rogue who could be rough or refined as his largely illegal activities demanded: and my father and Uncle George, one prosaically anxious for a modest sort of respectability, the other more adventurously in search of more spectacular manifestations of it – I thought myself doomed, by way largely of the grammar school, to belong at the aspirant end of this scale; but secretly thrilled to Uncle Will's wonderfully assertive vulgarities, the smell throughout his house of pigfood, apples in store and a general rot of vegetables and fruit. When I was very small, before the polarisation between the brothers became acute, I'd be allowed to help him with the pigs on Sunday mornings. His jesting intimacy with those bulky snorting pinknesses, the thick green smell of the swill, the incomprehensible jokes he shared with me his small companion – in a general way I took them to be disgraceful, and laughed with as close an approximation to Uncle Will's throatiness as I could manage – caused in me a great love for him, which never lessened: it was, I guess, a curious secret product of my character, as my mother's love for him was of hers. These brothers had come out of the Paddington slums of the nineteenth century divided into those who would seek in the twentieth to become Blishens remodelled, decent citizens more or less dulled, and those who clung to the other element in the family temper, the stubbornly coarse and spiritedly unaspiring.

And here I was, in 1985, in Havana Street, Wellington, and here was the Motley Photographic Studio: and here, in the plumb centre of the window, was a photograph I'd never before seen of Uncle Will, aged about twenty-two. He was grinning, as throughout life he grinned, baring his good white teeth: his hair was parted in the middle: he was as handsome as any early film star. Twelve thousand miles from home I was precipitately, profoundly, at home. I felt my mother's heart leap inside me. The photo was surrounded by others that looked at first glance of the same vintage: but then it became clear that he was there to give an authentic touch to a current local taste – for being photographed in garments that might have been worn by the sitters' grandparents. Inside the shop my cousin Peter, white-coated, busy with a customer, waved us in. There was the instant feeling of deep recognition that follows when you meet a close relative not seen for forty years, followed by its reverse: I knew him all right, but he was at the same time a deeply unfamiliar stranger. We entered the studio itself, in which hung the costumes and other Victorian and Edwardian accessories in which customers liked to be photographed. There was a row of bowler hats that would have taken even Uncle Will, who made a jocular social feature of his urinary needs, a long time to fill. We were greeted by Peter's wife, a New Zealander by birth. Then Peter came in: and took me in an embrace of startling intensity. I understood from it how cut off he felt from his family: from which some might have been glad to take refuge – but then your family, if you're in any sort of exile, must seem a warm centre: an institution to which, even if you didn't belong, you belonged. That dizzying inadvertency of blood relationship! I felt, at that moment, desperately inadequate. I was, after all, from the aspirant branch: bloody scribbler, as Uncle Will might have said. I had no hat he could have pretended to believe was for pissing in, but he'd have thought of something I had, the use of which could be similarly misunderstood. I wanted, in Peter's embrace, to be of the earthy Blishens, to smell of pigs and rotting apples. I wanted not to be the guest of the New Zealand

Library Association, about to be picked up here, and taken for lunch, by a publisher . . .

On a wall in the studio was a collage of photographs, and I realised that many of them were of scenes in Barton, forty or fifty years earlier: and among them, one of 4, Sutton Villas being demolished. It was the home Uncle Will and my father, cycling at a venture out of London, had found for their widowed mother, in 1913: a Sunday morning excursion out of which, amidst much more, my own lifelong residence in Barton had sprung. I remembered it in terms of my grandmother's everlastingly complaining Cornish voice: of a batteredness of furniture that I now think might have come from many years of fraternal chair-throwing: and, as in the case of Uncle Will's house, of a bruised general air of urine and apples. Perhaps my nose, remembering these things, exaggerates: but there was surely a not displeasing proximity of the odours of waste and fruit. What I remember perhaps is the general thick atmosphere of a house before the arrival of refrigerators, aerosols, all the modern apparatus of refreshment and renewal of air. In the photograph on the wall in the studio in Wellington, 4, Sutton Villas was laid open, a poor torn shell of a semi-detached house. You'd think there would have been room for barely a single person to live there, where the six brothers and their sister had squatted alongside their mother: and had found space even for two lodgers. I remembered the lodgers: they formed, I think, for life my archetypal notion of two young men living in jocular friendship together: devoting themselves, as far as I could see, to wireless on a huge scale – the BBC studios with which I was now familiar seemed mere reduced versions of the front room at Sutton Villas, where those two young men had constructed what I remember as formidable consoles heaped with earphones . . . but largely devoting themselves to lifting me on their shoulders and trotting me about my grandmother's garden. I know nothing more of them: but part of me, perfectly

111

happy, will always be thrillingly balanced on their shoulders, ducking only just in time – but always just in time – as we flew, by some process more wonderful than mere running, under apple trees, pear trees – and a tree of which the smell astounded me: I think it must have been a greengage.

Another photograph on Peter's wall showed a row of cottages, and I suddenly remembered that, in one of those, George Straker's grandparents had lived. It had been one of the threads that had drawn us together as boys, our having elderly relatives who were near-neighbours. Old Mr Straker had been a watery sort of man, and was one of the large number of her acquaintances of whom my grandmother spoke with scorn. An opinion that she wrapped up in her usual fashion, for she had many indirect ways of being coarse – but I had a child's gift for unwrapping them – was that if a woman ever looked him straight in the eye, he'd wet himself. He'd been a clerk in the local gas office, which was against him. He lost points over Mrs Straker, too, who was holy. She belonged to a group that, as my grandmother believed or pretended to believe, were called the Desperate People. She was jammed up against Doomsday, I gathered, and about as thrilling to talk to as a wet herring. Mr Straker's fame was for never making up his mind. My grandmother held that he'd yet to take his first step in that direction: and I wondered now if George's appalling crispness sprang in part from a dread of resembling his grandfather.

Peter, though he'd lived round the corner, didn't remember the Strakers. He had an idealised memory of our grandmother – 'Fine woman!' – and faintly recalled Great Aunt Ada, that self-appointed guardian of the family morals. *She*, I knew, must have come on her visits of moral inspection to Uncle Will's as to the homes of all her nephews. I told Peter of an early photograph I had of Great Aunt Ada that would have interested him, given his trade and the local passion for Victoriana. In it she was to be seen as a severe young woman being unexpectedly winsome: her bosom a rampart, her large hat a kind of castellation: but she was touching her chin with the sportive curled handle of an umbrella. I thought of saying more about her, but saw that Peter recalled her as a fine woman. He wouldn't have remembered how she watched over our morals by way of the unremitting expression of dismay at our having none. 'He has no morals,' was how it was always phrased. This one had no morals, another somehow had fewer morals still, and as for Jack ... Uncle George was rarely mentioned in this context, for though he had been most spectacularly lacking in morals, in Aunt Ada's sense, he had been a worldly success, and lived in perhaps the largest house any Blishen had ever lived in. When I was small I'd had the appalled impression that Great Aunt Ada would have counted me in, among those whose moral content she was always assessing, except that she had no habit of measuring the moral inadequacies peculiar to schoolboys. She expressed the most tentative sort of hopes of me on the grounds of my wearing a cap with a crown on it. It was my mother who privately hinted to me that Great Aunt Ada's late husband, Ted, a wistful man on the edge of family photographs, had been driven by his wife's withering concern with morals to play the peeping Tom in Hyde Park. He'd been arrested for it. There'd been a sad little scandal, and he'd died soon afterwards. After hearing that tale I'd worried about Ted, lurking wistful and woebegone behind trees in the royal park. I wondered, here in Peter's studio among the stiff Victorian clothing worn for fun by Peter's loose modern customers, about that old photo of Ada, the tiny element of dash in the way she was leaning her chin on that really rather impertinent umbrella. How much joy had she and Ted ever had?

The publisher arrived: and off Kate and I went, to yet another talk. As the car drew away, Peter and his wife stood on the pavement outside the shop, waving. I looked back when we were some distance down the street, and they were still there.

'*Bloody* family!' my father had cried more than once: feeling, I guess, particularly plagued by mothers and swamped by brothers. Well, yes. But I remembered how as a child I'd thought of relations as amazingly pleasant possessions in the sense that they were persons willing, merely on the basis of the relationship, to give you lunches and high teas. They were also ready to unpack the family cupboard, which led to the occasional rattling emergence of a skeleton. Some were jollier than that, and pulled out little but skeletons, throwing them in all directions and laughing loudly. I loved sitting among them. That was when adult talk of any kind seemed wonderfully thrilling. Beloved, indiscreet, sixpence-proffering uncles, aunts, cousins, and some persons intimately but vaguely part of the web.

I thought, as we turned a corner and I could see Peter no longer, how all the sophistications in the world would never really purge me of those old sensations of perfectly irrational delight in the family.

6

What I'd looked forward to in Wellington, and imagined I'd do easily – it might be too easy, everywhere a much-beaten track – was to make a little journey round the world of Katherine Mansfield: who would have struck Great Aunt Ada, had they ever crossed paths in London some-where about 1908, as a brazen hussy, and not at all the type of girl you expected to have been born and bred in one of our dominions. I'd been in love with her ghost, though I had no sense of her being ghostly, throughout much of 1938 and 1939. Most of that time I was a reporter on the *Monmouth Hill Gazette*, in the opening months of my employment paying 50p a week for the privilege: it was held that I was being trained. It seemed to me that I was being, in some fashion, untrained. The paper had no use for the large cargo of words I was carrying. I was not much given to plain statement: the *Gazette* was given to nothing else. An account of a police court case must normally begin: 'At Highgate Police Court on Thursday, Mrs Emma Pease (57) ...' Reading Katherine Mansfield's stories, I longed to write of Mrs Emma Pease as she'd appeared at that moment in court: a crushed and bewildered figure, I remember her as being in one embodiment or another, summoned for falling into arrears in this matter or that. Poverty was distinctly the offence with which a procession of stunned and startled persons were charged, at Highgate. Or at Wood Green, where numbers of Mrs Peases were accused of failing to pay 15s 3d. Some had stolen objects valued at 4s 9½d. It was called petty crime, but petty was clearly not the word for the effect on many defendants. I wanted, in Katherine Mansfield's manner, to write about Mrs Pease, her hat, the way she stood before the bench, the brooch she wore: oh, her nose, her eyelids: what one felt she might have been as a child, or a young woman. I wanted – by implication, of course, entirely by way of storytelling, none of your sermonising! – to contrast the plump confidence of so many magistrates with the undernourished trepidation of so many Mrs Peases. I wanted to write with the full benefit of exclamation marks. Oh, that ejaculatory quality of Katherine Mansfield's notebooks, her diary, her letters! I walked with unsuitable slowness around my reporter's beat, reading as I went, and her eagernesses, her sharpnesses, her cruelties, the delicate precision of her observations – how each came (if not on her page, then in my head) with that mark of excitement! I doubt if the entire printery at the *Gazette* could have raised a single exclamation mark. My attempts to give what I thought of as colour and flesh – oh yes, and breath! and noses! and eyelids! and hats! – to the accounts of police court cases – or small fires – or church bazaars – led to furious encounters with the editor, Mr Trout. 'Look

115

here, young man,' he'd cry. 'What's this? I mean, this isn't *Peg's Paper*, you know.' I couldn't think what to say to Mr Trout, then or at any time – a man who confused newspaper accounts written under the influence of Katherine Mansfield (who'd written under the influence of Chekhov) with stories in a woman's journal of the lowest literary reputation! Later in my time at the *Gazette* Mr Trout came to favour the idea of my reaching for a remarkable word or two in an account of a concert, or some piece of amateur dramatics. He thought it gave some tucked-away corner of the paper a touch of style – defensible, if only just. But even then, exclamation marks were out. Once, angry, I asked poor Mr Trout to formulate his case against this item of punctuation. Oh, of course, I cried, with eighteen-year-old earnestness, I knew of the argument against its use as a feeble attempt to create excitement or drama not created by the prose itself. But he could hardly think that I (known reader of Katherine Mansfield and many others) was in favour of the exclamation mark at that level! Surely he accepted that there was a place for excitement and enthusiasm in the columns of the *Gazette*! As I remember, Mr Trout, who did not accept that there was a place for excitement or enthusiasm anywhere at all, and whose weekly column of jottings constantly advised Herr Hitler to weigh the value of composure and calm, returned with a sniff to his typing. Despite these wildnesses of mine, at a salary of minus 50p a week I was worth keeping.

But I wasn't drawn to Katherine Mansfield only by her exclamatoriness – the breathless quickness of response that was to be found raw, anyway, only in the letters and diaries – but also by her gift for catching at the mistiness of things, that quality of the physical world to which the Impressionists were sensitive, the tendency of the confidently tangible and visible to dissolve and become uncertain, and combining it with hardness and sharpness of definition when it came to describing an action, or the movement of a mind, or a sensation. And when I went to New Zealand I realised that many of my expectations about how it would look and how it would feel to be there were taken from my reading of the woman who wrote: 'Oh, I want for one moment to make our undiscovered country leap into the eyes of the old world. It must be mysterious, as though floating – it must take the breath.' (Exclamations, though as it happens without exclamation marks.)

Wellington was her home until she came finally to Europe in 1908, and I expected that it would be possible to visit one at least of the houses that had been associated with her. Well, there'd plainly be a little tour, well-established – to the family houses in the city at one end, and at the other the scene of that 'summer colony' she described in her story 'At the Bay'. In three years there'd be the centenary, and I thought things must be working up to that.

But instead, there was nothing much. Indeed, nothing at all. A friend in New Zealand radio found it necessary to inquire of the local historical society. They provided me with a typed account of Katherine Mansfield's Wellington, affectionate and full, and with its help, and if I'd been in the city for a week, I'd have been able to follow the writer around, from the birthplace (now divided into flats) to Eastbourne, the scene of 'At the Bay'. But for a hurried visitor there was no obvious quick way round the main centres of Katherine Mansfield's early life. It was only later I discovered that when I visited Peter in his studio, I was doors away from the site of the shop that provided the cream puffs that are among the chief characters in her story, 'The Garden Party'. 'Godber's were famous for their cream puffs. Nobody ever thought of making them at home.'

We did find Eastbourne and, from a distance, stared at the holiday bungalow the family had occupied: and looked out at the beach where Beryl in the story, demurring at being told she was a little beauty, nevertheless felt she was a little beauty: and beyond to the sleepy sea, still making the sound Ah-Aah! (The exclamation mark is Katherine Mansfield's.) And here and there, they said, was a plaque: and the Historical Places Trust was 'working towards' the preservation of the birthplace. A street near one of her homes had been named Katherine Avenue. But given her achievement, and that in the true atlas that artists create it was she who'd put Wellington on the map, I felt surprise at how little acknowledgement of her there seemed to be. Was it because as soon as she could she'd hurried to Europe to make her name? Was it because from Tinakori Road, Wellington, she'd written to a friend who was going to England: 'Kiss London for me – and tell it – that when I come back I shall live in a tent in Trafalgar Square...'?

What I found myself remembering, on a plane to Christchurch by way of which we were to catch a plane to Queenstown, was the effect, fifty years ago, of reading her. She made you value visions and sensations to which, because they were fleeting, you might easily have attached no importance. Well, I recalled such a moment amid the absurd despairs of those days – when I felt so disgraced by being a reporter, in such a place as Monmouth Hill. My flesh seemed the thinnest of packages for the great and aching disaster of my being. Was *this* life? Were my surroundings not inventions of my misery, which had spawned churches and chapels, banks and shops, villas, blocks of flats, and the printing works and office of the *Monmouth Hill Gazette*? I was walking down a road that a year later was to be torn apart by bombs, my nose in a book: and there on the other side of the street was a girl. And her skirt was full of sunshine.

It was all I saw of her: her skirt with its pockets and panniers of shining light. Nearly fifty years later I still see her.

It was like being flown over the open pages of a huge atlas, marvellously well-printed. We seemed to be seeing very much better than usual. Every wrinkle of rock, every thread of water was so clear that 'clear' seemed hardly the word. Here was a sort of super-clarity. I remembered how my father, drugged and recovering from a grave illness, had said he'd gazed at his thumbnail for an hour, perhaps more, seeing it for the first time and amazed and enchanted by it. Here beneath us was a thumbnail, indeed, and every change in the texture of the tilting scene, from the scabbiness of a mountain to the stained suede of a valley to the eccentric marquetry of cultivated fields, caught between great knees of snow, was entrancing. Kate and I, like my father, were drugged, of course: by travel, and by the mere notion of being at the other end of the earth to the one we were accustomed to. Kate said: 'When we get home I'm not ever going to be astonished by anything any more.'

Much in our present mood, I thought, they'd called the mountains at Queenstown the Remarkables. That suited us. Left to give names to bits of the planet, Kate and I would have raided the relevant pages of Roget: everywhere there would have been the Surprising, the Astounding, the Startling and Stunning: and exhausted we'd have named some forest the Ineffable, some marshy plain the Unutterable. The Remarkables fell down into Lake Wakatipu; and we were housed in a lodge overlooking the lake, part of it sportively built out of bottles. Queenstown was for tourists, which would have been fair enough, for who wouldn't have wanted to visit it, where water and mountain were so marvellously married? The trouble lay in the garishness of what was provided for us, all that ... well, I thought of it in terms of that name we'd glimpsed over a café in one of the plain little towns set in far from plain country through which we'd passed in a bus: Gobble 'n

Go. Here were the Remarkables, remarkable: here was the lake, their mirror: and here were the crude acres of Gobbling 'n Going. The light slid slowly up the mountainside, and I thought there was never a place with more overhead wires and cables of every kind. You'd have believed a hundred tramways were in operation. I imagined the grief the Maoris might have felt, seeing the beauty of the land so abused.

At home on Sunday mornings we often walked through Barley Woods to the Barley Hotel. This Sunday morning we walked down the Frankton Arm Walkway, on the other side of the lake to the Remarkables. It was not quite the same thing. Under the sun, the lake was a perfect mirror: you had a choice of everything, mountains, glowing trees, birds, small clouds, one way up or the other. Kate upright stared down at Kate inverted and said she'd really not have minded being a pioneer. We ate biscuits and cheese in the presence of astonishingly small gulls. It was a particular pleasure, to be the unremarkables in the presence of the Remarkables. Damn it, I said, it was hard going – the being, or feigning to be, or having to participate in the game of feigning to be, somebody. Well, there'd been the newspaper account that described me as 'tall, lean, silver-haired, warm and buoyant': which, a sympathetic university librarian had said, would have perfectly described an emaciated seal. That was all right, said Kate: I'd always be nobody to her: and she'd forgotten to bring the fruit that was to be part of our picnic. We turned as the walkway turned at the end of the lake, and walked back into another world. In a moment the weather changed absolutely. From nowhere came an angry freezing wind: the lake tipped and tilted and was turned into leaping rags of water: and then there was rain cruelly cold and sharp. 'It never,' they said when we got back to the lodge, 'rains like this in Queenstown.' All night it rained as it never did rain in Queenstown: and it was still at it in the morning as we started the long bus journey to Dunedin.

8

It was the best of such journeys, for much of the time through a landscape I couldn't identify but knew I'd once been deeply familiar with. I hit upon it at last – this was the phantasmagoric landscape of a Grimms' fairy tale. Or of all those tales, put together. I'd first imagined it in the safety of my bed in Barton, c. 1926. So, after many kinds of beetling brownness, there'd be a stretch populated with large green boulders: another in which every five yards there'd be a rocking stone: miles of rock colossally creased: a sudden broad occasion for orchards: a zircon-coloured river, wriggling: an area in which pale tussocks stood hairily shoulder to shoulder with pale tussocks, millions of them. The sun poured through sidelong sleet, and vanished. Quite different weathers occurred simultaneously. We were in an endless winding cleft. Here was the longest line of poplars I'd ever seen in my life, not noticeably associated with anything at all. We were in the baldest sort of moorland: and now, hardly out of one dull little town before we were in the next dull little town. The dullness was complete, except (as usual) for names: so that here we were, passing down Shakespeare Street, Milton. Then a never-ending grove of pale leafless trees, and in it, a limitless quantity of black-and-white cows. After that, an episode where all the trees had plainly been hastily constructed in the last five minutes out of miscellaneous bits and pieces. That branch didn't belong to that trunk, and so on. The leaves hung unconvincingly. And then we were in the outskirts of Dunedin. TAKEAWAYS, I thought, looked Maori, but wasn't. We halted, and Derek, a gentle and amusing librarian, stepped forward: for the conference, my guide and guard.

Dunedin, startlingly hot when we arrived, instantly became startlingly cold. As Kate prepared herself in our hotel bedroom for a mayoral reception, there was a knock at the door. I opened it and admitted a reporter and cameraman, expected visitors. Kate, half-dressed, stared at them, appalled. They, amazed, stared back. I tried to work out what I'd done wrong. Kate said, 'Please go away.' We went away.

We stood on the roof of a nearby high-rise car park, and I gave unsuitable answers to the reporter's questions. It was no use – professional interviewer, I found it difficult to be serious about being interviewed. I heard myself expressing amazement at being here at all. Couldn't for the life of me think what the Library Association was up to. Well, yes, educationist. Awful word. Had written a book about being a floundering teacher, that's how it began, so was taken to be an authority ... The young reporter grinned. I went back to the hotel in order *not* to prepare for the mayoral reception. Derek had assured me a tie would be unnecessary. He would not be wearing one himself. New Zealand was a shirt-sleeve sort of country. In the event, I had never seen so many ties, so much formal elegance. With my naked neck, I felt like an intrusive nudist. Could I have bared any other part of my body with ruder effect? People were charming to the visitor from London, but I felt like the Emperor in Hans Andersen's story. At any moment a child – or perhaps some senior citizen of Dunedin – would point and cry: 'But he has no tie!'

CONFERENCE SPEAKER HAS WEALTH OF EXPERIENCE, said the next morning's headline, under an indiscriminately chosen picture of an aged person. It took me more seriously than I'd taken myself. But at the conference that morning the reporter slipped into my hand the report she'd originally written: it had been frowned upon by an editor clearly resembling Mr Trout, of the *Monmouth Hill Gazette*. 'This is an awful country to be a reporter in,' she said. 'They have no sense of humour. I'm going to Australia.'

In this first version she'd included (as how could a lively reporter not have done?) the monstrous beginning of the interview ('Embarrassment all round') and the absurd car-park roof. '"How many of your subjects,"' her report went, '"have gone over the edge?" asked the star of the New Zealand Library Association conference as he leaned against the not too solid wire-netting fence. "I can see their bones below." But he wasn't really scared, this English teacher/journalist/broadcaster/reviewer/medal-winning writer of children's books and a long-running auto-biography/book-lover/husband of Kate/addresser of library conferences. He gave a running commentary during the semi-precarious photo session – about his face. "Wearing an expression I know is bound to be seen as idiotic in the extreme: the Face Abominable – here it is. The English face at its worst."

'Needless to say, he was easy to interview. He could have done it without me. I just kept writing and asked him to slow down sometimes when I couldn't keep up.

'"I was a school librarian," he said, just a little defiantly, when asked what his credentials were for addressing a librarians' conference. But then he owned up. "I'm supposed to be here because of my interest in children's literature. I do write for children sometimes – in fact, I won a medal for it once . . . with a friend. He's much more famous than I am."'

I seemed to have told her how I'd been divided between writing and teaching, and had concluded that I must stop being a teacher. 'That was 1959. Apart from two medals he has been going downhill ever since, ending up in Dunedin, inhaling the unpolluted air and admiring the open sky from the roof of Gardner's Motors' car park with the awful prospect of addressing four hundred and fifty-odd librarians the next day on the subject – "The Library in Education".

'... By the time we walked back to his hotel, discussing England's chances in the fifth Test, which Mr Blishen thinks look good, Kate had had her shower and was getting ready for the mayoral reception...

'Until she retired last year, she taught family planning and sex education in schools. "We should really give a joint lecture tomorrow," he said. "The Role of the Library in Sex." '

I've hoped since that she escaped to Australia, and that they properly valued her there. Covering Highgate Police Court in the thirties she'd have noticed Mrs Emma Pease's trembling hands, darned stockings, and dreadfully unchampioned bewilderment.

9

Having to address four hundred and fifty librarians was an awful prospect, in the reporter's words, only in that for my hour's talk on the first morning of the conference I'd been brought halfway round the world. If it had been a matter of mending a leak in someone's plumbing, or digging a garden, the nervousness would have been the same. It isn't quite like being invited to do something a mile from home.

And for all the comforting attendance of my friend Kate, I did feel I was among foreigners. I came away from New Zealand in the end feeling that the foreignness was accentuated by there being such a plausible appearance of familiarity. I think of the city of Dunedin itself. Here, in all directions from the statue of Robert Burns, sprawling huge somewhere in the centre with a morally ambiguous manuscript on his knee, was a sort of Scotland. It was what the Scots who first arrived there are said to have believed it was, only more so: they thought they'd come to some ideal form of their homeland as the result of an uncommonly roundabout journey. But they can't truly have believed that. Their acknowledgement of the Scottish nature of what they'd found must have been mixed with a frightful sense that Mercator at his most yielding could not have conflated those two territories. And the Scots were the source, after all, of those ballads in which we hear of innocents (usually drunk, but still innocent) who wander onto enchanted ground which, too late, they see for what it is. It is not homely country, after all. It is amazingly alien. Five hundred years later they escape from the world under the hill, only to find that in the other, comfortable world, all has changed and become uncomfortable. Nowhere, for them, is ever again quite to be home. They have strayed outside all notion of homeliness.

Of course my kindly New Zealand hosts were enchanted characters out of ballads. And yet, in a sense, I have to say, they were. I kept wondering what they were doing there. An absurd way of looking at them – but then, so much of what they were, and did, was of Europe, not of the Pacific. It was what, I thought, Katherine Mansfield might have felt – the unlikelihood of such Londonness, such Edinburghness, being found on the edge of the sleeping sea that made the sound Ah-Aah! She sent a kiss to London because London was the home of the words she used. Here the truly indigenous words (not WIREWARE, not TAKEAWAY) were not the English ones but similarly liquid and most beautiful words, Te Awamatu, Rotorua.

My anxiety, that first morning, was increased when I walked towards the conference hall in the company of a small fierce woman. She'd thought the opening address, which to my ears had offered a sharp view of local communications – the number of those in control of news and entertainment in New Zealand, the speaker claimed, had shrunk in twenty years to a quarter of what they had been – was vitiated by humour. He had gone in for jokes. They were, I thought, jokes of the most appropriately mordant kind, as if a cobra had guffawed as he bit you. But I suggested that seriousness and a feeling for the comic might be appropriate companions. That sounded, she said, like a typical male get-out. I suppressed the desire to tell her that Eva Figes, incorruptible feminist, had once (on a train travelling from Manchester to London) declared that I seemed free of male chauvinism. I was Eva-Figes-guaranteed, I wanted to say. In fact, since I had no gift for being serious except by way of detours into comedy, I felt depressed. My prepared talk was deeply felt, and as serious as I could manage. (There were times when I thought no one, anywhere, could be as appallingly serious as I was.) But it did hope to cause a chuckle – even, damn it, a guffaw.

I sat on the platform, desperate. *Of course*, what was needed on such an occasion was a sobriety that didn't rest simply on the avoidance of intoxication, but refused altogether the notion that insobriety might be possible. Oh, the four hundred and fifty-ness of the audience! Oh, the folly of coming so far to behave so inappropriately! Then, astonished, I heard the chairman read an account I'd written, in a diary I'd been contributing monthly to the *Times Educational Supplement*, of the arrival of the invitation to visit New Zealand. I seemed to have said that my impulse was to run up the lane where I lived knocking at my neighbours' doors and shouting: 'I've been invited to New Zealand! New Zealand wants me!' And so on. Instead, I'd taken Kate her morning cup of tea and with unspeakable dignity, laced with weariness, had said: 'Oh, by the way, they'd like me to go to New Zealand.' The chairman read at length these half-forgotten words of mine. Four hundred and fifty librarians, though the number can't have been as rounded as that, laughed loudly. I was beckoned to the rostrum. 'Fancy,' I said, 'being upstaged by yourself!' They laughed again, and I thought someone less modest might have thought they laughed inordinately. I shook myself free of the lady who thought laughter was a symptom of male arrogance; and

I began reading my paper on the Library in Education.

A dryish title, I said, for a subject about which I'd never at any time in my life felt remotely dry. How could I, essentially educated by libraries? I'd come from an unbookish home – though my first great memory relating to a library was of the copy of *Alice in Wonderland* my father had brought home for me from the Westminster Public Library. Bound in a severe green I still found thrilling whenever I encountered it, it had on many of its pages the name of the library stamped inside an oval, and a smell as of imprisoned paper: and I had a generally pleasant sensation related to the idea that this great institution, given to stamping ovals all over the face of literature, was trusting me, by way of my father, with that copy of *Alice*. And after that there'd been library after library: and I believed that I came to take my view of the world from the way a library is arranged. In the glowing forefront of things, fiction: and behind fiction, the grave areas of non-fiction, from any of which something might leap that made fiction look drab.

I had to stress random sensuous details of this nature because I believed one of the first importances of the library in education lay in what could be felt about the book as an object, and then about quantities of those objects, brought methodically together. What the library was as a physical space occupied by books ought to be one of the first educational effects it had. And very simply, a collection of books was astonishing. I spoke of Logan, an Irishman I'd once been taught by, usefully mad about books. Having been usefully mad about them at our grammar school in Barton, he'd gone off to be extremely mad about them in a public school. Being often too impatient to use the library ladder, and swarming up the shelves for a book instead, he'd been known as Monkey. Well, a library ought to be physically exciting, and it should be used excitingly: Logan being for me a model of that excitement. I wasn't proposing a general use of libraries as if they were zoos: but I had to say I thought I'd been lucky to be taught by a man who swarmed up the shelves like a monkey. I guessed being a librarian was like being a teacher: one's hair should always be slightly standing on end.

I talked of those of the children I'd taught at Stonehill Street who'd constituted the first little group of educational volunteers deciding to stay at school after the age when they could have fled. For them, opting for the swagger of continued education against the background of the downcast local philosophy, the library was the best assertion of that characteristic of education that had caused them to elect to stay on: for here was a large general offer of information, and of inquiry into the human condition, and of wisdom and folly, and of comedy and tragedy, and of things almost unbearably important and other things wonderfully unimportant: and of facts and thoughts springing out of the blue, and of connections between things to be run to earth in opposite corners of the library. Here was education. It has always seemed to me that the final state of education was the condition of being a freely self-educating person. In the end, you took the point, as it were: you continued the process for yourself. You might, of course, go on having teachers for this or that: we did not lose our need of teachers: but essentially you became your own teacher. The heart of the educated condition, I believed, was the habit of reference. You were minded to find out for yourself. You were constantly needing to know, and you did not like not knowing. It was not intellectual avarice: it was unwillingness to be uninformed if you might, instead, be informed.

I talked of how, as Stonehill Street's librarian, I'd tried, following the example of Logan, to persuade my colleagues that at moments of uncertainty in the classroom they should not supply the answers themselves, if they knew them, nor look them up and supply them later – or, dreadful teacherly tendency, hasten on to the next thing – but despatch an inquirer to the library. Alas, it had happened too rarely. It was so easy, being a teacher, to keep it all to oneself. It was so easy to suckle and suckle, and to forget that at the heart of education there was the need to wean the pupil away from the teacher: and so easy not to take it in, somehow, that one of the teacher's best aids in this process lay in the existence of the library.

And I thought that what might be suggested of the school library applied also to the public library. In a sense it applied even more intensely to the public library: which could be seen as a symbol of freely continuing education, a symbol planted outside the school, and a statement by implication about the connection of the school with the world beyond the school. Of course, there were respects in which public libraries might not wish to be thought of as actively involved in teaching processes. Among other things, they were guardians of the great orderliness and system of literature: they were experts on its availability, and on access to it. But they couldn't help being also important elements in the entire activity, begun in the schools but only begun there, which constituted education. Well, I offered myself as evidence. Truly, I had been substantially educated by libraries. Not only by their offer of general collections of books, but by all those largely silent services that lay behind their existence. When I'd first become a library-user, they were narrow services. I remembered Mrs Griffiths, round about 1930 the head librarian in Barton, a lady of notable moral severity, given to a particular kind of librarian's frown that was called into being especially by noise anywhere within the building (oh the terrifying thrill that followed from one's dropping a book!) or by a less than perfect cleanliness of the hands of a small person ('Come back when you've had a wash!'). I would not have liked to suggest to Mrs Griffiths that she was part of the general enterprise of education. Her own great field was the tracing of stains – tea-stains, tomato-stains – and especially the making of comments in margins, whether in pencil or ink. She'd once interrogated me fiercely about a note shouting 'Rubbish!' in the margin of a book I'd returned – I, who abhorred the idea of writing in books, was a prig about turning down the leaf to mark the page you'd reached in your reading, and anyway didn't think 'Rubbish!' was, in this case, a sensible comment. But since the days of Mrs Griffiths, whom I remembered with nervous affection, the services offered by libraries had increased, and many in essence were educational. As a school librarian, I'd valued public librarians as colleagues with a difference. It was useful, when I took the children I taught on a visit to the public library, for them to feel that they hadn't gone outside the school as much as all that, but still they *had* gone outside the school.

My vision was that, bit by bit, the schools and the public libraries would, between them, positively increase the number of real, lifelong readers. There were born readers: and there were those who grew into the habit of reading because of the nature of their studies: and there were great numbers of human beings who might or might not become lifelong readers, the question being resolved early on, and depending on experience in which both school and public librarians had a vital part to play. Someone – best, some network of adults – somewhere within the situation had to be lively, vivid, welcoming as to books. Well, welcoming. Education had always been at its best when there was someone who made it irresistible to come in. It was part of the role of the library in education to make itself increasingly difficult to resist.

I had to say something, of course, about our old headmaster, Percy Chew. He'd believed that the bottom had fallen out of the human enterprise somewhere about 1850. In the great library checks we had at ends of term, much looked forward to by us boy-librarians, a chance to plunge one's arms up to the elbows in books, as a miser plunges his arms into his gold, Percy Chew would wax satirical about the neighbourhood of this writer with that on the shelves. It might be Rider Haggard next to, or close to, Aldous Huxley. Though active after 1850, Haggard was exempted from Percy Chew's various acts of literary excommunication: it was all right to read Haggard, as it was all right to read John Buchan, because they had managed to get themselves erroneously born after the fatal middle of the nineteenth century, as had Percy Chew himself. It wasn't their fault. Making his terrible jokes about the impropriety of having the excellent Haggard cheek-by-jowl with the indecent Huxley, Percy Chew was surrounded by young librarians reflecting on the perfect propriety of it. It was a major virtue of a library that it didn't mind who was in bed with whom. There was this immense bed of existence, and there was no other bed. So, healthily, said the library.

10

In such an absurd venture, nothing better than having risen to the main occasion. Well, I seemed to be beamed upon. There were queues of university librarians to kiss Kate – an odd consequence of my address, I thought. Kate transferred to the Antipodes seemed to have become a willing magnet of kisses. She was taken here and there, tenderly, and, while I sat in on talks about cataloguing, was introduced to some of the shyest fauna and flora of the island. Reclusive birds stood boldly on branches and sang for her: wherever she went, uncommon flowers chose to bloom. Which of us, I wondered, was the monarch, and which the consort? 'It's the nearest we'll ever get to that situation,' said Kate. 'Is it all right to enjoy it? I do have to struggle now and then with the desire to wave, graciously.' Having, she said, a month earlier been among those never knowingly embraced by a librarian, she was now surely (someone must be compiling statistics) near the top of the list of those rarely out of a librarian's arms.

We ate Chinese, Traditional, Italian. We were introduced to the mayor so often that we began to suspect that 'mayor' was a title conferred generally on citizens of Dunedin. (The mayor may similarly have believed that the town was suddenly full of persons from London.) Everywhere we were surrounded by familiar people from the milder quarters of Barton and Barley Wood: but the physical world they inhabited was as far as could be imagined from those temperate streets back home. We drank tea, and talked small, and across the way was a headland where not much more than a hundred years earlier a Maori stronghold had proved not to be strong enough. Under siege, they'd posted dummy sentries, and the trick had been discovered. The few survivors had escaped down the cliff on ropes made of the tendrils of vines.

Well, was mildness not to be preferred to such murderous heroics? I turned the question over when Luke Moss and his wife Sue took us to their country places. She was a librarian: Luke, appearing for the first time at the wheel of the car in which he picked us up, was almost absurdly unmistakable for anyone but a farmer. He even had a sheepskin on his chin: a very large, jutting and yellowing beard, set at such an angle that it gave an impression of having been glued there. He talked at first sparingly, as a farmer might have talked: but the subject-matter didn't suggest agriculture. I thought he sounded improbable: something like an academically learned hayseed with a bent towards the classics. In fact, as it turned out, he was a lecturer in classics at the university, with a bent towards arboriculture. I suspect he enjoyed misleading us. He specialised in the Romans and their language, but much preferred the Greeks and theirs. The Romans, he said, the pelt on his chin twitching disdainfully, were second-rate people. I thought how they'd come to Britain two thousand years ago, and wondered if there'd been in their behaviour an insipidity that might have seemed duller than it was against a background of painted

132

and glowering natives. Were the white New Zealanders a sort of Romans, rewritten?

Luke and Sue, it appeared, had two country places. In one, largely Luke's, an old hay barn with land attached, they kept sheep: but not at all as we'd seen sheep kept, elsewhere. These were, so to speak, half a dozen intellectually limited members of the family. They seemed to live entirely for their owners' visits, and were lined up impatiently behind the gate as we arrived. They were mostly large, and brown: they liked to be fed by the Mosses, and one, known as Calpurnia, refused to feed by other means. The biggest of the males, Nero, was enormous, and had developed quite unsheeplike qualities: he heavily pursued Luke and Sue and, with a sort of cumbrous playfulness, butted them. It was like nothing so much as visiting a group of profoundly woollen grandchildren. When we could escape from their clumsy attentions, we followed Luke across the plantation he'd established, to the rear of the barn. There were hundreds of tentatively successful trees, and hundreds of distinctly disastrous ones. He was, I thought, in the Chekhovian sense, a wood demon. Somehow, his nature was such that he was deeply stirred by the idea of being the founding father of a forest. Sue was sceptically encouraging. *Her* country place was more orthodox, a cabin with books high above a creek that when the water was out displayed such tints of almost green and nearly pink and not quite blue as baffled our previous experience of colour. We talked of a print Kate and I had bought, of a bold boat on a bold beach: it reflected some of that unfamiliarity of familiar colour, and we'd be glad to have it hanging in Barley Wood, reminding us of another atmosphere. Sue Moss laughed. A boat on a beach? Every exhibition of amateur art in New Zealand was dominated by paintings of boats on beaches!

They took us to a headland and we saw the jigsaw of the coast continuing, mild bay alternating with fierce cliff.

Everywhere we looked, I thought, were bachs, these seaside homes, cabins and converted barns: and, of course, boats on beaches: the land that so recently had been the scene of epic and tragedy now clutched to itself a hundred weekend retreats.

11

There'd been amusement at the idea of us going from Dunedin to Christchurch by train, as if I'd proposed pushing Kate there in a wheelbarrow. I never understood why New Zealanders were so derisive of railways. The Southerner was slow and comfortable, and offered, as attendant scenery, for much of the journey, the Pacific Ocean: and for the rest, the New Zealand Alps. It yawned through level crossings, which tinkled like sheep bells as we passed them, and muttered in its sleep across a scene suddenly pale, growing paler as the day ended, and then darkening with the onset of night. Near sunset the sky was marbled like endpapers: above the snowy teeth of the mountains was a stretch of delicate blue and washed-out apricot, one of those long stretches characteristic of this landscape. There was rarely just a little of something, and then a little of something else. Fascinated, we observed that we were being accompanied for the last hour by a single cloud that, beginning the size of a giant pillow, became slowly a giant bolster, and then so huge that no simile fitted: it was simply an improbably elongated bag of cloud that became, as we went, more and more deeply peach-coloured, and towards the end, when we were in the unusual position of finding a cloud not only awe-inspiring but also rather laughable, outlined itself in black.

12

We stood on a cheerfully funereal hillside in Akaroa with my distant cousin Agnes Mild, and she told us about the dead who lay there, under sloping slate-coloured stones. Here, for example, was Mrs Trunk, who as a child was known as Candlelegs, for her white stockings. And here was old Mrs Pall, whom no one remembered as young Mrs Pall, and had seemed immortal: to the end of her life she'd walk the length of the beach picking up pieces of paua shell as she'd done as a child, ninety years before.

And over here, under the full glare of the midday sun – which made the sea, into which the cemetery appeared to tumble, flash like a signalling mirror – was Bateman Thomas Missen, who'd arrived in New Zealand in 1851, and was the son of Harriet Missen, née Blishen, of Sutton in Surrey. 'He's all right,' said Agnes, running a hand down the face of Bateman's stolid tombstone. 'But I reserved a plot for my grave last year, and what do you think? I went to look at it, and it was thick with wild onions! Well, *wild onions*! I've spent a lifetime rooting them up in my garden! I could do without having to do that when I'm dead!'

She struck the tombstone playfully several times with the flat of her hand. I thought she'd certainly regard that as a not particularly indirect way of slapping Bateman Thomas Missen on the back: and thought also that she'd be furious to be lying at last under her wild onions, on the grounds that the most disadvantageous position possible for an historian is to be dead, and so merely historical.

Agnes was in a constant tangle of memories, her own and those of others, being indeed the local chronicler, and seeing history as a tireless heaping up of anecdotes and striking facts. Even to unstriking facts she was hospitable. Lately she'd missed what she saw as a desirable opportunity to possess herself of half a dozen sacksful of sermons by a nineteenth-century preacher who'd lived somewhere in this assembly of bright bays and green hills. They'd been burnt before she could get to them, and she grieved as if it had been a matter of the burning of the library at Alexandria. But I guessed that the very idea of the sermons being stored as they had been was consolation for her. *Sacks of Sermons.* I could see the heading in one of the pamphlets she was perpetually having printed.

John Aubrey, I thought, was a seventeenth-century antiquary living largely in London, and not a twentieth-century spinster with a passion for graveyards, roses and bacon-and-egg pies, residing in New Zealand: but otherwise they seemed much the same person.

Agnes had written to me years before, having read a review of one of my books. 'I'm afraid it was unflattering,' she said, and I could see how it would have been set down in her brisk mind: *Harriet Blishen's Distant Relative Unflatteringly Reviewed.* She'd never before heard of a living Blishen: so, if I was a living Blishen, would I write and say if I was also a relative? I told her in reply of the letters I had of my Great-Great-Uncle Harry's—ending with the one he'd written the day before he was killed at Sebastopol, perhaps by the 'Muscovite' with whom he'd been swopping shots from morning to evening in the spirit of two boys with catapults – which spoke of 'our Surrey cousins'. I'd discovered that there were these parallel families in the nineteenth century, the line that I came from living in Paddington, the other in various places in Surrey. Each, curiously, had its own tradition in the matter of Christian names: they had Marys, we had Sarahs, they had Johns, we had Henrys, and whereas we had Marthas, they had Harriets. Agnes flooded me at once with random Blishens she'd come across in her researches: along with Blushens and Blishings and Blissings, and totally improbable persons such as John Blishen who was thirty-five in 1851, a butcher at Worplesdon: he and his wife Caroline, thirty-four, had three servants. I wished my father could have been alive to be told of that. Ours was so profoundly a family given, on the female side, to being maids, cooks, housekeepers and ladies' companions that the idea of any Blishen at any time having one servant, let alone three, would have been as astonishing to him as it was to me.

Agnes's letters bustled: as – we'd discovered at this first meeting – did she. Using airmail forms, she was always astonished to find that, still bursting with news, she'd come to the end, and sometimes beyond it. They were attics rather than letters, crammed with unconnected items: visits to Rose Conventions or old gold mines or newly discovered and delectable graveyards. There were recipes for hot quiches; and there'd be sudden stories: like that of the Norwegian who'd escaped from a whaling ship and *later* (distrustful of the unhistorically minded reader, Agnes underlined the *later*) hanged himself. They found a tin of sovereigns hidden under his bed. He'd married an English girl, and they'd had a huge family. *At a subsequent date*, one of his sons had been buried next to another with whom he'd not for years been on speaking terms. 'So early one morning a neighbour of mine helped the gravedigger to dig him up and replant him further away,' Agnes wrote. 'Highly illegal, of course, but they knew the men and liked them, and knew how unhappy they'd have been if they had to put up with each other's company in the grave.'

'Never believe historians,' she'd said startlingly in one letter. It followed from an account of a rival who'd invented names for roads, and then provided backgrounds for the invented names. Agnes herself was clearly the most honest of women: but she was no fool, and I believe she distrusted even her own honesty. She knew how the creative element in memory, always ready to give a helping hand with the facts, together with the historian's impatience to bridge a gap in a story, may lead to convincing sensations of accuracy at the very moment when one was being most inventive. But Agnes set store by being as reliable a witness as could be. She'd have frowned at

137

anyone who'd turned those six sacks into seven. I'd noticed as we scurried round Akaroa that day how she'd said things twice, for my benefit. In letters I'd told her of my view that everything was fiction, men and women not having the capacity for non-fiction. 'Accuracy,' I'd thundered on some airmail form or other, 'plays a small part in our daily lives; which is just as well, since we find accuracy difficult if not impossible to achieve. Most of what we report to each other and to ourselves is coloured by feeling, and in the nature of things we register only this or that fragmentary aspect of the events we are involved in.' And so on. I think Agnes knew I was perfectly capable of inventing names for roads; and that if I wrote of her, I should provide her with a more suitable name than her own. It was to this unprincipled ear of mine that, on that sunny hillside among the sloping graves, she addressed the story of her struggle to have a project accepted for the marking with stones of the graves of early pioneers. The council employees who mowed the grass had objected on the grounds that it is easier to mow a cemetery without stones than with them. The council had decided in Agnes's favour. 'Just as well!' cried this gently fierce woman, square in shape, busy, essentially a person from Surrey who'd found herself at the opposite end of the world in a setting now famous for holidaymaking, but once groaning, shrieking, bent of back, prematurely white of hair, as the pioneers struggled with the intransigeant soil and the beautiful, baleful sea.

In that cemetery, side by side, names French and names English. For it was here in Banks Peninsula that a shipload had arrived, eager to claim New Zealand for France. It came a little late: the place was already in the hands of descendants of the Surrey Blishens, and others. Rather than make the tedious return journey, the French pioneers had settled beside the British: and here was a graveyard that was a sort of necropolitan English-French dictionary. When it came to the naming of roads, the one Agnes lived

138

in had its French name: but Agnes, snorting, said this had existed only since the onset of tourism. Well, as we hurried about Akaroa, trying to see everything ('Notice that tearoom – it was built as a fort against the Maoris!'), she was scornful of more than one instance of this sort of renaming. Never believe historians: never believe tourist boards.

Agnes's house dated from just after Bateman Thomas Missen's arrival in New Zealand. (He was a stonemason, she said, as all the Paddington Blishens had been once they'd stopped soldiering.) It was a pioneer cottage built of pit-sawn totara wood, with cob walls. Its garden was like Agnes's mind, or her letters: a lumber room. What were stored here were old roses – 'I welcome every newly opened rose,' said Agnes, and I thought she probably did, the historian anxiously present at an event, even one so repetitious – lilacs, snowball trees, bluebells, forget-me-nots, borage, periwinkle (the major and the minor), honesty. 'The cottage is wreathed in buttery yellow banksia,' she'd written: but the truth was that the cottage was wreathed in a score or more of plants. 'Oh, oh! I long to be twenty years younger! – or it would do if I had the arms of an octopus!' she cried. She'd made a maze of roses somewhere, but it had taken its own course and become, she said, a mess of roses, instead. Inside, the cottage smelt like so many of the houses of my childhood – sour-sweet, with little local mustinesses: a kitchen mustiness, and a very particular lavatory mustiness. I lifted the lavatory seat and it fell sideways and out of sight. Agnes had heard the bang of it: 'I mean to have that done,' she said. 'There's a carpenter – ' But then she had to tell us about the carpenter's forebear who died one winter night trying to bring rum across the hills to Akaroa from the nearest tavern, which was then thirty penitential miles away. In the local restaurant where Agnes had taken us to lunch, she'd joined with me in consuming a very large carafe of wine, drinking it as if it had been an unusual distillation of genealogical data. Now she worried because the wine at times blotted out some tiny urgent fact she wished to communicate. In honour of our coming she'd tidied the cottage: which meant she'd cleared a minimal space in its wonderful and touching confusion, which followed from its being a sort of freelance and unsubsidised museum. Some of her neighbours, she said, were left cold by her passion for the past, and repelled by her delight in grave-yards. ('At Little Akaloa recently we had our lunch sitting on the curbing of the graves! Little Akaloa had never been seriously looked at before!') I thought they might have preferred Agnes the Girl Guide, as she had been: or the valiant wartime WAAF. She'd seen the world, when it was at war, and had most thoroughly honoured her obli-gations to the New Zealand Air Force: but she'd been glad to be home again. 'I don't take,' she told me, 'to the seamy side of life.' I thought how odd it was, that her concern as a collector of historical dust covered a great range of human sordidness – the pioneers had not only hanged themselves and made caches of sovereigns under their beds, but they'd been incestuous and rapacious and mur-derous, and Agnes knew and hoarded all the stories. Yet there was a sense in which her appetite for human frailty, which was boundless, operated only within Banks Pen-insula. I thought of Emily Dickinson, touching the extremest edges of human experience in terms of her never being at home anywhere but in Amherst, Massachusetts. This sweet bustling Agnes, my belatedly discovered, remote but distinct cousin, was in the same mould.

She served us with little cakes, walnut bread, biscuits with pickled walnuts embedded in them: resisting the desire to pass on each recipe. What was at work in her, given these visitors, was simply the wish to tell all she knew. I thought how marriage at least quietened this persistent human urgency. Indeed, sitting there, I felt there was a kind of unfairness, in that Kate and I had no ambition to display everything, our entire existences, and

140

Agnes had clearly so great a need to do so. Amid the soft mustinesses of this cottage at what for us counted as the end of the earth, I felt a helpless love for this blood relation of mine, who had, I thought – and perhaps large numbers of New Zealanders had – a quality as of a castaway. In a sense, Agnes's bustle was like Robinson Crusoe's: it sprang from the attempt to impose order upon the anarchic experience of being lost in the Pacific.

I remembered the driver of the bus who'd brought us here. Dressed in the bus company's uniform, green jacket, green shorts, he was a Maori: and when he stopped on the brow of the hill that overlooked Akaroa, so we could blink down at that sunshot jigsaw of bays and inlets, I thought his offer of a view didn't rest on the usual suggestion that this was a conventionally suitable place from which to take photographs, but sprang from a deeply wounded pride in the quality of a landscape that, to him, was not merely landscape. The truth being that he had the constitution, physical, moral, imaginative, that was at home down here, in these amazing islands: whereas the Europeans, my dear cousin among them, would always be astray here, their sensibilities incurably trained for other scenes, other views of the inner and outer worlds.

Before we left, Agnes produced a photograph of Harriet Blishen. When we saw it, Kate and I gasped. It was taken perhaps about 1860: a portrait of a woman born in 1800. It simply happened to be a perfect photograph of my sister, born in 1924. It was not a mere matter of outlines and features being identical. Harriet was smiling: and her faintly lopsided smile, with a very particular order of diffidence about it – a special disposition of the face to suggest amusement combined with uncertainty – was exactly my sister's smile.

141

13

We drifted northwards again, at every halt a meeting to address. We found ourselves at Bring-a-Plate parties (you were expected to bring something on a plate, but we met a charming woman who'd been new to it, and simply brought a plate). A friend drove us among crinkled hills and alongside the ocean to Nelson for a teachers' conference. On the way we picnicked on crayfish in a curious wayside dust heap provided with tables: I went to pee under a bridge and discovered, late, that I was subject to survey from a ship at sea, passing cars and a train. The conference began with a Maori welcome. Haphazardly dressed, with the reverse of a grand effect, two groups parried traditional jests, comments, bursts of song, and what appeared to be teasings. I wondered what might be said in a language unknown to most of the audience. The mayor, once this ethnic obligation was completed, was officially to open the conference: I noticed his fingers beat an impatient tattoo throughout the fidgeting mystery of the welcome. His own welcome had the character of a television commercial, and presented this extraordinarily pleasant town, sitting on the edge of a spread of splendid bays, as if it were an amalgam of emporia, and nothing better.

I loved the conference. It began with a battered teacher telling the stories a battered teacher tells: of fertile disasters, and of pieces of teaching that, in going wrong, go right. Suddenly, on this journey that raised so many questions as to the way people could be misplaced, I found myself among my own kind: part of the universal nation of teachers.

Rotorua. Katherine Mansfield had hated the town – though she thought it might have been because of the smell. 'Sulphur City,' said the librarian who picked us up at the airport. She was plainly preparing us for olfactory miseries for which the performance of the most dramatic geysers in the world would not compensate. We found ourselves in a motel room: and in the walled yard into which it opened was our own plunge pool. We didn't know that was the name for it until we walked into the town. Rotorua was designed for the simultaneous enactment of a hundred *High Noon*s. It has streets overwide, at this time of the year empty. We walked past such nervously competitive motels as we'd never imagined, each making promises designed to be a fraction more frantically irresistible than those made by its neighbours. Waterbeds were offered, video, plunge pools. One establishment alleged of itself that it was run by PURVEYORS OF THE FINEST MOTEL ACCOMMODATION. On the edge of town, the earth gasped, its breath sulphurously visible. Kate and I, bemused, suddenly particularly aware of being remote from Barley Wood – 'I find myself thinking we seem twelve thousand miles from home, and then I realise we are,' said Kate – introduced ourselves to our plunge pool. It was circular, a plastic container whose burning walls it was best to avoid, and an odorous steam rose from it, perpetually. The trick was to turn a cold water tap and temper the pool until you dared to enter it. It was heavy, this sulphurous water, as well as supportively hot: you lay out in it and became a human water lily. When we first entered the pool – which thenceforth we occupied as often as we could, since the pleasure of it resembled no other pleasure we'd known – it was gently and rather warmly raining. As Kate said, to take a bath in the open air, in water so buoyant, under such a tender storm of rain, was to feel one was misbehaving in some entirely novel fashion. There was a touch of decline about it, if not fall.

We went to see the geysers. It seemed an odd visit to

143

make, simply as sightseers, to these acres of the earth that wept, gasped, fumed, and produced great showers of water and spume obeying some buried metronome. It was like going as a tourist to one of the outer tracts of hell. I'd not expected anything so strangely, grossly beautiful. There were, for example, the pools in which a thick mud, here plain chocolate, here milk, simply spat and plopped. It made round mouths, and you watched with a sort of daft delight, trying to guess where these impolite mouthings and spittings would next occur. In some places there'd developed a sort of general mouth, slowly heaving, and it would have made a crust for itself, of sulphur but much else: so each would have its own complex colouring, brilliantly gangrenous, poisonously blue, amazingly rusty. The geyser park was arranged so much like a gentle Japanese garden, and the flowers it contained were so ungentle ... that spitting mud, those high thin wavering screens of steam, those fine spouts and leaping sprays of burning water – here and there, little groves of steam, a stretch of vaporous shrubland – all obeying the regular irregularities of the timing mechanism that set them off.

I thought there were perhaps few more effective ways of causing an uneasy human being to feel fragile and transient. And in a corner, indeed, were Maori tombs, from the lids of which wisps of steam wandered. It struck me that death came close here to being a sort of cookery, and then wondered sadly if the image would have got me into further trouble with the young Maori novelist met in Auckland.

We walked next day into the forest: or the Forest Park, as this remnant of a wilderness was now called. In no time we were among immortals, great redwoods, and more fugitive plants of a spectacular kind, the giant tree ferns, which when it rained hugely offered us an ambiguous sort of shelter: we stood under their great leaves, amid the apparent litter of inner tubing that is the debris of these untidy giants and, the purest rain dripping off our noses,

144

smiled helplessly at each other, obliged to hole up in what remained of a Pacific forest. What on earth were the Blishens, from Barley Wood with its silver birches, doing in this rump of a great paradise of giant ferns, which lowered rain to the earth by way of an audible escalator, leaf to leaf to leaf?

Close to the motel was a complex of single-storey houses that had been taken over by Maoris. The litter was dismaying. Unable to be at home inside, they'd brought their furniture out of doors: there were rotting sofas, collapsing tables and chairs. A nearby hotel offered the rooms overlooking this complex at a reduced rate. I thought of the superb orderliness of the reconstructed Maori *pa* a mile away, in the geyser park. The sordidness of these houses had clearly nothing to do with Maori character. It must have had much to do with inconsolable defeat and dispossession, and with the demand that a people accustomed to living according to the broad gestures of the land should live instead according to the narrow gestures of a world of competitive motels.

A voice on the radio said that, in proportion to their number, the Maoris were the second most imprisoned people in the world.

14

It was a Maori guide who conducted us through the upper caves at Waitomo, a handsome man given to the foolish jokes that everywhere guides in majestic places are tempted to make. I thought that, as in afterlife we approached the fields of asphodel or the lakes of fire and brimstone (that ultimate Rotorua), we'd not escape such jesters, making their duties endurable by the constant polishing and improving of facetious comment. Thirty or .forty of us made our way, tittering, exclamatory, through these superb spaces: icy stomachs and throats, with intestine-like means of descent from level to level. We'd been swallowed, I thought, by some refrigerated whale: and then wondered if I were any better than the guide, unable to avoid making comparisons. These slowly-formed and frozen pink-and-white spaces were what they were, and not like anything else in the world.

And then we came to the lake at the roots of the mountain. A boat waited for us, in black water, under a glowing roof. The place was a silencer: nobody spoke: even small children stepped into the boat without a word, watching as the Maori boatman reached up for what we made out to be ropes fixed to the roof: by pulling on them the boat was made to move. It was a silent movement, not so much through water as through as complete a liquid blackness as we'd ever known. The constant light offered by the glow-worms seemed always likely to fail, and never likely to fail: it was composed of a million intermittent gleams: it was a huge pulsing light that held its brightness to itself. Slowly, in absolute silence, we moved from throat to throat of this final cave. I thought the silence was caused by awe, understandable enough: blackness of such an unfamiliar degree, light so unlike any other light imaginable: the mysterious obedience of the boat, for although we knew the boatman's hands were on the rope overhead, still our movement seemed difficult to explain. But I wondered if that silence weren't also caused by a deep response to an old image, which some in the boat might not have encountered but that must invent itself in any mind, being so deep and so accurate. This was Lethe, he was Charon, and over there was Hades.

Over there was the bus, waiting. But next time it might be otherwise.

A dragonfly
Split the sun:
One sank,
And one flew on.

146

It was our son Tom's poem, arriving in New Zealand in a letter from Greece: and here we were in that most monstrous of all dragonflies, a Boeing 747 (but I admired it always, such a gorgeous expanded insect, and particularly fine in the livery of Air New Zealand). We'd set out from Auckland in order to arrive an hour earlier in Los Angeles. This week we would have two Wednesdays.

New Zealand. A literate community (more books are bought per head than in any other country in the world) that feels distant from the general literary scene. Well, there was this general sense of being remote. To oversimplify the story, huge numbers of people from Cambridge and Lichfield, Winchester, Richmond, Wakefield and Wanstead (I take the names at random from the map of New Zealand) travelled across the earth's diameter and found themselves among an alien quantity of tussocks. They sought to repair the damage by creating alternative Scotlands and surrogate Home Counties, but could never (for all that passion so sturdily felt for Katherine Mansfield's 'undiscovered country') feel anything but at the furthest end of the road. Those Scots arrived at the south of the South Island had thought they'd simply gone the long way home. I tried to imagine that it had happened the other way round. Maoris had taken over Britain: and Cambridge (until a late change designed to appeal to tourists) was renamed Oamuru, and Lichfield became Kaikoura, and Winchester was Taumarunui. The Maoris tried very hard to feel at home in this other island closely associated with clouds, but it wasn't the same, nothing could make it the same: all the affection in the world couldn't transform the wildest beach in Cornwall or the west of Scotland into one of those profound beaches north of Auckland, to which Kate and I were taken by our last hosts – beaches with a sort of blackness about them, a touch perhaps of lava disseminated throughout these southern waters: a huge oceanic quality alongside which the greatest of British beaches had an oceanic quality of an altogether smaller kind.

A few weeks before we'd arrived in New Zealand the Greenpeace ship, *Rainbow Warrior*, had been blown up in Auckland harbour, causing a death. The sense of insult was deeply felt throughout the country. It was partly that it had been done in such a manner that even the police, not famous for their detective skills, had known within half an hour that it was the work of the French. If, people said, they'd left on the scene of the crime a long loaf, a beret and a bottle of Medoc they could not have been more insolently careless. The deeper cause of distress was that the French had displayed such contempt in general for a small and distant country.

We had, for the moment, and on the basis of dozens of pleasant encounters, a sense of being New Zealanders by proxy. Greatly in favour of the French, we were temporary Francophobes. But here we were, about to become (having vaulted over a couple of Wednesdays) inhabitants by proxy of the USA, and then surrogate Canadians.

15

OUTDOORIUM. It was a word we'd caught sight of over a shop somewhere in New Zealand. And here we were, in what must be one of the world's great outdooria. It was near the end of a well-known journey, from Calgary to Jasper Park, in the Canadian Rockies, and back. Smooth car, smooth roads.

The fact is we were on a tremendous floor among tremendous mountains. My sister when a child had amused us with her exaggerations: in a field, she'd say, there were millions of buttercups. The scene here included, coolly, millions of fir trees. The road wound across the huge space, along with a great, largely dry riverbed. Ahead of us, as far as the eye could see, were mountains of unspeakable size. There was no real way of dealing with the problem of expressing the vastness of the setting in which, tinily comfortable, we moved.

Everywhere, rising walls of fir scattered with the grey splinters of fallen timber. Everywhere, entire arboreal graveyards. Everywhere, water coloured by rock flour. On the mountainsides, whole meadows of red and gold. But each was a giant of a meadow. Each quarter of the scene was a breathtaking world in itself.

Kate said she badly wished to have eyes with wide-angled lenses.

Who could have guessed at the infinite variety of mountains? That great one over there was a profound pink, and there were several shades of rust represented in its gargantuan neighbours: and here was a gold one, and here one purely green, and another that was a pinkish grey. Each took an age to appear, to take shape, to pass. There were clouds on them, like other mountains hanging upside down. Man had tried to make sense of it all by giving names to aspects of this enormousness. Beauty Creek. Tangle Creek and Tangle Falls. Sunwapta Falls. Maligne Canyon. Pyramid Lake (next door to Patricia Lake). The Athabasca Glacier, which was close to dipping its immense dirty toe into the highway.

You could stop, in this geological hugeness, and drink at the Grizzly B'ar.

Every turn of the road offered a new wonder in the way these great things lay. Here was a redfaced mountain swimming in a general sea of sunshine and mountains. 'To say I feel like a flea,' I said, 'is to understate it.' 'I married a flea,' said Kate.

Suddenly, a succession of vast tilted slabs, as if the earth's innards were hanging out. And then, a multitude of little plum-yellow forests. Here we were, in an extreme of sunlight, and we looked ahead (a hundred miles or so) to visible great slantings of rain. As I thought that the world ought to be full of rainbows, perhaps a thousand rainbows would fill the space adequately, I saw that we were driving between hosts of little trees as yellow as some quite other sort of sunshine.

We slept, exhausted by majesty, and suddenly were back in Calgary, stripped of it. Mooseburgerville.

16

My cousin Bobby had a sense of perhaps being about to be famous – or not. At sixty-five he'd been required by the university regulations to retire: but it had struck him that this rule ran counter to a recent national enactment that forbade discrimination by sex, religion, racial origin ... or age. The offence involved, Bobby had no doubt, was ageism. We discussed it strolling through Toronto, which would have delighted our Uncle Arthur, I thought: he'd been a plasterer, but also a glazier, and as a child I'd loved to watch him at work with putty. He'd never walked through a glazier's paradise like this – whole buildings of glass. Bobby said he was greatly excited: for what he felt lay ahead was the possibility that he might enter the history books. Gaining such entry had been a dream of his since, an unhappy child whose home was breaking up around him, he'd spent days in the public library in Southsea, reading of distant places whose general name might be Peril – you could be frozen to death, shot or hanged or scalped, devoured by bears or drowned in frightful torrents: but in these stories there wasn't a single quarrelling mother or father. The boy's dream, in a nutshell, was that future atlases might note the existence of Mount Blishen, the rapids-ridden Blishen River, or a small, rough, parent-free township, Blishenborough. Things had not turned out like that. The standard table of social mobility related to racial origins bore his name: but there were no rapids involved, and if pioneering had entered into it (as it had), it was what could be done in a study. The little war with his university, in which he was supported by his professional union, brought hope alive again. His father's attempt to secure him the fate of a nameless hobo by sending him to Canada at fifteen with five pounds in his pocket (actually, he said, double-pinned to the lining of his jacket), would be defeated: he would instead become a prodigious legal footnote. One of his daughters, herself a lawyer, had married into the law: and Bobby confessed that he dreamed of emerging onto the steps outside the great courts of justice in the Canadian capital, Jess on one side of him and Jim on the other, and being borne through the city on the shoulders of a group selected from the waiting millions. It would be a sort of *Mr Smith Goes to Washington*: except, he said anxiously, that it would of course be *Professor Blishen Goes to Ottawa*.

And friends of Bobby's reopened their weekend cottage for us, having shut it down for the coming winter: it was alone on a small tortoise of an island on one of Ontario's thousands of lakes. The island had originally been called Syndicate, being owned by two or three families together: Hugh had inherited it from an uncle, who'd renamed it Singkettle, that being his childhood understanding of the name. The cottage was a sort of wooden kettle, indeed, boiling with books. We'd come to it in Hugh's boat in bright sunshine, and as the sun set, needing half the sky to stage the burning drama in, Hugh took Kate and me out in turns in a canoe. It must be an addictive delight, we thought, such silent progress, such closeness to the thick swell of the metal-coloured water, such a need to measure each movement and mostly to be still. It was an experience of profound silence to set beside that in the Waitomo Caves. You could have heard – and I thought I did hear – the sigh of a fish. Kate and Hugh made their noiseless return to the island under the moon.

And it was under the moon that we returned across the

lake to our cars: Bobby required to shift his weight from back to front of the boat so that we aquaplaned, thick moon-shot wings of water rising behind us. I thought back across the gabble of the past two months, Gabble 'n Go it had been, all that talking, all those dinners, all that feverishness of cities – though four had been such beautiful neighbours of the Pacific, Sydney, Wellington, San Francisco, Vancouver – that rhodomontade of higher and fatter buildings, as in Toronto, swollen condominiums, towers of glass glaring at towers of glass: all that human coarseness, all that Gobbling 'n Going, all those fully licensed paradises: and I hardly knew how to thank our hosts for that evening of chosen silences on that scrap of an island on that fragment of a lake.

17

Being home again was like when you were a child and spun yourself round and round to see if it made you dizzy – and it did. Well, it was like the aftermath of that. The world continued to spin, a little, and you found yourself rather faint on your feet.

There were cuttings of interviews with us in New Zealand. 'Oh my God, I'm warm, soft-voiced, unruffled,' Kate groaned. But I was worse. My eyes had an almost elfin sparkle: and, not satisfied with that, they also had a tawny glow.

PART THREE

1

'It'll become two little bags, like your father's.' It was what my mother had once said, I guessed round about 1930, about my immature scrotum. I'd remembered it at this moment, a few days after the completion of our circumnavigation of the globe, because I'd run into George Straker, in the High Street, and he was telling me about New Zealand. There was nothing to do but gaze into the nearest shop window. That was full of bathrooms in the modern manner, baths of bizarre shape, lavatories designed for persons without legs. Notices stuck on the window were anxious to know when we'd last restyled our bathrooms. And I suddenly recalled the never restyled – indeed, never styled – bathroom at our old home. I'd been standing in it, childishly scraggy – in fact, in our old-fashioned bath-shaped bath – when my mother made that astounding statement: having become suddenly hilarious, as she always was when brushing up against the facts of life.

'It's all very well for Mr Lange,' George was saying, mispronouncing the New Zealand Prime Minister's name, 'but I know one or two reasons not known to those who merely read the newspapers' – he fixed me with an angry eye, and I realised my crime was worse: I'd merely been to New Zealand – 'for saying that his anti-nuclear policy will not do.' George paused to admire this last phrase and clearly liked it. 'Will not do,' he repeated.

I could see that the first stage of his Saturday afternoon lecture was nearing its close, and that he would soon be turning to the question of the Maoris. The fact that they had problems threw some light on how they'd been super-seded by a more enterprising race as effective rulers of New Zealand. That's what he'd be saying in a moment or so. I decided I must continue to think of the bathroom at home.

It was a whole world. There was a washstand with a top of grey mock-marble. There was a cupboard in which my mother kept the box containing some huge device intended, as I understood it, to make more comfortable a condition from which she'd suffered since my birth. I'd once found in the cupboard a pamphlet on birth control, with illustrations drawn by someone whose natural sub-ject-matter was sewage systems: he'd turned the inside – and much of the relevant outside – of bodies into a repellent matter of great pipeways and sluices and U-bends, and you'd have thought, studying it, that making love must involve much work with wrenches and suction cups. I think I felt about it that it described what suitably took place between parents, and parents only.

'... I'm sorry to say this,' George was saying without any evidence of sorrow, 'that being a Maori, a ... um ... Australian aborigine, a ... um ... North American Indian, becomes an end in itself. There is no wish for absorp-tion ...'

From 1938 onwards the bathroom cupboard had con-tained my *New Statesman*s, of which I never threw away a copy until about 1945: I can't think why my father permitted this unsuitable use of the cupboard, but he did so, growlingly. The focus of the room was provided by the geyser, the explosive roar of which, when it was lit, always made the entire house nervous. As a boy I'd admired my various skinninesses in its shining brass belly. With care one could oblige the distorting surface to make this or that part of oneself dismayingly small or dis-gracefully large. When my mother was still bathing me she could be relied upon to bring these narcissistic moments to some prosaic end: as with her reference to my scrotum.

'. . . and you were in Calgary, I gather,' said George, 'and probably didn't realise while you were there . . .'

I'd checked with the suddenly ridiculous brazen reflection and decided not to believe my mother. It did seem the sort of thing she might well get wrong. At the same time, I remember, I was uneasy: it seemed also the sort of thing that, the soul of indiscretion, she'd blurt out to a neighbour in my presence. 'Teddy's . . . you know what I mean . . . has become two little bags, like his father's.' It would be worse, of course, if my father were present, too. I imagined, at any rate, that he would also blush.

George, in his demolition of any claims I might have been tempted to advance to an understanding of any spot I'd visited during our recent journey, had reached Toronto. He remembered my cousin Robert, could not recall the university he taught at, was uncertain about what he called Bobby's discipline (I thought of a moment during that visit when Bobby and I had somehow drunk a bottle of wine between us whilst washing up), and appraised the Canadian city in terms, as far as I could make out, of its having been, from the beginning, badly sited. Well, George couldn't be everywhere, I thought, and the Canadians had certainly had to do without his advice in the early years of the seventeenth century.

I wondered what methods would be chosen to take me down a peg or two at Bush House.

It is not widely known (to use a phrase of George's) that when you cross the main entrance hall at Bush House, you are treading through the ghostly walls of John Donne's dining room. He lived in a house on that spot in 1612. True, you could walk nowhere in the centre of London without stepping on the toes of famous phantoms: but, having read and loved Donne for half a century, I felt whenever I made my way towards the BBC's multilingual lifts that I was in the presence of a very special coincidence.

I'd brought a tape back with me. It was of an interview, recorded in Nelson, with the novelist Maurice Gee. I'd said that I thought as a writer he was made particularly happy by human unhappiness. He said he must make a note of that. It was right. It wasn't that he enjoyed the spectacle of misery, but that somehow his gift responded to whatever was downturned ... Walking with Kate in nearby public gardens after the interview in a studio at Radio Nelson, I'd thought how true it was that, for some, disaster was sustaining. Perhaps the only happy man or woman under the whip of the Ancient Egyptians was the one who saw there was a novel in it. And take Nell Shilling. If you looked through Nell's work for extracts that might be used in an anthology designed to cheer us up, on any front whatever, you'd look in vain. If there could be such a thing as cheering us down, that was Nell's field. Yet somehow the effect – of Nell and Maurice Gee – wasn't dismaying.

That was because a skilful account even of calamity and mishap was invigorating, owing to the fact that it was ... oh, damn it, skilful?

Here, on my first day back, was a writer who'd just won a huge literary prize. 'Poor man,' I said, 'you must have been interviewed to death.' 'Yes,' he said. 'But it's much better than not being interviewed to death.' And here, to follow, was a novelist who, I knew from previous experience, could not give a short answer to any question. To him, a question immediately suggested a range of answers, some complementary, some in conflict, all to be welded into as satisfactory a response as possible, given that it would be absolutely tentative: for he did not trust his own conclusions, massive though he made them appear. It was as if, my first question asked, he at once began selecting, and bolting together, the sections of some immense construction – usually a dome, I'd think – measuring the space to be covered with an eye at once confident and anxious: swarming across the great surfaces of the answer as they

were assembled, suddenly finding a rivet necessary –
sparks would fly – the dome already filled the space
between us, but he did not altogether care for it: he began
to move back across it, unbolting, removing rivets – allowing an entire section to fall with a clatter to the floor. This
morning Stella, my producer, was looking anxious – she
wanted, good Lord, at most four minutes thirty seconds,
and this answer was already twice that length. I opened
my mouth, but, seeing only those gleaming surfaces, he
was now swarming at fantastic speed round the recon-
stituted answer, hammering, tightening, loosening. And
then came the sigh of despair with which he always ended,
the throwing up of hands. It was the best he could do, but
. . . not good enough, not good enough!

'Ah,' I said: and, avoiding Stella's eye, asked one more
out of the half-dozen questions I'd absurdly chosen as
those that *must* be asked.

Bush House, accustomed to people arriving from the
round earth's imagined corners, seemed to have little of
George's disposition to get in first with information about
the places I'd visited. But the suggestion that my eyes not
merely sparkled but glowed, making me perhaps the only
pixie engaged in broadcasting, had appeared in a radio
journal widely read on these premises. I tried travelling in
the lifts with my eyes shut, but this did not prevent me
from hearing a small Hungarian remark that I was saving
them for the Kiwis.

2

No doubt about it: the 1980s belonged not only to George
Straker, but to my father.

Cheering her on from his armchair, my father might
well have forgiven Mrs Thatcher for being a woman. As
for my mother, she'd have been driven time and again to
perilous displays of insubordination. 'Yes, dear,' she'd

murmur, at pauses in his encomiums, in Mrs Thatcher's favour, and diatribes, on the subject of her enemies. But there'd be a quiver in her voice. She found him so very funny, at times: so pompous . . . And when that happened, the attention she gave to his monologues – in which he moved awkwardly from phrase to phrase, hammering language together in a fury of split wood and bent nails – would be flawed with a faint giggle. My father had become expert in detecting its presence. The monologue would halt: 'I don't know why I bother!' My mother would say, in a curious satirical tone she reserved for these occasions: 'But of course, dear! You're right, dear! No one's saying you're wrong, dear!' When she knew (though I don't know how she knew) that the risk could be taken, she'd add: 'We wouldn't dare!' He would leave the room, furious, and she'd do an impertinent little jig. I guess it all went back a long way, to early moments in their relationship: at fourteen under one of the lampposts where she said so much of their courtship occurred, he'd be the humourless boy giving an overlong account of some dispute he'd had with a brother, and Lizzie would giggle and jiggle, and love him and deplore him, and the evening would end in his black gloom, and her tears.

Through the eighties I cheered myself by imagining how she'd murmur, just within range of his hearing: 'Oh you and your Mrs Thatcher!' And when we were alone she'd say: 'I wonder he doesn't go and live with her!'

We even found ourselves now evading the Bostocks, glimpsed anywhere in Barton or Barley Wood. They'd long been good friends: and always, until now, in circumstances free of politics. I knew that Godfrey, whose true love was the bat – since boyhood he'd been a tremendous expert on this creature so commonly loathed, and had great tenderness for it – could not be a political ally. He'd been a successful businessman, in a family firm, and as long as I'd known him as a friend had been spending much of his time dressed for the City: a piece of the local

160

clockwork, going to his pinstriped work and returning from it in one or other of his large cars. The Godfrey I actually knew was the off-duty man, in shirtsleeves or sports coat, always eager to talk about books – his reading was narrow but intense, with W. H. Hudson at the centre of it – and the enthusiast for bats, to whom it was not imaginable that his passion was unshared. Nelly, his wife, had perfected various ways of stopping him before he could invite utterly unsuitable persons, famously squeamish, into the room where he kept his specimens. There, in the gloom he cultivated, were to be found his friends, suspended, as if years ago someone had done away with, shrunk and hung upside down the entire staff of the grammar school, in their black gowns. There was a shining of little dead eyes and a gleam of tiny sharp teeth. There'd be something new, always, or something new to relate about something old. I believe a visitor had once fainted, but Nelly liked to exaggerate the number of such casualties. Given a bump anywhere in the house she'd say: 'Godfrey's taken someone into the battery!' 'Could you ever haved imagined that Godfrey was drawn to bats, of all things?' she'd say. 'I mean, they really don't try to make themselves attractive, do they?' Godfrey would blush uncomprehendingly. 'Oh come on, Nelly!' 'He kept it quiet while we were courting. But then, mark you, I suppose he could hardly say: "What I really do is collect vampires."' 'Oh Nelly!' After thirty years of failure to get Nelly to distinguish between bats and vampires, Godfrey seemed always to feel that the latest attempt would succeed. 'Nelly, a bat is . . .' 'Oh Godfrey, you really don't need to tell me . . .'

I found it odder to think of Godfrey as a squadron leader – and a valiant one, as I knew he had been. Now he was a man gently exhilarated by what he took to be the divine inventiveness that lay behind the creation of the bat. 'Do you know . . .?' he'd exult: and make some point about a variation of wing-span, some newly discovered nocturnal oddity of habit in a creature that, in respect of its behaviour after lights out, one would have thought could have no fresh eccentricity to add.

They'd been our friends since the years just after the war, though we'd known Godfrey much longer. When we were all children he'd lived in one of Barton's avenues, in a house that filled me with awe for being so casually large: spreading itself in what I imagined (from my reading) to be an elastic arrangement of lounges: breakfast rooms and so, presumably, tea and dinner rooms: sculleries *and* kitchens: bedrooms numbered or named for the colour of their walls: multiple bathrooms, bootrooms, and certainly a billiard room: as a child scrumping apples in their positive kingdom of a back garden, I'd seen waistcoated men, bent at acute angles, and the stab and thrust of cues. Coming from 10 Manor Road, with its few cramped rooms, I was dazzled by the thought of accommodation so reckless of space. Godfrey went away to be schooled, and later became a scarfed figure in a sportscar, accompanied by young women who plainly went away to be courted; for none of them came from Barton. I sourly admired this contempt for the local, in education and love. There was no rising superior to *that*.

Nelly had been a WAAF: and, settled in with Godfrey in that once vast house, which seemed to have shrunk since my childhood, joined the amateur dramatic company Kate and I belonged to. Our producer was always running short of grand ladies, to play grand ladies: and Nelly was capable of tremendous grandeur. She played Lady Bracknell splendidly, except that she gave the strongest impression of being twenty years younger than her daughter. I'd not liked her at early encounters, for her patrician habit of crying: '*Mark you!*' 'If she says it to me again . . .' I told Kate: not finishing the statement, for I knew that if she said it to me again I should merely describe the offence sternly in my diary. Kate said that under those habits of hauteur there was a very different Nelly, and so it was: like

162

our friend Sally Roberts, she had inside her a chuckling urchin. Late in life I enjoyed being the victim of one of her cries of '*Mark you!*' Now, rather older than Lady Bracknell, but still looking rather younger, she'd accompany the exclamation with a dig to your ribs of her spectacles, which she seemed to carry for this sort of purpose more often than she wore them. There was something incurably young about both the Bostocks, and I saw this as a further measure of the extravagance of their upbringing. Godfrey in his battery was, in the faintest rheumatic fashion, the boy he'd once been in the same room. Their children having dispersed, Nelly was rapidly reverting to some amused creature she'd been before she ever met Godfrey. She re-read the favourite books of her childhood and youth: she added to collections she'd been making most of her life: she played Lady Bracknell yet again, and now seemed her daughter's slightly older sister.

We were caught up, I'd think sometimes, not only in our own but in other people's synopses. Heavens, there were scores of lives we knew in this summary fashion: to the open stretches of which could be added stretches more or less shadowy. So there were Godfrey's infidelities: and – with someone so like Godfrey it hardly seemed worthwhile – Nelly's one large infidelity. Kate said she'd heard Nelly's lover had been different from Godfrey in one huge respect: he had no interest whatever in bats. But, never the closest friends, we'd been through the years warmly in and out of their synopsis, as they'd been in and out of ours. We'd met always in those small but pleasant areas of our common existence where liking had no difficulty in thriving. And now we couldn't meet without the emergence of an unmanageable difference between us. They were delighted that what they thought of as the world of the open-necked was in retreat. Liberalisms of every variety were being cut down in every direction. Sloppinesses of social benevolence were being removed. Oh,

163

hurrah for cuts falling where they did! Oh, hurrah for such overdue severities of budgeting in the field of the arts! Oh, hurrah for the defeat of the miners! Oh, hurrah for this and that demonstration that the British lion still had teeth! I said a sharp thing about the British lion, and about teeth (my own were causing me great discomfort, lately), and about bats and *their* teeth, and then wished I'd kept quiet, for Godfrey looked wounded in a way that had nothing to do with the British lion, but much to do with the long amiability between us. Nelly said, gesturing with her spectacles: 'Mark you, I don't think they see things in quite the same way . . .' 'Oh, we've always got on,' said Godfrey, 'though we've always known there were subjects to be avoided . . .'

We'd moved into a time when those subjects could not be avoided. All that could be avoided, alas, was the Bostocks by us, and us by the Bostocks.

3

The other car began, astonishingly, to waltz across the near-midnight road. It obeyed some sort of silent music, dangerously jolly: and it was waltzing across the road, in wider and wider musical sweeps, until it became clear that it would strike us. This it did, with an outrageous crash and crunch, and then it steadied, the impact with us had enabled it to stop waltzing: and it went, enormously quickly, and we were left to make two major discoveries, slownesses emerging out of the hideous pace of those previous seconds: we were alive and unhurt, and the car was a ruin.

At some point – it remained difficult to return to any sense of one event preceding or following another – a car set off indignantly in pursuit of our assailant. At some point, it returned, rueful, having been outsped. At some point, from the steak house, a similarly indignant Greek waiter appeared, to offer brandy, and to inform us that we'd been hit by an orange Volkswagen. We'd been aware of what struck us only as a calamitous waltzing blur.

And once again I knew what it was Kate would say as the world ended. Smoke and flame rising from cracks in an over-strained planet (I'd always had the feeling that, simply, too much had been asked of what was essentially a straightforward ball of clay), Kate would cry: 'Oh, *no*!'

It was what she'd exclaimed on both occasions when our car had been struck by another. Faced with a strong possibility of our extinction within the next few seconds, she was mildly aghast, and drew on the language of domestic expostulations. Well, she'd said last time it happened, it might not be of the quality of Flamineo's final observation in *The White Devil*: I have an everlasting cold upon me. It was not an observation like that ventured by Hamlet, that the rest was silence. Given a scribbling pad and an hour or two between the approach of the other car and the actual impact, she might have produced something worthy of the occasion. As it was, I'd have to put up with an ejaculation that, if it lacked drama, at least had the merit of sincerity. 'When someone has behaved idiotically in such a manner as to threaten us with death,' she said, 'my attention is obviously drawn to the simple silliness of it all. Thus this cry which gives you so much literary dissatisfaction.'

Actually, I thought 'Oh, *no*!' would do, perfectly. It was what all the rest of that splendour of last words amounted to.

Certainly silliness was the mark of the behaviour of the other driver, in each case. On the first occasion we were in one of those suburbs of London that have a sort of mortuary lighting, so that the late-night street seems full of refugees from graveyards: and were astonished, being on a main road, to see a car drive dreamily out of a side street into our path. 'Oh, *no*!' cried Kate, applying her brakes: the other car, a Morris 1000, struck us a surprisingly tremendous blow – you'd not expect two objects of limited mass to come together with such sound effects, as if an opera by Wagner and a symphony by Mahler had reached their climaxes together. There was a general impression of two motorcars, together with their occupants, being reduced to particles none of which was more than a square centimetre in area. Astonished thereafter to discover one was shakily intact – though there was an enormous sensation as of things that had been bowling along becoming things that would never move again – one shifted from contemplation of one's end, an eternal matter, to a very brisk, temporal desire to read someone or other an immense lecture. As this thaw proceeded, from the frozen moment of impact to the hot sensation of simple indignation, I left the car by a door that had burst open of its own accord, and crossed to where the Morris stood, looking oddly like some blunt-nosed dragon, its bonnet in the air, smoke rising.

Kate said she observed my departure and what followed with, at first, considerable satisfaction. 'I suppose I thought you were going to thrash the living daylights out of someone,' she said. 'It's not your kind of thing, but it seemed appropriate, at that moment, and I think I hoped you would manage it.' In fact, reaching the Morris, I looked inside (both its doors had burst open) and saw a very young woman, weeping. She cried: 'Oh, what will my father say? He gave it to me for my birthday. I've just been to see my boyfriend. I wasn't thinking.' As far as insurance was concerned, it was our case in a nutshell. But I wasn't thinking of the law, or the slow filling in of forms and the establishment of facts. Putting my arms round the quivering enemy driver, I said: 'I'm sure your father will understand.'

Kate said it was, if one had to refer back to drama, as if Hamlet had embraced Claudius. Sitting in the ruins of our car, she'd scarcely believed what she'd seen. When later she upbraided me for my behaviour, I had one consolation only: that if it had been she who'd taken those angry strides across to the Morris, it would have been she who'd made every effort to comfort the young woman. Kate had no greater gift for revenge than I had.

Kate was always the driver. She'd come from a pioneering family in respect of the motor car, and had herself been driving for nearly fifty years. The progress of her childhood had been marked by her father's purchase of dying cars, none costing more than five pounds, which he had a gift for marvellously rejuvenating. One day Kate and her mother would look out with dismay at the wreck he'd brought home, one of the ruins that Laurel and Hardy might have knocked about a bit: and the next day they were looking out at an object spick and span and gleaming, ready at a turn of the starting handle to purr with promising life. Early photographs show Kate in this or that dickey seat, halfway between a daughter and a postillion. At the first legal moment, if not earlier, she'd become possessed of an Austin Seven of her own. It had cost £35, and Jim, her father, said she'd paid seven times too much for it. It had a tendency to progress by leaps and bounds, and was known as The Flea. When I met her in the mid-1940s she'd progressed to another sort of Austin, smelling of leather, with pockets on the insides of its doors in which I longed to keep the manuscripts of novels, and would have done so had I written any. It was, in those days, when there was little doubt about sexual roles, difficult to be the non-driving man courting, as the term was, a driving woman. Kate felt it strongly: asking me, on evenings when she took me for what were then called spins, and as our emotions mounted, what I would do if I were in charge of the vehicle. I remember on such an occasion – we were in a lane on the edge of Barton – answering that I would draw into the gateway of the next farm. Kate did this: and sexual differentiation, as we didn't think of it then, was able to proceed as usual.

This was 1946: we have travelled rather more than forty years since then.

So I found myself married to a woman with a positively romantic view of driving. I had no wish to drive, and felt a curious pleasure in that being Kate's mysterious province. As time went on, and driving became generally less romantic, and Kate grew older, I was sometimes sorry I hadn't learned. And my regret, on that evening when it was she who had to confront the waltzing Volkswagen, was increased by the fact that it had been, curse it, a bad evening out, spent under the Houses of Parliament.

I'd been asked to speak to a group of persons disposed to be rational. I was greatly in favour of rationality, and was pleased to be asked to address them on the importance of giving the head some say in affairs. The disposition to accept such invitations had led at times to my talking to groups of humanists. Those who, like me, leaned in this direction, tended – if given to turning up to evening meetings – to be curiously dull in appearance. Alas, alas, there seemed never to be a vividly dressed, or simply pretty or handsome, or sportive, or Tom Foster-like humanist. I felt I'd have justified myself in the light of that philosophy if I'd turned the King of Greengrocers into an essentially unsober person who agreed that the sober use of the mind ought to occupy something like the forefront of human activity – not as an extinguisher but, in the chimney sense, as a damper. I knew that important intellectual and emotional revolutions had been brought about by persons indifferent to appearance: but I couldn't believe that, among all the rifts that opened up between human beings, this one was inevitable. Damn it, must the Devil have, not only the best tunes, but the best faces and the best costumes? It made me sad to think so, for there seemed a distinct unreasonableness about it: but the sort of rationality that led to attendance on such occasions – in crowds of up to half a dozen at the time – went hand in hand with remarkable mousiness.

It had been rather better in that room in the bowels of Parliament, for some of the captains of humanism were present, and if there was anything of the mouse about them, it was a brisk and even brightly painted mouse. Kate was seated next to a publisher whose list was a tremendous rebuke to the frivolous: and heard him say something that baffled her. In fact, she'd been telling me about this a second or so before we were incredulously impressed by the certainty that this other car was dancing across the street, and that it must hit us. It was rather later, and after we'd managed to damp down the helpless and consuming indignation that rages in your soul after you've been struck by a driver who doesn't stay to see what damage he has done, that Kate told me what the publisher had said. Or had seemed to say.

'*Cubism*,' she thought she'd heard, 'seems lately to be making some progress.' She could not think this to be true, but wondered if some title he was about to publish would demonstrate that, while her back was turned, the relevant artists had staged (largely from the grave) an immense revival. She made some confused reply, she said, which she'd rather not try to recall: and only as we made our rather downcast way home – indeed, on the very brink of collision – had she realised that it was *humanism* he thought was on the up and up.

4

My cousin Bobby had told me, on that recent stay in Ontario, how perplexed he'd been at some moment of family stress to find he'd set out grimly walking with his father's stick in his hand. That's to say, a stick Uncle George had cut for himself on his last visit: with his name jauntily carved on it. GEORGE ADOLPHUS BLISHEN, said this stick, marching angrily alongside Bobby's anger. (I remember whispers during my childhood about the origin of that unlikely name, Adolphus.) Am I, thought Bobby, simply my father very slightly rewritten?

Sometimes, decadent twentieth-century Blishen who'd not drilled anyone or, since the day of Sergeant Clinker, been drilled by anyone, I found myself behaving like a nineteenth-century Blishen. Perhaps, I thought, like my paternal grandfather, who'd died young, but spent seven years out of his short life in the Army. When in 1883 he joined the First Battalion of the Royal Fusiliers he was holder of a Third Class Certificate of Education, and George Straker would have been delighted to observe that this involved none of those educational loosenesses I'd encouraged in my own pupils, seventy years later. In Reading and Writing from Dictation, Henry Blishen had reached Standard II: he had Requisite Proficiency in Numeration, and had mastered the first four elementary compound rules and Reduction of Money. (I thought for a man who, on discharge from the Army, produced my father, my five uncles and an aunt in rapid succession, appreciation of the way money reduces must have been particularly valuable.)

His account book shows the amount due to him and from him at various stations from Colchester to Cairo, with rather a lot of Hounslow: they are mostly tiny sums, so that in January 1885 his services to the Army seemed to have been valued at three farthings, while in August of the same year he received nothing but made a donation to the Army of one penny. Over his years of service the circumference of his head appears to have grown by half an inch. The only characterisation of my grandfather in my possession is in the form of a testimonial given him on his discharge by Major Fred Tottenham, who was no great shakes at making a man come alive in words: saying only that my grandfather had served without any crime being entered against him on his Company Defaulter Sheet, and that the Major believed him to be a respectable sober man.

He added that Henry was a clean smart soldier: and it is this characterisation of large numbers of my family, on the whole avoiding the commission of crime in Kettering, Hounslow, Cairo and the Crimea, and being always clean and smart, that I have felt surfacing in me from time to time. A kind of ghostly cleanness, and phantom smartness.

We'd been to the pantomime, taking our son Dan and our grandson Tim. There'd been discussion of what sort of pantomime it might be, Tim's first. Should it be one of those revivals of an earlier form, gentler, prettily knock-about: if at all coarse, then respectably coarse? I was against that. The more vulgar, I thought, the better. It was a quarter of a century since I'd been the father of small boys, and Tim astonished and delighted me all over again with the range of his indelicacy.

Aladdin. A theatre in which you could feel two different kinds of nervous expectation: that of small children, and that of their parents. Tim was now a tough six year old and veteran of space odysseys who took in his stride the elimination of curiously constructed creatures from Mars by curiously constructed creatures from Saturn. A moment came, quite early, when a comic policeman was thrown between the rollers of a mangle: and was retrieved, flat. That's to say, he dived through the mangle, to shrieks, and a flattened cut-out of a policeman emerged in his place, to a deeply uncertain theatre-wide taking-in of breath. And I felt the six-year-old sophisticate and master of interstellar weaponry at my side vibrate with grief and despair. The situation was saved by an instant display of her knickers by the Widow Twankey. Joining in the huge general guffaw, Tim was saved from reflection on the fate of the comic policeman. Well, common sense would tell you that it was a cut-out: he wasn't really flattened. But common sense doesn't deal with all the questions raised by such an event. Some dark dread of being flattened, present in the mind of every small child, must have been touched off by this moment of slapstick. There can't have been a child in the theatre who didn't, for a second or so, feel personally squashed.

Well, wonderful, we thought: small children reacting in a primitive way to primitive humour! The villain, the wicked magician, was played with marvellous energy by a black actor: and watching him, I remembered precisely why I'd loved the pantomime as a child, and understood why Tim was loving it now. Of course, it was *rude*! There was that shameless stress on the existence of knickers! And there was the knocking of people over the head with plainly soft truncheons: and the comic policemen intending to rush off the stage in pursuit of wrong-doers, but turning towards each other, always, and cannoning off each other, and falling down with their legs in the air. There were jokes like that, offered not once but gloriously over and over again! The place was filled with a profound gratitude for repetition! But there was, above all, the exchange between stage and audience: at its best, here, between the villain and all those enormously amused children. They booed when he appeared: they hissed when he spoke of his diabolical plans: they answered his rhetorical questions: and when he appeared at the back of the stage, unseen by hero or heroine, they tittered immense, general, urgent warnings. More than anything that afternoon, they loved hating him. And he loved hating them. After the interval he asked how many had eaten ice cream. The theatre was a forest of hands raised. Hard luck! cried the villain. He'd poisoned every one of them. And the theatre screamed with disbelief – edged with belief. I knew when Tim was nervous, and Tim was nervous. Oh yes, I remembered the main beauty of those earliest visits to the theatre: the never absolutely resolved uncertainty as to whether it was only a play . . . or *not* only a play.

And so we came home to Barley Wood, a little bit beside ourselves, as my mother used to say. 'Dick, they're beside themselves!' I had a vision, when small, of actually, as a result of inner excitement, being my own riotous

172

companion. We walked from the station onto a quiet path between trees leading to our house. I said to Dan and Tim: 'Bet you I'm first home!' We set off, still under the spell of Abudnazar. And through a wicket-gate and on the home straight, we heard a cry from behind us.

It was Kate. Someone had come up behind her, softly swift, and tried to wrench her handbag off her shoulder. She'd clung on, shouting: 'You *bastard*!' And he'd fled.

And there were Dan and I, twentieth-century Blishens, both inclined to pacifism, taking off punitively, our minds hot with anger. I was the entire First Battalion of the Royal Fusiliers. I was responding to a frontier incident: I was intent on preventing the Muscovites from reaching Constantinople. I was my grandfather, that clean smart soldier.

Failing of arrest and restored to our milder selves, Dan and I looked at each other ruefully. 'It strikes me,' I said, 'if we want to stick to our principles, that we're lucky neither the Kremlin nor the Pentagon has yet had a harsh word to say about your mother.'

Tim hadn't liked Kate being attacked, of course: but there was an aspect of the affair that, for the thrill it offered, threatened to overshadow the pantomime. He was practising the story for Monday's playground. 'And then she said: "You *bastard*!"' It wasn't what could be reported of every grandmother.

And then, it was just before Christmas, Kate stood on a chair to take something festive out of a high cupboard. The chair slipped. Tim was elsewhere that day, but Dan was with us. We found Kate on the floor, groaning: her shin had been laid open: there was a terrifying amount of blood. We made a hasty bandage: and then, Kate so white and the wound so awful, I said to Dan:

'Get the car, get the car! *At the double!*'

In my agitation, I didn't know I'd said it. Dan made no reference to it until we returned from the hospital, with Kate starting the long weeks of inaction that follow from breaking the flesh over the shin. We'd not known the complications that could result from doing that, where there's so little to cover the bone: an example, it seemed to me, of a desperate cutting of corners, or expense, by the designer. I'd had some grudging admiration till then of the human machine, on the whole so tough. FRAGILE, we might all have been marked: but an astonishingly large number of us got through the day without important damage. It was perhaps this that the pantomime celebrated for the benefit of its particular audience, flattening policemen, causing large numbers of persons to collide and fall: only too aware of their fragility, children were presented with bizarre instances of survival. Kate's mishap was a reminder that sometimes flattened policemen *are* flattened.

'I didn't,' I cried. 'Dan, I didn't say: "*At the double!*" Why, it's what my father would have said – and I guess what his father would have said to him! No, I can't have done! It wouldn't suit me!'

Kate from where she lay, worrying about a hobbling Christmas, said: 'Well, I heard it too. You said: "*At the double!*"'

I felt aware of a large number of ghosts within me - everyone of them respectable, sober, clean and smart – every one of them, grinning.

5

Never having known a grandfather makes one very curious about grandfathers. Of my mother's father I've not seen even a photograph. Of Henry Blishen, several. His hair is parted almost centrally: it's dark, and is drawn back at the brink of his forehead in two licks. It's as if somehow he'd autographed his brow in black ink. He has a marshalled face: in one photograph he has under his arm a cane, seeming another manifestation of his body's crisp alertness. He has the general air of a mild flagellant: though he was not mild, as I gathered from my father, with his sons, whom he treated like a little army. Every day followed a military pattern. Every son was repeatedly cashiered, flogged, and sent running round the parade ground under full pack. They all grew up with memories of being cowed, and ready to cow others. They all, I believe, thought of fatherhood as a brief period of absolute power, to be made as much use of as possible.

My own poor father! In the little army of *his* family, there was one soldier only, and he exhibited every intention of being undrillable!

I wondered what my grandfather, cane under arm, with his moons of licked-back hair, might have made of a scene in Barton Market, eighty years after his premature death. The stall at which I was standing was always bright with fruit and the less prosaic vegetables: cabbages, potatoes, parsnips were sold in an adjoining booth. In midwinter, the square into which the stall was divided with vivid green paper were assorted displays of sunshine. And the colour of the woman who presided over it was appropriate: she was generally as brown as onion skins, though parts of her flesh were pineapply. Her dresses were the leaves in which she was loosely wrapped. She had hair the colour of peaches, and roguish eyes, a faded blue that might have been too much in the sun. She was altogether edible, and had a voice greatly roughened by crying her wares: as she did incessantly, making large claims as to their superiority over anything to be purchased at Harrods. Her scorn for Harrods was unexplained and immense. She seemed, in her deeply relaxed fashion, to be anxious that if she fell silent for a moment her customers, actually deeply loyal, would at once rush into London and buy worse at much greater cost.

To her for years, for my habitual Saturday morning purchase of mushrooms, I'd been Mr Mush. Well, the place was awash with brevities. Bananas were bans: and there were straws, bloods, navels, toms, pots, poms and cus. At the desperate end of the day you'd be offered a pot 'mum for next to nothing.

'You look well, Mr Mush!' '*You* always look well!' 'I always *am* well!' I'd master my desire to vault across the stall and devour her. 'Half a pound as usual, Mr Mush?' 'Half a pound, please.' It was a banal exchange that gave me great delight. I had, after all, known this market for more than sixty years. It had been a cattle market, once, and as children we'd rush to it after school in order to watch the pigs defecating. I carried round with me from those days a no longer particularly useful knowledge of how to sneak out of the place by way of an unorthodox exit or two. Recently on a stall that specialised in deeply dilapidated books I'd noticed a book of my own. It might have begun as the property of a family of chimney sweeps, and have passed to another with a straightforward hatred of the printed word, who'd kicked it round the garden before offering it to the dog, who'd bitten it once or twice and then refused it. It still didn't seem as bad as seeing one of your books remaindered.

It was just before Christmas (Kate had still to fall off her chair), and there was a long queue at the stall that morning. There was a man ahead of me, a generally big man, who said how busy the market was. I said yes, it was. And the queue here was very long. Yes, it was. All this talk of unemployment, he said, but there was plenty of money about. It would be different in the north, I said. No: he and his wife (a generally small, very uneasy woman at his elbow) had been there. There was plenty of money in the north. Well, how else could the miners have afforded to be on strike for nine months? There was plenty of it! That was obviously untrue, I said. It was what came of charity, he said. Too much charity. His experience had taught him that if you gave people charity today, they'd be back for more tomorrow. The miners, I said, were moved by fear of losing their work: they were afraid for themselves and their children. Did I know Norfolk? he snorted. The farm workers there had lost their jobs, but they'd taken it. They'd accepted it.

The edible lady had glanced in our direction. The man had become generally bigger, with hatred for me and the miners, and his wife had become generally smaller, with what looked like regularly practised alarm at her husband's belligerence.

We should be thinking what to do for people whose occupation was threatened or gone, I said. Couldn't do that for the miners, he said. They were thick. The further south you came, the more intelligent people were. Everyone knew that. It was how the country was divided. The thick north, the smart south.

I said we had better stop talking, because I was becoming very angry. His wife tugged at his sleeve. People didn't want to work, he said. That was untrue, I said. Well (and the voice and manner were suddenly my father's), perhaps he had simply more experience of the world. I said: 'I've been a teacher and . . .' Well, he said. That explained it. Teachers were always behind it all. Teachers were responsible for everything that had gone wrong. 'Now I think you should stop,' I said. I had never hit anyone, in a market or elsewhere, having neither the temperament nor the skill for it, but I thought I might do it now, if he went on speaking. He was silent until he'd bought his pound of oranges: then, as he moved away from the stall, he cried: 'Sorry you couldn't take it! Perhaps you'll learn!' 'Hallo, Mr Mush – what's going on?' said the golden stallholder. I was shaking with a rage that had its roots in my little wars with my father, tangled with some of my experiences when teaching in Stonehill Street: there were boys there whose whole talent was for finding the rawness in you and then touching it, again and again. 'You're an impertinent person!' I found myself shouting. Then, to curious faces: 'That is an impertinent person!'

'I hope I guessed right, Mr Mush,' said my edible friend, handing me half a pound of mushrooms in a bag hardly more brown than her fingers. It was only then that

177

I thought of hoping that my opponent hadn't taken that to be my actual name.

I wonder what my unknowable grandfather would have made of it. Alas, for I foolishly wish to make him a member of my army, I fear he'd have been on the other side. Unless, that is, there had been a miner or two among his friends in the Royal Fusiliers.

6

Was it really only eighty years since my grandfather had died, and my father, taken by his mother to identify the corpse, had been astonished to observe that liquid of some sort could still run out of a dead nose? With two world wars to come, and the appalling madhouse of the thirties, and the bomb, and the colonial collapse followed by the neo-colonial recovery: and lately, the factories in which not a human being was to be seen, only the huge claws and blind trolleys of automation: and, where there *were* humans, their being the servants of row after row after row of computers, lunatically swift, which translated the slow beautiful world into information too rapid to be experienced? Was it, indeed, only ninety-odd years since my father was born, in Acklam Road, Notting Hill, now at the centre of the miserable hostilities that followed the merriments of the Carnival?

Well, how old we all had become, in the twinkling (in our time, such a stormy twinkling) of an eye!

'*Ancient bastards!*' It was, said my brother-in-law, what the young shouted at him and his friends, playing bowls. It amused him wryly – for the touch of unexpected grandeur about the insult. Remembering the old men on the bowling greens of my childhood, in Barton's recreation ground, I thought the temptation to utter such a shout might be perennial. Drake's famous moment of delay might have followed from his having to chase cat-calling boys off the

Hoe before giving his attention to the Armada.

But when all that was said, an ancient bastard was clearly what one was becoming. On our way to and from Barley Road School, c. 1929, we'd readily mocked anyone over sixty. In the comics, the old were the natural victims of footballs adrift, or falling buildings. Their very slowness of movement made them legitimate targets of our cheerful scorn.

I had new teeth. They seemed enormous, made for some mouth twice the size of my own. I used them first in the Friar's Holt, feeding them peanuts. These they consumed as if without my collaboration, with terrible efficiency. But within minutes they'd filled my mouth with torment. They seemed to be made of iron. They were cruel teeth. I had filled my mouth with cruel uncontrollable teeth.

Having given up smoking, I now had a non-smoker's cough, the harsh bark of it making people jump, and causing some to look for other seats on the train. There was arthritis in my thumb, at times so vicious that I'd yell with dismay. I was an ancient bastard given to scaring people out of their skins with my cough, and alarming them unspeakably with my sudden howls of pain.

The arthritis made its way into my back, and I sometimes groaned when getting up from a chair. I was also inclined to sigh loudly, following some melancholy thought: and at times I'd caught myself talking to myself. Worse than that: on one occasion I'd caught myself talking to myself talking to myself. I'd been clumsy, and had told myself off. 'Oh you silly idiot!' At once I heard myself offer a rejoinder: 'Don't you talk to me like that!'

And of course I was still seeing Mr Baynes, the consultant surgeon. 'Well, let's see how things are,' he'd say: and we'd see (in fact, *he*'d see) how things were. His tendency to follow the inspection with some general talk about literature made me uneasy: it could be that what he'd observed barely called for comment, or it could be that he was inserting literary generalities between me and

179

some fatal pronouncement. In fact, the threat remained where it was: and I'd begun cautiously to believe that it wasn't possible to despair, continuously, in respect of a danger that remained at a distance sniffing the air but never quite seeming to catch one's scent. It didn't seem very bright, or valiant, to have been so scared for a while, and then to drift into being so indifferent, simply because nothing had happened. But I decided that if I'd come out of it badly, it was a kind of . . . coming-out-of-things-badly I'd be quite glad to repeat, if need be.

Fifteen years before, my father had said, whenever we met: 'I hope you grow old! I hope you find out what it's like!' At the time I was struck by the readiness with which he assumed that I had no sympathy to offer. It was as ever with him: at the first hint of the understanding he longed for, he'd lower his head and charge. Now, as I grew more and more to look like him, I thought how he must have hated the way he'd been vandalised by age.

That's what it was! Good God, I could not now rely on myself to identify, with certainty, music I'd known most of my life!

Kate wished to destroy this photo because it showed an indeterminacy of chin: that one, for a crease in the neck. I had a tender sad liking for her emergent defects, these symptoms of subsidence in the human frame. They were what time did to the structure of a being for whom I felt more grateful love than I was ever likely to feel for anyone else. I remembered once during our holiday in Provence looking across at her and thinking: There's time doing its damnedest to make Kate ugly, and failing! I'd found a photo in which, a year old, fat and astonished, she'd been sitting at her mother's elbow, in a great and promising innocence of lace and linen. In sixty-odd years she'd hurried slowly from that smooth and rounded amazement to her present state. The original skin mildly, and mostly wisely, rumpled. Why, I wondered, should an inevitable extra chin, a wrinkling only to be expected, cause her so

180

sternly to insist on the destruction of a photograph? Almost at once I was provided with the answer by way of a photograph of myself. It made much of an illusion of white-hairedness, and of an optical libel in respect of my appearing ... large. I'd always been slight. Slight might have been my middle name. But, monstrously, this photo suggested a general enlargement: as if furtive expansions had occurred in almost every quarter. The round brass belly of the geyser in our old home would now never accomodate my reflection! 'I don't think we should keep this photograph,' I said to Kate. Kate raised her still unvandalised eyebrows. She welcomed me, she said, to the ranks of those given to destroying portraits of themselves on grounds of candid vanity.

I made some wretched comment about photographs being lies, anyway. One's identity was to be found in the constant mobile action of one's features. A frozen view of one's face was a simple frozen lie.

Kate sighed, and did not ask why I'd not demurred at preserving so many lies of that kind, photographs of myself at any age short of sixty.

Now, when I was about to use a camera, she'd cry: 'Give me proper warning!' 'Why are you smiling?' I'd ask, on any non-photographic occasion: and it would be because a smile lifted the chin and made difficult – if it could not guarantee to make impossible – that general grimness of facial outline that becomes the drift of any ageing profile. I'd feel a nineteen-year-old lightness of heart within, and remind myself that, without, I might be suggesting a terminal melancholy. I would smile. 'Why are you smiling?' Kate would ask.

We agreed that this question, as one never to be put, should join others, such as: 'Why do you mumble?' Neither of us mumbled. Our ears had simply joined the conspiracy. 'Dear mug!' I'd said on some occasion – it was in a lift in Greece, we'd had a happy day, Kate looked suddenly exactly as she'd done when I first knew her, forty years earlier – and she'd been desperately offended. She'd heard my affectionate exclamation as a derisive cry of 'Beer mug!' I'd chosen the image because of her ears, she thought, adjudged to be large by small shouting boys on the way to and from school ... c. 1929. At one end of the town I'd been mocking old men, and at the other small boys had been mocking Kate.

'You talk too much about being old,' people said. I knew it, and understood that it was not an attractive thing to do. But I was simply struck by the discovery of this process, to which all human beings who'd survived youth and middle age had been subjected – and always to their outraged astonishment, whatever face they put on it – the process that took the thing you were and roughed it up. There was, I saw, an understandable taboo on discussing it: but I couldn't help believing that even those who pretended it wasn't happening were deeply concerned with it. They could hardly be otherwise. It was a tragi-comic evolution not easily ignored.

And it was funny, *funny*! Out of our dismay so much laughter sprang! There'd been a moment in Barton High Street when Kate was telling an acquaintance how she'd been to see an ancient uncle, living in Wiltshire and barely able to get about. 'In Wiltshire, you say?' said the acquaintance. 'No,' said Kate. 'He's still able to walk.' We had to hurry away as quickly as possible in order, in such decent seclusion as we could contrive, to laugh ourselves to exhaustion.

Met briefly in the same High Street was old Cragg, whom I'd known at Barley Road when he was young Cragg. When he was eight and nine there'd been this fierceness in his eyes, which had never come to much, and had clearly come to little since then, for he'd had a respectable career as a local government official. But now that he was retired, and had become a carrier of shopping baskets for his wife, his fierceness had intensified, had become an angry glare. 'Bloody kids!' he growled, as two

girls brushed past us without ceremony, moving awkwardly in the skirts they wore, which encircled the tops of
their legs like elastic bands. 'I'd like to give them a good
thrashing!' Unaware of their peril, the girls bumped past
a slowly moving old lady. 'Blame their parents!' Cragg,
I thought, was actually vibrating, as if on the point of
explosion.

Well, I couldn't think how the notion of a harmless old
person got around. Consider what, by the mid-sixties, was
crammed inside any of us! All those hostile chemicals:
emotions, memories and false memories: many bits of the
mind and heart corroding with age or misuse or by some
internal misfortune of contact with one another: the marvellous computer hopelessly in need of servicing, now
subject to an accumulation of errors and simple failure of
vital components. Small seethings, precariously main-
tained securities converting back into the stuff out of which
they were originally made! Inside, one morning, a dull
roar as an entire structure of suppositions collapsed! Ani-
mosities long held in, suddenly on a much shorter lead!
Sexual suggestibility, for so many years capable of being
merged with reasonable satisfactions, becoming a dangerous absurdity: flickers of power in the powerless!

I thought uneasily that it might be as well to avoid
Cragg, in future.

7

Agnes Mild wrote from New Zealand: she'd discovered
Australian Blishens, sprung from William Blishen, basket-
maker, and his wife Caroline, who'd come from Stepney.
They'd outbred Uncle George, with sixteen children, half
of them having the briefest of lives, and among them
Edward, who'd lived in New South Wales from April 1865
to February 1866. Given that it's not the commonest union
of names in the world, I was much moved by the thought

of this fugitive forerunner of mine. And how strange it altogether was, this giving way of part of the blank cliff of time, and the tumbling out of ancestors, with unforeseen occupations (how *had* we got into baskets, who'd always been in stone?), and unexpected points of origin, and a new set of much-repeated Christian names: here Frances, Emma, Amy. Florence Elizabeth, who'd died of consumption at the age of twenty-eight, the year after her sister Frances Caroline died of the same disease, had been a teacher. They'd married bootmakers, harnessmakers, tailors. Suddenly, on a single sheet of paper, and never to be more than paper, were twenty or thirty cousins: simultaneously, brand new and hopelessly old.

I was asked to talk to Barton's Historical Society – a group of local Agnes Milds. They hadn't Agnes's memorable eagerness, so that she'd be forever my image of the true, passionate archivist. Some clearly preferred the past to the present on the grounds that the past didn't answer back. (Though to someone like Agnes, it was perfectly capable of doing that: among the qualities I admired in her was her understanding that the past could bite, and could tumble your conception of the present into new shapes.) But on the whole they were committed to admitting the past into the present, as a part of the present: they saw that the present lost half its meaning if the past were excluded. I'd thought of these things when teaching, in Stonehill Street, what was numbly called History. Well, numbly because, for the children I taught, the term was without life. It didn't, to them, hint at its own meaning. I wanted sometimes to replace it with a word like Remembering, a phrase like Looking Back. Perhaps we could call it Yesterday and the Day Before That? Anything to establish that what we were doing was thinking of earlier chapters of a tale in which we ourselves had become characters. And now, talking to the Historical Society, I thought how the trend was toward the promotion of some kind of all-satisfying present. If the past, as part of the present, was the Red Lion, then the present that excluded the past was the Dandy Lion? The *Barton Press* would print an occasional page of old local photographs, but in such a way, and with such a commentary, that the past was held at a distance, was seen as a quaintness. Barton High Street with a single toddler walking down the centre of it, following a horse and cart, was represented as waiting impatiently for the storm of motor traffic to arrive. I thought it was like George Straker's view of our school-days, and his appraisal of Sergeant Clinker. Damn it, we'd been in the past, he and I, and it wasn't quaint, and it had no need to wait for future storms: it had been, like any period ever, a storm of its own!

Oddly, at this moment I found myself reading a new collection of poems by the Australian, Peter Porter: it, too, was concerned with our readiness to obliterate the past, in the name of a materialism that wanted us every day to start afresh, to wipe out what had gone before: buy a new car, move on to a new detergent, scrap yesterday's wardrobe in favour of today's, which we would scrap in favour of tomorrow's: restyle our bathrooms. He'd called his collection *Fast Forward*: and when I interviewed him said he'd thought he was the first to recognise the ironical resonance of this phrase from tape recording, but had discovered that everyone had used it. 'I'd chosen a cheap catchphrase for a title!' I told him how the drift of his poems had coincided with the drift of my thoughts after talking to the Historical Society. He reminded me then that the mother of the muses was Mnemosyne, the Titan who personified memory.

I asked him if there was anywhere in past or present another poet with an echoic name like his, and he said no, there wasn't, and how ironic that such a sportive name should have been visited on him, a man with a tragic view of things!

8

At some point in this scribbling life I'd become subject to VAT. And now the VAT man rang to say he'd call, and inspect my records. Such an aim filled me with alarm. I kept accounts as well as I could, but had never thought of them ponderously as records. The term, together with the whole style of the man's announcement of his intention, made me certain I'd not pass muster. I had no book-keeping skills. I was naturally not given to tidiness: and had reached an age when I thought I could fiercely defend the relative disorder in which I operated as a valuable (as well as irreversible) condition of my character. It was not simply a reaction against my father's enormous neatness either, or his belief that if everything was folded and stored in its right place, all would be well with the world. With him it was a religion, it was Neatism; he was an Exclusive Neatist. The phenomenal scope of his insistence on order, covering every aspect of my childhood and youth, had certainly acted as a sort of aversion therapy: in that sense, I had been cured of any inclination to be tidy. But I didn't think I'd had much inclination, to begin with. What I believed was that my nature required me to expose myself to the higgledy-piggledyness of life, and to let the pressure of that be felt in the one department in which I loved and required order as my father did: which was in writing. As compared with my father, I was a Higgledy-piggledyist, working up to regular feats of Reformed Neatism.

Kate tended to be critical of this theory of mine. It was another aspect of the argument we'd had in Ontario, about promiscuous photography. Kate said that, for reasons it might be better not to go into, I was a compulsive hoarder whose passion outran his gift for the use of filing cabinets, cupboards and bookshelves. I said if it came to com-pulsiveness, she was driven (for reasons it might be better to leave alone) to discard, to hurl away: to cave in at the

186

merest twitch of her neurotic dread of clutter. Without
people like me, I felt bound to point out, there would be
no History. History was an activity made possible by
hoarders. Did she remember an occasion when we'd
moved dazzled from case to case in the British Museum's
manuscript rooms, and I'd said if it had been left to her,
the whole lot would have ended up on Barton's garbage
dump? Shakespeare, I said, warming to the opportunity
to restate our old quarrel in majestic terms, had clearly
been a victim of a concatenation of Kates. Her answer to
all this was that my squalid proclivities might have helped
History on its way, but it would rapidly have been halted
by my inability to lay my hands on anything among those
millennia of bumf. History books would have been full of
phrases such as: 'I know I could show, if only I could find
the relevant document, that ...'

It seemed to me that it might be useless to explain all
this to the VAT man. He would be an elder of my father's
church, and indifferent to the argument that the sin of
untidiness was, in some subtle way, also a virtue.

I underestimated him. He might even have found my
father sloppy. Fetched by Kate from the nearest Underground station, for he had no car, he settled down with
the box in which my papers were kept. I worried too late
about this box, of pickle-smelling wood, which bore a
legend saying that it came from the Grape Valley Market
in California, and stressed the availability in that excellent
market of strong cheeses and stronger spirits. But I left
him at it. In an hour or so I was summoned. He was
cold. 'These records,' he said, 'are below the standard we
require.' 'I have no skills of the kind you have in mind,' I
said. 'We insist on certain standards, however, and you
must keep to those standards,' he said. I wrote, in my head,
rapid letters to *The Guardian*, *The Times*, *The Author*: I
prompted an indignant speech or two in the House of
Commons. 'It seems to me,' I said, 'that I shall have to
ask my accountant to look after these things for me.'

187

'That's as may be,' he said. 'Our demand, I have to say again, is for a certain standard. And I have also to say I've found one or two errors in your arithmetic.' Fifty years back, the chalk fell from Miss Baker's astonished hand. Her most promising pupil, c. 1929, remiss in *arithmetic*! It had all been a flash in the pan, I wanted to tell her – not really me at all. Anyway, with her at Barley Road it had been hundreds, tens and units, or pigs, oranges, potatoes: it was arithmetic with a colourful edge. If the BBC switched to paying me in sheep, buns or pins my accounts might well show an improvement. . .

'Fortunately,' said the VAT man, 'those errors are in your favour. I calculate that we owe you just over £40.'

9

It was another reason for my feeling of closeness to my grandson Tim: the difficulty of being young was so like the difficulty of being old. In fact, perhaps it was the same difficulty, looking at itself in a mirror. Out of chaos, the child was being driven to create an ordered creature: out of his long years of order, the old person was slipping back into chaos.

I'd try to say it once, as a sort of poem:

Difficult, being a child
Everybody ready to judge you in terms of conduct,
wondering where, today, the incontinent mercury
of your spirit will soar, or sink.
You being raw human matter, the stuff undiluted.
Condition, unstable.
                    Theoretically, easy
to handle, being small, reliant,
needing assurance, assistance, guidance, a stream of
definitions.

Difficult, being a child: seeming so helpless,
being, in fact, so appallingly powerful.
What can be done when a child explodes?
Observe the confusion caused: the panicky swing
from righteous indignation to frank terror.
A child out of hand is the human fire unbanked, the
human flood
rapidly rising in the absence of all sandbags...

In the life of adults
charged with children, there's a touch
about every day of the desperate, doomed
attempt to assert the human dam, the efficient
employment of sluices, the measured rise and fall
of waters contained.
               And every day
spent with children spells out another message:
maybe there is no containing embankment:
no sluice: no engineer:

and maybe growing up is merely an illusion
of control, a lie: a self-deception:
and in the end we are all
               children berserk:
children refusing
all decent pretences, cool restraints ...

which (incidentally) is why
it's difficult, being a child

'Now watch, gentles and ladymen,' said Tim. We
laughed. Within seconds he was crashing through the
jungle, leaving a trail of blood. There were enormous
griefs: and the call for patience among the search party
was tremendous.

'We left Daddy walloping in the bath,' said Tim. We
laughed. Mildly he asked to have the joke explained to
him. It was explained. *He* laughed. He swung between
Kate and me, enchanted by his own error.

He made me realise afresh, and with fresh alarm, how much of childhood consists of the imitation of elders. Or, to put it a little differently, how the child moves within a confusion of examples set by his confusion of parents, uncles and aunts, teachers and neighbours. So Tim was much taken by my central activity: which was that of typewriting. One's grandfather typed. An amusing machine: difficult to decide if it was more entertaining in its electric or its non-electric form. Amazing possibilities, anyway, of causing words, or failure to achieve words, to appear on paper. Gratifying possibilities of making mistakes and screwing up the ruined pages, fulminating, in the manner of one's grandfather! And, as time went on, impressive possibilities of writing *Robin Hood*, by Tim Blishen: *Treasure Island*, by Tim Blishen: and, on the strength of a reputation secured by these two successes, *Dracula*, by Tim Blishen.

It was interesting, I thought from my end of the world of writing, that a story had to be brought to a conclusion, *any* conclusion. Tim's earliest draft of *Dracula* struggled through the prime sensations of which, to his mind, the tale was compact: and within half a page he was desperate for a curtain. A boy called Jonathan Harker: a castle: a vampire (met at a bus stop, Jonathan on the way to school): Jonathan's resulting enervation: his being heavily punished at school for what the school did not understand to be scholastic impotence brought about by loss of blood: a final encounter at the bus stop. 'He felt Dracula's teeth in his throat,' Tim said, trying it out on me. 'Of course, Tim.' 'And that's the end. He died.' 'That's a tragic end!' 'What's "tragic" mean?' 'It means terribly sad.' 'Oh, that's what I want,' said Tim, breezily embracing his destiny as a sombre sort of chronicler. He typed out 'The End', cursing because he'd forgotten to make a gap between the words, and rushed off to play a form of football which involved losing the ball in, and disastrously attempting to recover the ball from, the deepest local ditch.

I was asked to talk at Tim's school about being a writer. I sat in the hall on a chair waiting for the children to assemble: Tim was among the first, and squatted at my feet. 'I like your shoes,' he said. 'Oh good,' I said. I talked about the richness of the English vocabulary, all those words, so many of which they, though so recently arrived on the scene, already had stored away. 'How many words are there, I wonder, in English?' I mused, rhetorically. A small boy had an answer based on the amazement in my voice: three billion and a half, he said. I said he'd quite taken the wind out of my sails. Building on *that*, a small girl said, carefully: two hundred and seventy-nine.

At question time, Tim's was among the hands that went up. 'Are you famous?' he asked. I hastily imagined the background to that. 'My grandfather's coming to talk this afternoon. He's famous!' 'Your grandfather's not famous!' 'He is!' 'Bet he isn't!' 'Bet he is!' And so, this question. Even for Tim, I couldn't tell a swingeing lie: I certainly couldn't present children with what would have seemed a display of appalling self-regard. But I had somehow to save Tim.

'Well, sort of . . . quite well-known,' I said.

I thought, from the way he looked along the row of classmates, that he might just about scrape by on that.

10

One thing I'd noticed, watching Buster Keaton or Harold Lloyd with Tim, was how to my grandson the simplicities of storytelling in early films had become sophistications. Accustomed to modern forms of editing, swift and cryptic, Tim was puzzled by narrations intended to make everything clear to the slowest-witted. Buster would race from spot to spot, in that frantic exaggeration of haste that made me laugh helplessly still, and he did it not once but twice, and if need be more often, until that old audience of which,

191

c. 1928, I might have been a member, concluded that the events occurring in the first spot were to have their sequel in the second. Tim thought there must be some reason why we were seeing much the same sequence over and over. 'Don't you love the same funny thing happening more than once?' I'd ask. Tim would sigh and tuck himself under my arm: at the moment, the best means he'd contrived of dealing with adult absurdity.

I felt something of this confusion myself during the scene in which at last, and I supposed finally, we lost our tempers with George Straker. We were elderly sophisticates, surely: and yet between us occurred a scene that might well have been a fragment from a silent film, with captions occupying the screen long enough to be understood by the slowest reader.

It really arose from George's having become, over the years, a sort of born-again prude.

Though this had come about gradually, like a very stealthy Ice Age, it still surprised me, remembering how, in the mid-thirties, George had stood with Barbara in the shadows at the bottom of the road where I lived: he with his school cap in his pocket (that in itself, in our headmaster's eyes, was a phenomenal crime), she with her school hat behind her back. To be standing, as they were, face to face, very close, everything about them declaring their desire to be closer, was a cardinal offence under the rules of both our schools. Kate and I (Kate having been a contemporary of Barbara's at the girls' grammar school) were sometimes wistful for the excitements of forbidden love we'd missed by not meeting before our schooldays came to an end.

Far from beginning as a prude, George as a boy had had a powerful if vague reputation as a sort of schoolcapped plaything of passion. This was, I now think, largely an accident, resulting from his fame among us for the scale of his genitalia. In the early days after the school was shifted from cramped historic buildings at one end of town to roomier unhistoric buildings at the other, and showering and bathing after PE and games became possible, the news that George was to be seen in the changing room spread fast among his small classmates. As time went on the legend that his sexual behaviour was directly related to his genital grandeur was not contradicted by George himself. And in the erotic annals of Barton, in the 1930s, that long-ago Barbara, latterday chatterbox, is surrounded by some of the awe accorded to George, it being taken that (whatever was involved, and most of us were wildly uncertain of that) she must be similarly prodigious. I think now that George was never a convincing libertine: but in those days he was not averse to being admired as one, and to having it thought that, of Barbara, as of so much that lay ahead of him, he knew every inch.

He was now more or less opposed to sex itself. Sex had been a recent invention of enemies of the state: they'd paused in the creation of comprehensive schools and the showering of honours on pop groups (George appeared to believe that what had happened to the Beatles had happened to all other pop stars, and that the country was awash with Sir Michael Jaggers) to appoint certain Director-Generals of the BBC and give licence to certain novelists, poets and painters. Sex was the result. George frowned on it all. Among other things, it was a conspiracy to bring his daughters low.

George's daughters were pleasant, alarmed girls, not too much seen: when we went for dinner, they appeared while they were still at school fleetingly from some harem of homework at the back of the house. George would question them sternly on the progress of this bit of French, that after-school dose of mathematics. 'Oh *Daddy*!' one or the other would sometimes murmur, moved to protest by the generally untrusting nature of George's inquiry. There was no doubt of his love for them: and no doubt that he hoped, with overloads of Latin and algebra, to ensure that they never stood, school hats behind their backs, close to some modern George or other, who'd not even possess a school cap he could stuff into his pocket. George thought of them as surrounded by enemies: and lately, I'd realised, he was more and more inclined to think of Kate as one of those.

This was because, stirred as I was by the memory of the moral distress of our childhood, when the fact that human delight was inseparable from human danger was seen as a reason for the cultivation of ignorance, Kate went into schools to talk about sex. Having been sexually educated by her myself, I knew the kindness and imagination, and due sense of comedy, that went into it. When the going was difficult, she'd remember that anguished need of information that one child or another had confessed to, often outside the formal occasion of a visit. 'Oh God,' she'd cry sometimes, coming home from a school, 'it's as if we let people go on the roads without learning to drive!'

George had always frowned when there was an allusion to this activity of Kate's: once or twice he'd made an icy inquiry about some detail, and frowned again. Kate, who worried about George's daughters, was anxious to carry the argument into his camp: but he'd move, sometimes with an effect of violence, to another topic. 'Some time we're going to talk about this, George,' she'd say. 'Not,' George would reply, 'over coffee.' It was one of his more curious beliefs: that coffee and controversy were incompatible. But then I'd known him offer a similar view in respect of *coq au vin*, a bottle of wine, and even a box of chocolates. I think George knew he was always skirting the edges of other people's uncontainable indignation.

The evening had begun badly. I'd recently recommended Bernard Shaw's musical criticism to George: who now declared he'd found it simply dull. Not a patch on Bernard Levin. I thought, whatever allowances one made for taste, this was an extraordinary judgement. Bernard Levin himself would have been abashed. But it was the way George offered it that angered me. He *could* have

194

said: 'I'm very sorry ... I know you're an enthusiast ... but I don't quite share that enthusiasm ...' Instead: 'Simply dull, simply dull!' he said. Further discussion was not invited. Not willing to have Shaw thrown aside as easily as that, I said Shaw's latest biographer, struggling with his subject's immense output, had told me of his calculation that Shaw wrote ten letters a day throughout his adult life: and if, for some reason or other, he had to miss a day, he'd write twenty letters the next. The biographer had just come across a letter ten thousand words long, almost certainly written in the train between Welwyn Garden City and King's Cross, passing through Barley Wood. 'The ten letters a day leaves me cold,' said George. 'It's what businessmen write. And don't think,' he continued, making the precise gesture of a man nailing another to the floor, 'that they are without wit. Businessmen, as I am in a very good position to know, can be very witty. *Extraordinarily!*' 'You mean as witty as Bernard Shaw?' I asked. George ignored the question and asked Barbara when she was going to stop talking about the girls' grammar school. Since she'd been there with Kate, it was a natural subject between them, but George had a general view of his wife as a woman who blathered. 'And Barbara was blathering, as usual,' he'd say, in the context of some anecdote. It wasn't an entirely inaccurate word for what Barbara did, but it was applied ruthlessly to any statement of hers lasting longer than thirty seconds. 'Barbara, don't blather! Come to the point!' On Barbara's behalf, tiresome tattler though she was, I'd imagined her, at a score of such moments, darting across the room and planting a knife in George's guts: and Kate and I helping her to conceal the crime.

And here, a few minutes later, was Barbara saying that one of their daughters had found a flat in London, a development she and George did not regard without alarm. 'Oh, *not* alarm!' Kate cried. Surely they'd not frown on the girl's pleasure in her independence. 'I would not accept the word "frown",' said George. 'I think Barbara and I are not given to frowning.' He was frowning frightfully as he said this. 'But we make no secret, if that's what you mean, of our concern. We wish, frankly, that she had stayed at home. As any responsible parent would.' Kate, I knew, was thinking of the pleasure with which we'd seen our sons fly out of the nest. That's what they were for – flying! Of course, we'd not known the special feelings one might have about daughters ... But letting your children go – it was, in Kate's view, the ultimate parental duty. 'However, Barbara intends to drop in on her once or twice a week ...' *'Once or twice a week*, George?' 'Do you find something wrong with the arrangements we choose to make?' George demanded. Kate said: 'She won't want to be made to feel, surely, that she needs ... oh, constantly checking on. I mean, have you thought how untrusted it might make her feel?' 'Untrusted?' said George. 'When the streets are full of young men taught by you to ...?' 'More coffee, anyone?' asked Barbara. 'What have I taught them to do?' asked Kate. 'As I understand it ...' 'You've made little effort to understand it, George.' 'As I understand it, you've taught them that there's nothing wrong in indulging themselves whenever they like, with anyone they like ... my daughter, if they want,' said George. 'That,' said Kate coldly, 'is something I have never taught anyone, and you know me better than to believe I've done so.' George said: *'Sex education!* They'll be teaching them next how to ... knock old ladies down. I'm not sure that they don't!' 'Are you willing to discuss this calmly?' asked Kate. 'It is not a subject I choose to discuss, calmly or otherwise, over coffee in my own house after an agreeable dinner,' said George. Surrounded, I wondered that he hadn't added, by a fine garden, kept in trim by an elderly and respectful gardener employed for half the week. I'd never before heard such extensive reference to the proximity of one's personal possessions as a reason for curtailing debate. I made a last attempt to prevent THE END from appearing on the screen before some final smoothing of the story. Buster Keaton must arrive among us, having as always at the last moments of the film understood what it was all about, his innocent expressionlessness becoming a knowledgeable expressionlessness: he'd fall out of the chimney, or emerge from one of those great occasional tables, and we'd laugh amid the credits. 'George, George!' I cried. 'You've known Kate for donkey's years – you can't possibly believe that when she was due to go into a school, the children would say to each other: Oh good, French this afternoon, and then Fornication with that lady!' 'That is exactly what I do believe,' said George.

We left at once. Barbara said: 'But George – why are they going early?'

As we agreed, we all became our own dungeons. In search of any sympathy I could rally for the sort of prisoner he'd become, I thought of everything I'd known about George over the years. In the end, the balance of his qualities had fallen one way rather than the other: the seeker after freedom had fled, leaving the authoritarian to pace round and round the cell and scratch the record of his captivity on its walls. I thought Kate and I were rather more right than he was on the issue that had finally split us. All you could say of human beings was that they could not make use of themselves and their energies without risk, and so must be given all the aid possible, in the form of knowledge and understanding, in order to face and, if possible, outface that risk. Of course George should be watchful on behalf of his daughters: but only within the bounds of the perception that to parental watchfulness there were clear limits. Among other things, in the hope of saving your children from disaster you must not be caught breathing down their necks. And even that was to leave aside the thought, not easy for any parent to accomodate – but still necessary to accomodate – that disaster itself might be a vital experience for a particular human being. Altogether, love called for such a delicate combination of concern and detachment: of not concealing that one was ensnared, and setting the other free from the snare as often and as much as possible. I thought how Kate and I were happy to be together, but also happy to be apart. Small separations permitted the exercise of characteristics submerged in marriage. Prisoners, again! The most pleasantly married couple were, in some sense, each other's prisoners. Little bursts of parole helped.

So I had to think that we were right, and George was wrong. And in feeling that, I was helped by a very simple – in Buster Keatonish terms, naive – fact. I loved Kate in such a way that I had an inward, if not an outward, readiness to beat round the ring anyone who behaved to her as George had done. At the same time, I saw that we are, all, imprisoned. The drifts of our lives, across decades, had brought us to some final, and limited, space. Kate and I were prisoners of our wish to extend freedom, as George was a prisoner of his wish to curtail it. And within us, a huge cast of ancestors were at work, continuing, in these derivatives of theirs, the interrupted debate of their own existence.

I was fighting for, and against, my father. Against the stern prison he'd devised for himself, worse than George's, and against the experiences – including childhood in a London slum and youth in the trenches of the Great War – that had made him seek that prison. I was fighting largely for my mother, an eager soul who'd barely ever been in a position to profit from her eagerness. I thought George, like my father, was governed by terror: and that in his case, this terror sprang from a background of ineffectuality. Old Mr Straker, his grandfather, had been limp: and they said younger Mr Straker, his father, was limp, too: and George's aim in life had been narrowed to that of determining that *he* would not be limp.

My grandson Tim, floundering when it came to Buster Keaton, had a natural conversancy with computer games. I thought he was at home with those as much as, sixty years before, I'd been at home with the sometimes cryptic pages of *Kinema Fun*. Children are always clever in the style of their time. It struck me that Tim would have understood, in computer terms, exactly what was going on in the genealogical jungle: how my grandfather Blishen, who was said to be marvellous at lifting pianos from a prone position in pubs, might have been behind my writing of books: since writing a book has a very close resemblance to the effort of raising a heavy object in the air, and keeping it there with as little betrayal as possible of one's instinct to let it fall to earth with the dullest of thuds. Or how Kate's father was at work in her when, a naturally diffident person, she steeled herself to go into a school and talk about human sexuality. We had the letters written during Jim's courtship with Dorothy, and their freedom from every kind of sexual and emotional realism was dismaying and moving at once. Jim, who'd met Dorothy when he was wounded in France in 1917, had got no further, after childhood and youth in a country town and young manhood in an unspeakable war, than was involved in writing to Dorothy as if she were a fusion of ideal qualities, mounted on a fusion of ideal pedestals. It was possible to think of the marriage that followed as a slow process of education, appallingly late, which left both of them, under the surface they cultivated, aghast. Kate's need somehow to talk to children of sexuality and what it is and what it does to a human being and how it may be managed and how its huge pleasures may be reaped and its huge miseries avoided – that need sprang, I thought, from a deep wish that as many as possible should be saved from being Jims and Dorothys, caught as her parents were caught: in a belated exercise in realism which happened to be their marriage.

It was as my friend Ben Fletcher had said, after his

honeymoon forty years ago. All his knowledge of physiology, his own as well as Marie's, he'd told me, seemed to have vanished. 'I needed a handbook, one of those in several languages, with diagrams! Well, I needed a course of evening classes! And I thought how we'd spent seven years learning Latin, you and I, and hadn't spent seven minutes being instructed in how to make love! That's it – I knew more about Latin than love!'

11

I'd recalled *that* two years after Ben had said it. It was in 1948, just before our marriage, when we'd set out on Kate's first journey outside the shores of Britain, and my second. We were accompanied by an old schoolfriend of mine, John Race. John himself had intended to be accompanied by a Miss Newby, whom we'd never seen, but she had dropped out. So, each carrying £35, the most we were then allowed to take out of the country, we'd boarded the ferry at Newhaven: and Kate, as her mother had foretold, was instantly seasick.

Kate's mother had opposed the entire enterprise. It was to take the quite unnecessary risk of exchanging a familiar setting for an unfamiliar one. It was to invite numerous disorders of the stomach. It was to fritter away a sum of money that might have bought us some serviceable stick of furniture. It was – Dorothy never said as much, but her uneasy looks spoke for her – to be tempted to anticipate the amusements of the marriage bed.

She was right, not only about Kate's seasickness, but also about the pressures of temptation. We made our first stop in Paris, at a tiny hotel in the rue du Bac I'd discovered the year before; and there we were robbed of felicity by Kate's continuing queasiness and by the reflection that it seemed hard on John if I left the room we shared with some polite murmur that would not have deceived him as to my destination. The absence of Miss Newby weighed heavily upon us. John was resigned, but had clearly not adjusted to a situation that made him, not only our expert on transport – he had a deep love of trams, buses, trains and the timetables that offered clues to their movement – but also a temporary eunuch.

From Paris we took the train to Milan: by way of a stop in Switzerland, at Brigue, where at the station buffet we found that cherry jam was on offer, and a variety of butter we'd not met with since 1939. There was a long queue, and when it was announced that the train was ready to restart, we managed only by seconds to give our orders, receive our rolls oozing with jam and butter, and run to re-enter the carriage. It was absurd, we thought, to be so excited about jam: but ... about jam, at that moment after the austerities of war, we were excited.

John was thrilled by Milan, in terms of its having an extant tramway system of great complexity, and timetables worthy of being mastered. The edge seemed to be taken off his sexual discontent. We went from tram to tram under his entranced instruction, observing with wonder the labours of the conductors, who, the Germans having taken and melted down all coins, were required to make what they could of infinitely tattered notes: sitting at the rear of the vehicles, they disengaged one clingingly dirty note from the next with the help of a ridged rubber thumb-guard, and then set to the work of repair with sticking-plaster and tape. It was like being among restorers after some great artistic calamity. With all this John seemed in such high spirits that we felt mere sexual opportunity could have provided him with no further happiness. As we drank coffee outside our hotel, I handed Kate a note asking if I might join her that night. 'I'm going ... else-where. Perhaps you'd rumple my bed for me,' I muttered as John brushed his teeth: the form of this request depend-ing a great deal on my recollection of appropriate passages in literature. Prompter, the programme might have said, Aldous Huxley.

And, having embraced with trembling enthusiasm, Kate and I fell instantly asleep. It had been a long and exhaustingly interesting day. In bed together for the first time, we slept profoundly.

I woke to find Kate expressing her interest in me in an unambiguous fashion. Well, some such foolish statement was needed: for the fruit of my long education in being an unnatural human being, trained – by characters such as Sergeant Clinker and my father – to dread his own appetites, was that I was at once uncontainably excited by this simple proof that my friend had sexual hungers, and that they were of a certain plain kind, and unable to accept the discovery with the remotest grace. Next day I found myself flooded with a frightful meanness and spite. As a small child might – and at that moment I was a very small child – I behaved towards Kate as if I'd caught her out in some humiliating action. The fact that it was an action capable of giving me profound pleasure, and that the thought of embarking on complementary action was immensely pleasant, too, had no effect on this feeling at all.

Well, I was the classically repressed person classically relieved, and at the moment of rescue behaving abominably to his saviour. Poor Kate! If she remained my friend during the days that followed, it was entirely due to that refusal to be my enemy to which I have ever since been indebted.

I've sometimes thought, looking back on that moment, that it was as if I'd been obliged to wait till I was twenty-eight before uttering a single word. And it was then that I remembered Ben's confession of complete bewilderment.

Ben was the brightest human being I knew. He seemed to make sense of considerable quarters of our confused world. All these years later, I see how odd it was to have built as much as I did on the lucidity of a single human being in the midst of the general darkness of the 1940s.

But if human destiny was ever to be improved by the possession, by some, of brightness of mind and spirit, here was such brightness! That Ben, so buoyant of mind, should sexually have come so close to sinking, gave me some measure of the difficulty I was faced with. He and I had been brought up under the same monstrous pretences, as to one's nerves, one's senses, one's readiness to be high-spirited! (And high-fleshed – there must surely be some such word!) When we were seventeen or so I'd written to him, saying how unhappy I was because my life, which earnestly I supposed should be a temperate matter of intellectual discovery, was shaken by great sensual storms. Briefly, I had an awful suspicion that I would become a full-time masturbator. Ben wrote healingly to say that my present excess was something to be proud, not frightened, of. I walked round for some time strengthening myself with the recollection of this statement. Later Ben told me he could hardly believe he'd made it. He'd been in a much worse state than I was. 'There were many moments when I felt that Percy Chew would tap me on the shoulder and I'd spend aeons in detention.' In a world in which Ben scored '0' for sex, what hope had I?

The hope, as it turned out, lay in my encountering Kate, who had been more pragmatic than I was, and had sensibly regarded shyness as a curtain to be drawn aside. There had not been a vast deal of it, but enough to make her such a tutor as I needed. It was as if, in Ben's terms, the Latin master had turned out to have read Virgil, and to know one conjugation from another. I wasn't, when the actual ground plan was made clear, particularly unteachable: and in Paris, on our way home to continuing austerity (in all fields but this), I might be said to have had my sexual eleven plus within reach.

Though it was not as pat as all that! Artificially reinforced shynesses take ages to disperse. Something in me, I'd think in my sixties, having begun so unnaturally, would remain shy forever.

And we'd gone to Florence, at that distant date. The Italian railways were only roughly recovered from the war, and in the immense fascist shed that was Milan station we sat on the edge of the platform, legs dangling, with dark-suited businessmen, patiently waiting (oh, the patience we'd learned by then, from 1939 onwards!) for some train or other to be assembled, item by item: and so we had experimentally bumped and clinked towards Genoa: where we'd found refuge in a deeply seedy hotel. The proprietor warned us against playing games of any sort, with dice or cards, with any of the youngsters who squatted on the pavements, the stairways, the very roads. In the morning, having had no difficulty in following his advice, we made our way clinkingly towards Pisa: where they robbed us of our engine: and after hours during which we did not dare to visit the Leaning Tower, for fear that the capricious railway would hastily assemble a train and make off without us, we drifted to Florence. There we'd booked rooms with a lady living on the hill up to Fiesole, who'd been so appalled by the price she was asking (the equivalent of 50p a night) that she'd offered us Italian lessons as an extra. Florence was then a great city knocked sideways by a disgusting war. We were absolute novices, to whom much the same thing had happened. The beauty of the place, still seeming profoundly endangered – to this day I cannot think of a confident Florence – bowled over its scarcely prepared admirers. That's to say, we'd had a general notion that we might expect to be amazed: but we were amazed beyond measure. Our headmaster, Percy Chew, had certainly spoken of Florence on one of his special afternoons, intended to make us conversant with European civilisation. He had made the place seem yet another obligatory boredom, in that chain of boredoms that, à la Percy Chew, was the history of an entire continent. What I remember from this holiday was that the eviscerated reality of Europe in the wake of the Second World War had a vigour of which none of Percy Chew's second-hand lectures, c. 1934, had given a hint.

In the aftermath of war, Florence was beautiful as it were by weary habit. Never since had Kate and I had such an experience, finding ourselves as it seemed accidentally in the midst of wonders. Here was a Duomo, here a Piazza Signoria, here a Boboli Gardens, here a Giotto, here a Botticelli, here a market stall entirely made of melons: here an office in which, in the course of a long morning, the major part of our food coupons, each covering a year, a sort of intricate ludo board, was cut up with immense scissors in order to set aside (sending the rest to Rome) the tiny section that ensured for Madame Farlatti the butter and sugar she provided for us during our stay. And here was Fiesole itself, and the monastery perched on the hill, and the tiny cell which, gesturing with a skull on a table towards death (then for us, even after a long war, a purely formal idea), and with a window gesturing towards life, the great sky and a selection of vines, I chose at once as a place to write in. In the crammed room in which I write in Barley Wood I think still of that blank room in Fiesole, a white box in which the light pulsing on the wall was green. And there, in the Villa Collina Ridente, Kate and I slept in a space in which the 'Lancers' might have been danced. Long long ago we spent nights together in a great box of shadows, up the hill from Florence, three years after the most lunatic of wars, in a shattered fragrance that was only partly of flowers and shrubs!

And here again, feeling far from home, I found I was still tangled in the branches of the family tree, as I was to be nearly forty years later and further afield, in New Zealand. For semi-permanent guests in the villa were an English couple, he forever a colonel, she forever a colonel's wife, who deplored us for being temporary and loosely enthusiastic, and for not dressing for dinner: as well as for not being refugees from Clement Attlee's Britain. And from their conversation it became clear that more desirable visitors to the city than us, another couple they'd encountered and who were recognisable at once from the monstrous claims he made for them both, and that she was not yet given to bluntly refuting (in later years she'd mutter 'You *didn't!*' 'Oh, the stories he tells!' 'You *never did!*') were Uncle George and his second wife Jane. My senior uncle – 'my elder brother' as my father would carefully categorise him – was also escaping from post-war Britain, but temporarily: the more earnest refugees, the colonel and his lady, remembered how their tastes were first found to coincide. '*Della Robbia blue!*' They'd all loved it! Britain stodgily afloat under her dismayingly subfusc skipper, Attlee – and these refugees united by an admiration they were confident he would never have shared! '*Della Robbia blue!*' A marvellous colour indeed, this was for a long time, for Kate and me, a synonym for conservative kinds of escapism. In Barley Wood, in the early 1950s, may we be forgiven, we thought this reactionary citizen or that was to be dismissed with a cry of '*Della Robbia blue!*'

And by way of the helter-skelter of the Apennines, we'd gone on to Venice. So ingenuous that we'd not known of the waterbuses, the *vaporetti*, and had found ourselves on arrival in a gondola. It had taken us to the Hotel Savoia, where the gondolier's request for immense augmentations of his fee led to his peremptory dismissal by John Race. *Allez-vous-en!* cried John, drawing on what Kate and I only just avoided: a sense that all continental languages were the same language. We spent the night in the Savoia, enormously alarmed by what I recorded in my diary as 'its apparatus of waiters and chambermaids', before escaping next morning to alternative lodgings in a humbler hotel not half a minute from St Mark's.

I think now of the lower-middle-class terror we felt everywhere, unaccustomed to hotels, unaccustomed to restaurants, unaccustomed to foreignness! Inside us, such a sense of being doomed to be gauche! Such a rage because I'd be returning home to my father, who believed Paris was an enormous brothel and Italy the home of comically cowardly soldiers and vendors of ice cream, and Kate to her mother, who'd ask about those three weeks only anxious hygienic questions. Uncertain and certain of each other at once, we longed to discover what could be learnt from living together: if we could, to venture away from the gauche: to set up our own penny world! Kate said she'd caught me, at the most intimate moments, thinking of the girl I'd prefer to be with, a fusion of Ginger Rogers and Virginia Woolf. She tried not to hate, but did hate, my writing in my diary, a greater intimate than herself. I tried, but failed, not to lean the pages away from her if she came close when I was writing. We were greatly happy: my gooseberry of a diary says that I declared in that land of pictures that Kate's body, in movement, made pictures in thousands. My twisted displeasure had vanished, and now I was free to be astonished, for the first time, by the variety of delights offered by the smallest shifting of a knee, raising or lowering of an arm, that naked standing, naked sitting, naked lying – a sudden yawn doing to the body such things that my heart almost stopped. It was another journey into breathtaking foreignness.

And we were greatly miserable, not knowing what would come of anything, or if what we proposed as a relationship was wise or rash!

And meanwhile, here we were, in this marvellous waterborne maze, made up of *calle*s, *ramo*s, *salazzada*s, *sottoportico*s and sudden small *campo*s. These words for this variety of alleys and archways and branchings and glades of stone entranced us. The light on the lagoon was at times too intense to be easily looked at. I'd blink at Kate, stepping round a corner and turning into a blazing golden girl. The sunshine was of a quality beyond our experience, pouring into the dark alleys and into the thick stale water of the canals. 'Never before,' I wrote, 'have I seen a country where everything is influenced by constant sunshine: where sunshine is burnt into the very stone, and

207

any dark, enclosed space is like a draught of water. And never before have I been among people who are creatures of sunshine, as I'm a creature of rain and cloud.' And I thought our happiness sprang perhaps from 'the curious narcosis of day after day in the sun in strange and beautiful places': I was terrified of what might happen when we went home to Barton and 'reason returns'.

It was, good Lord, years before the package holiday was thought of!

On our last night in Venice we went to the film festival, enjoyed a film we didn't understand, called *Sotto il Sole di Roma*, and left before the screening of *Primavera in Park Lane*. We stood in the Piazzetta. The palace to our left was a lace of stone against a sky that had been upholstered in the richest and thickest black material available – this wasn't the thin night sky of home! Across the lagoon there were long lines of light. Light unafraid to show itself was still amazing to us. At their moorings, the gondolas slapped and sucked at the black water. We looked up at columns and towers, all that pale geometry in the air. It was well after midnight, when to be abroad in Barton would have been an infamy: here, the warm wakefulness enchanted us. Kate wept, very happily. Later, having seen and felt too much, we lay in bed without sleep. The outrageous Continental night, of which Percy Chew had never spoken, was half over before the noises in the narrow street below us died away. We'd asked for a call in the morning and, startled out of late sleep, I'd fallen into John Race's vagueness of language before Kate could clap her hand over my mouth. Out of '*Grazie*' and '*Merci*' I made an Englishness, 'Gramercy!' 'But you shouldn't have spoken at all,' whispered Kate, and we were back with gaucheness, not knowing if, in a Continental hotel, it mattered or didn't matter if you were in the wrong bed. I heard Sergeant Clinker cry that it was drill detention and worse for being found nocturnally astray.

And it *was* difficult being home again, in the two or

three months before we occupied the penny world of marriage. My diary said: 'Between the old English existence which was interrupted three weeks ago and the new one which is beginning, something has been interposed, shining, complicated, rich in colour and detail, something heavy and beautiful sunk into the thin texture of the time that surrounds it.'

Forty years later, I could not forgive George Straker for wanting to reinforce ignorance and gaucherie in the young.

12

In his lodgings one night in 1937 our English master, Williams, had challenged me to a contest in translation. We would see who'd done best, after half an hour, with that poem of Catullus's that begins *'Odi et amo'*. I hate, and I love. The lover's ambivalence. I have no memory of our attempts, but think from time to time of Williams in relation to that tremendous opening. At that moment, as I half knew, he was in thrall to a woman he deplored. When Kate and I were caught in that mesh of certainties and uncertainties that formed the early phase of our relationship, I'd feel the need for a tempering of Catullus's painful cry. I love, and I am uncertain that I love. I love, and I am afraid of my love.

In a hundred circumstances, over the years, a hundred variations of the phrase had been in my head. Oddly, nowadays, one of them was present whenever I went to see Mr Baynes, the consultant surgeon. I like, but cannot wholly like. We had discovered a shared pleasure in cricket. We talked of Ian Botham. Mr Baynes was irresistibly drawn to the surgical aspect of the game. The fingers, the elbows, the knees – these most endangered parts of the cricketer were not in his province, but he had views on their treatment, especially in respect of that vulnerable hero, Botham. At times I'd imagine a test match held up while, on a hastily erected operating table round about mid-off, Mr Baynes set to work on the all-rounder with his saw. He told me he had the use of subtler instruments, and would certainly, if the worst came to the worst, seek to employ them in my case. But I preferred to imagine the gruff sound of a large, practical saw, making it possible for Botham to resume some epic of bowling or batting without leaving the ground.

I liked Mr Baynes, but the occasion for our encounters set bounds to my enthusiasm. Having resumed my clothes, I'd come out from behind the curtains to find him at his desk, making notes. 'Do you think,' I said once, my thoughts (perhaps because of Catullus) reverting to ancient Rome, 'it might help if you simply turned your thumb up or down?' He said he thought it might be difficult to reconcile that with the dignity of his profession, though when he said as much he recognised that the gesture had a simple directness that might help him through bad moments. I was beginning to worry, now, that I was so much at ease with the situation. Was it possible that I'd once felt I was, in some way, no longer part of the world? (My diary said so.) Had I, not so long ago, had the nervous need to tell the story to myself, or to imaginary persons, over and over again: much, I supposed, as a murderer might be driven to make a non-stop narrative out of his crime? Could it be that I'd thought an essential ingredient of ordinary happiness was a sense of safety, and since I didn't have the second I couldn't have the first?

Was it possible that what I was left with was my interest in the natural history of a morbid experience?

I thought often of that brush I'd had with the young Maori novelist, who'd clearly believed there was some indelicacy in the view that, in the end, everything that happened, however odd, intimate, grotesque, shameful, or absurd, was matter for a writer. Did he have in mind some true crudeness in the European approach to a story to which, being European, I was insensitive? I'd think, then, of newspapers. And my thoughts would be carried back to the days when our local railway was still a steam railway and, coming back from teaching at Stonehill Street, and later from this or that piece of broadcasting, I'd find myself among men and women returning from their day in the city, and they'd all be turning the pages of an evening newspaper.

They, those newspapers, caused me a dismay that for some time I didn't understand, until I realised it sprang from horror at the callous energy with which journalism fed upon the daily ration of disaster and dismay. There was this unremitting tone of mechanical excitement, as poor *homo sapiens* was recorded as reeling from calamity to calamity. In the carriages of the 16.55 to Hitchford, stopping at all stations including Barley Wood, these brutally enthusiastic sheets provided almost everyone's reading. I thought what an odd way of life it was: to go to be exhausted in the city and, returning home, to relax with what might have been discarded chapters of the Book of Job rewritten in the most brittle and heartless prose.

Oh, those evenings, before we went hesitantly electric, when the train came groaning and squeaking out of the tunnel to where, white-faced, we waited on that platform under which, it was said, Boadicea was buried. Concern for her would sometimes compound the misery of those evenings for me. First the Romans, and then eternity under platform 14 at King's Cross! Smelling of intense concentrations of sulphur, the train would twitch to a halt and make itself available for the everlasting struggle with door handles. Having broken into a carriage, a cell in which air had been replaced by some dense chemical mix, you murmured apologies amid a reluctant contraction of thighs: then found yourself perched on some tiny area of seating, wishing you had neither elbows nor knees, and flinching from the news-sheets that, on all sides, were stretched wide for the turning of pages. Dismaying items of news would come into focus and out of it again. OF TWO KILLED. BOMB BLOWS. NOT RAPE, SAYS.

211

THQUAKE DEATHS. FLOODS DRO.

A mild handful of us would descend and disperse at Barley Wood; and I'd observe my companions as they surrendered into the hands of waiting wives and children and, their heads stuffed with mayhem, horror, outrage, crisis, disaster and disgust, would make their way home to green evenings in the garden.

I could see that my Maori friend would hate *that* use of human experience by storytellers, and hoped he didn't see European literature as simply a grander form of our popular journalism. But it was difficult to know where literature ended, and prurience began.

I was in the Marquis of Abergavenny, with Rufus, and we were discussing a recent trip we'd made to the north, to talk about the books we'd written together. The body concerned had lodged us in the most disastrous hotel we'd ever entered. It wasn't merely that it was deeply grubby, and smelt of ancient meals, and was decorated in a fashion that would have made one wish to turn one's face to the wall, if the wallpaper hadn't been so appalling. It was also that at some time or other the hotelier had clearly been pressed by the relevant authority to provide well-marked avenues of escape in the event of fire, and had indeed provided them, with an indifferent madness that offered one an exit through the blind wall of a lavatory, or, by way of a series of fairly illegible notices, through someone else's bedroom window. In the corridor outside our rancid rooms was a blackboard, worn almost to whiteness, on which you were to name your preferred breakfast: using the chalk provided. This chalk was an eighth of an inch long, and even if grasped between the fingernails made no impression on the greasy pallor of the blackboard. Rufus and I had come back one evening, a little but not very late, to find the hotel closed: so that we had to take desperate measures to gain entry to a place we'd have been glad never to enter again. Having without result battered at the door, we struck the ground-floor windows with keys

212

and other objects, and found that we'd wandered to the windows of the hotel next door. The proprietor of this hotel, when we asked how we could attract the attention of his neighbour, said our activity with keys and other objects, addressed to the windows, was standard practice, though it was sometimes necessary to follow this up with the hurling of bricks. His own windows, he said anxiously, could be distinguished from those of his neighbour by the simple test of his being clean, and the other's not being remotely clean. Admitted at last, we found the bar at our hotel was open until halfway through the night. It was perhaps to prevent the discovery of this fact that it was turned so early in the evening into a fortress. We sat in it ourselves, fascinated by the intoxicated griminess of the place, and by the notices warning us against attempting to assault the proprietor or any member of his family. Large numbers of those behind the bar had eyepatches and variously sited bandages, and we concluded that these notices were fairly ineffective.

And so we sat in the Marquis, reminding ourselves of the displeasures of that trip of ours, and I found I wasn't listening closely: my attention being caught by a couple in a corner. It must have been a case of hopeless office love. She was tall, with a long plain face, and wore a long overcoat and a fur hat. He, perhaps in his mid-forties, was handsome in a faintly florid way. They were not striking, except for their deep dejection. He'd sunk his head on her shoulder, her head was sunk on her breast. They said nothing. Then she'd lift her head a little and look down at him with large dark eyes, very sad, and would smile, the smallest of smiles, and he'd put up his hand blindly and feel her face. The pub buzzed hugely, Rufus and I laughed at some twist of that awful recollection of ours: there was a cannon-fire of laughter, a sudden shrieking by a whole group that was like a firework display of sound. The man and woman sat, without speaking: and she touched the top of his head. They seemed like children.

213

Would it be all right, I wondered, in my Maori friend's eyes, simply to report that?

Or the occasion when I was travelling down an escalator in the nearby Underground station? Coming up towards me were a couple most intensely engaged. London, all eyes, could ascend and descend on escalators all round them: they were lost to the world. He was conducting a census of the parts of her body. He was assuring himself that her left elbow was complemented by her right: that below her waist was her bottom. She was astonished by his having a head, and could barely credit the ingenuity which which his legs were attached to his trunk. Each was the other's sexual abacus.

And as they drew level, in the sealed container of their amazement at each other's existence, I saw that she was George Straker's daughter.

13

A slalom of engagements and commitments: that was how I thought of the work I did at Bush House, where I attempted (watchful of arthritic shouts) to present the image of a man in his fifties with the physical vigour of a man in his forties, and the mental energy of a thirty year old. I'd hear my father uttering one of his favourite cries: 'Not a bit like it!' (Oh, how as a child I'd loved those phrases he used predictably on predictable occasions: 'I believe you – thousands wouldn't!' 'Can't do it – got a bone in my leg!') He'd smuggle into my head his own vision of the BBC corridors, full of officials detecting cases, however concealed, of ageing. In his own working corridors in this or that department of the Civil Service, decades earlier, he had always imagined conspiracies to discover in him defects on which demotion or even dismissal might be based. 'McLagen came into my room today. I wonder why that was?' My mother, who was of the opinion that McLagen had come into my father's room because McLagen had come into my father's room, and there an end of it, would sigh. She had had to endure many hours of paranoiac analysis of the movement of my father's colleagues about the, to her, detestably familiar building occupied by the Tithe Redemption Commission.

Well, I'd point out to that ghostly commentator, weaving my way in and out of too many books I was still on my feet in this downhill dash. It was still exhilarating. An uneventful life, some said. But a book was an event. All my life that had been true, for me.

So, here I was wondering if my moral duty involved writing a letter to one of the world's great cellists, confessing that my feeling for his wife was warmer than it should be. That was after I'd talked to Galina Vishnevskaya about her autobiography.

By the time I'd read the book I'd felt extraordinarily uneasy about interviewing her. Before I opened it I'd known what everyone knew, of the refuge she and her husband Mstislav Rostropovich had given to Solzhenitsyn in their *dacha* near Moscow, and of the cost of their courage: exile and the loss of Soviet citizenship. From records I knew the beauty of her voice – like a black wind suddenly silvering, the poet Akhmatova had written – and from a television appearance her personal beauty, mischievous, fierce, silver, black.

The book was consistent with all that – but added to it marvellously. She had a wretched childhood, abandoned by her parents: came close to dying during the siege of Leningrad, alone in a flat with a dead grandmother (she recalled hearing the *clink* of frozen bodies being thrown into a cart in the street below): made her way, with this great voice she had even as a child, into the Bolshoi, then Stalin's personal theatre: married Rostropovich after four days during which he wooed her with lilies of the valley and pickles: while they were on honeymoon was wooed again by Bulganin, then Head of State, whom she desperately kept at bay by taking the tormented cellist with her to every dangerous Kremlin dinner or entertainment: was a close friend and ally of Shostakovich: stood side by side with her husband when he gave Solzhenitsyn a home: and backed him again when she was unable to dissuade him from writing his letter to four newspapers, crying out against the treatment of the writer and protesting that his novels ought to be published.

Her portrait of that brave, bustling, impetuous man, Rostropovich, was a model of affectionate candour: she made it clear that when she couldn't save him from the consequences of his generous unworldliness, she resigned herself – but it was the resignation of a tigress – to doing what she could to limit the damage. I couldn't think of a more fond, proud and exasperated portrait of a husband by his wife.

As for the pages in which she excoriated the Soviet authorities, they expressed a ringing anger and scorn, out of which came now and then a coldly precise phrase: as when she spoke of what had become in the Soviet Union 'the traditions of betrayal'.

How did you interview such a person, politely, for a few stilted moments in a BBC studio? An undramatic Englishman, in the presence of such a witness to foreign tempests? How did you present her with your small, obvious, inadequate questions?

I felt nervous until I found myself face to face with her. Tosca, Aida, the tigress – they were all there, in her dark gaze: pride on a grand scale, with a certain mocking quality in reserve: together with the warmest possible readiness to be friendly and amused. She wouldn't risk English – had an interpreter with her, a subtle man, who somehow made it seem that we were talking without an intervening language. Her attention was sharp, her response vivid: at times I thought I'd understood her before a word of English had been offered.

I said it had been a bad start, and then a difficult journey

216

through life – at forty-seven, at the height of her fame, her name had been erased from the story of Russian music – but she was, I'd gathered, fierce enough to cope with all that. Her eyes flashed with pleasure at the thought of her own fierceness. Yes, she had decided from the beginning that she would not easily be put down. Mustn't an operatic lady have found the Bulganin affair a little too operatic? But *second-class* opera, she cried. Had it been under Stalin, the husband, great musician or not, would have been sent to a prison camp or shot.

She spoke of Shostakovich – 'that persecuted Titan' – with sorrowful pride. Without him there'd have been no twentieth century in Russia, no Soviet art. And exile? Well, that was not how she thought of it. What she thought was that the world was her home. Though as to that, she had to say that, until she came to the West, she'd not understood what was meant by the phrase: 'A home of my own'.

The interview was over. I was sure, I said, that she had other engagements. Grateful to her for giving so much time. She collected from corners of the studio what in my entrancement I thought of as a large number of capes, shawls, stoles, scarves, and coiled herself in them to what were surely sounds of music. The studio, I thought, would take a long time to stop being dizzy. She made a huge-lettered affirmation of her love and good wishes inside my copy of her book: and left the stage.

My conclusion as to the moral problem was that if everybody who found himself in my condition wrote apologetically to Rostropovich, the poor man would be drowned in mail.

And here was H. G. Wells's son, Gip: hero of a story of his father's I'd read in innumerable classrooms, 'The Magic Shop'. I'd read that in such circumstances so often that it was rather like meeting Jim Hawkins or Huckleberry Finn.

At sixteen and seventeen I'd been a parasite on Wells. It had infuriated Percy Chew, to have from a juvenile this ghastly echo of the voice of a man he destested. 'Self-important little pseudo-scholar, gentlemen! Only sensible thing he ever did was to become a draper's assistant! Should have remained one!' I'd imitate many of Wells's devices, including his way of breaking a story into numbered sections: I'd pontificate and lay down the cosmic law, in his fashion. I used words as he did. I turned myself into the unheroes of Wellsian stories. As in one I submitted to Percy Chew as a weekly essay, at the end of 1936, ignoring the title under which we'd been required to write: 'Architecture,' I think it was, 'is frozen music. Discuss.'

'The gym period was over,' I wrote. 'He ran to the door with the lightness of rare nudity.' (At this point, I imagine, Percy Chew knew it was not going to be about architecture.) 'McDonald and Lash were behind him: if he got into his shirt quickly, they could not take it as they had last time. He pulled off his vest: but the light of madness was in McDonald's eye: that strange light, the candle of some altar deep in him ... He clutched at a bare leg: and the artist in him rose, an ectoplasmic observer, out of his body, and saw the group on the floor, of which he was one: the two quick and derisive, and his own abased form. And then ... a voluptuousness of impotence ...'

'This is impertinence,' Percy Chew had written underneath the story. 'This wilfulness will not get you into varsity.' (He spoke so often of my wilfulness that I thought of myself as a sort of medieval king: Edward the Wilful.) I had not intended to be impertinent: I had simply needed to write about a moment when Ben Fletcher and a boy I remember as Flame, though I think he must have been Frame, had discovered that I was easy to tumble onto the changing-room floor: I was there for the tripping up. I remember the humiliation of it: worse for Ben being, when we were alone, a fellow Wellsian, given to the quiet exchange of ideas. It was my being so opposed to athletics

218

and the notion of competition, I now see, that irked Ben, himself intensely athletic, intensely competitive. Nearly fifty years after the scene in the changing room we climbed together to the top of that great rock in the middle of a marvellous plain in Sri Lanka on which old kings (and old, though here the adjective seems unsuitable, dancing girls and wives and near-wives) had their summer palace. I suffer from vertigo, but make myself climb: as here, where the final yards were a matter of creeping from one time-smoothed foothold to another across the shining summit of the rock. I thought I'd done well, making rather a thing of clinging to whatever was to be clung to, but also making jokes about it. When the world is spinning round, the worst joke offers some faint stability. But Ben told Marie, who told Kate, that he thought I could exercise my will, if I really wished to, and rise quite superior to vertigo. It was a matter of determination. I was astonished to be reminded that, in a very few matters, Ben was of Percy Chew's mind.

I read, and reread, and read again, the *Experiment in Autobiography*. It was, I think now, a little as if I *was* Wells. I certainly think of those two volumes as an account of one of my own lives as well as of his. And now here was *H. G. Wells in Love*, the addition to the autobiography of that thread that could not be included in it in the 1930s. Here was Wells saying straight what I'd understood him to be saying obliquely in his account of himself: that, as I'd have thought of it at the time, he was enormously given to ladies. He'd made it clear in the volumes as originally published that he'd been enormously given to breasts, and I'd extrapolated the rest. It was another example of that distance there was throughout my childhood between the reader and the actual human being. I had a sense, as a result of reading Wells, of, so to speak, taking breasts in my stride, when I was in fact not a mere virgin, but as it were a virginal virgin. I was of the original stuff out of which virginity was confected. I sigh now, fifty years later

... I was made of paper, made of paper!

And here, following the arrival of *H. G. Wells in Love*, was G. P. Wells, who'd edited the volume. I knew of *him*, of course, and was, from that old sense in which I was H. G., a sort of father of his. I knew him also as the hero of that charming short story with which I'd tamed awkward classes in Stonehill Street long ago. And here he was, in the studio, large, round, like his father, and old and tired. And he had forgotten half of what the book contained, and more than half of what he'd written as an introduction. I had to remind him, and he said: 'You know far more about this than I do.' 'I think what is happening,' he said after he'd failed to remember the name of one of his father's mistresses, 'is that I am interviewing you.' I said I'd not expected ever to meet the hero of 'The Magic Shop'. 'It never happened. It's an invented story,' he said anxiously.

And a few days later, moved mysteriously, he went to Sandgate, on the south coast, to look again at Spade House, which Wells had had built with his first literary fortune (something over £3000) at the turn of the century. Voysey, the architect, wanted a motif for the house, which would determine the shape of knockers, door handles, lights cut into shutters. From the pack of cards he chose hearts, but Wells said he didn't care to wear his heart on his house, and so they had spades, instead. In Sandgate it was rumoured that he was the very man who broke the bank at Monte Carlo, and it was with the ace of spades he'd done it.

So, Gip Wells went to look at it again, after many years: and returned to London: and died.

And C. L. R. James, who'd written so beautifully about cricket and revolution. That slim Trinidadian, his slimness now that of a man in his mid-eighties: a man, I couldn't help thinking, most elegantly fatigued: coming to be interviewed in Bush House, sitting with his straw hat on his knee: and later having to be interviewed in his office, which was also his library and his home, and was where he'd always been, in the thick of things: now, Brixton. He'd been so many people, sports writer and literary critic and art critic and historian and political analyst and much more, and I asked him what he was most glad to have been: and he stroked his knee with a slim hand (would you see the coffin spots on a black man's hand or were they features only of a white pigment?), and said it was being eighty-five. That was his best achievement. But he was very tired. It's the envelope, I said, that wears out. Yes, he said, if only part of the envelope could be renewed: he'd be awfully glad to have brand new legs.

And this man who was aggrieved. I'd been using words that embodied a value judgement, he said. Well, incredulously he'd heard me use that despicably soiled word, 'good'. What had 'good' ever *precisely* meant? In interviews in BBC studios, as elsewhere, he'd like to see it replaced with the term 'maximum potential'. I said I supposed this meant that the word 'evil' must be replaced with the term 'minimum potential', and that the prophet must be understood as crying woe unto them that call minimum potential maximum potential, and maximum potential minimum potential. He was in a tremendous hurry to leave, but said this did seem to him to bring about a measurable increment of signification.

Sometimes, interviewing, I felt like Mr Baynes. I thought the author of this little book on language should come and see me at least twice a year. ('It could become ...*rather nasty*!') But it hadn't been an unthrilling encounter. He was determined to scrub away from words the emotional filth with which they'd become coated by centuries of squalid use. To my helpless plea that the sound of words was part of their meaning, and that an accumulation of use created a sort of everlasting novelty, since every word had the freshness of what it had most lately become, he replied that he was sorry, but that was sentimentality. All emotive words must be replaced with unemotive words. (I tried to imagine how the Act of Parliament might have been drafted.) I thought even my cousin Bobby, with whom I'd had those gentle disagreements about the language of sociology, would have flushed furiously at this point. Bobby, tormentingly shy, had wooed his wife Jane with the '*Liebestod*' from *Tristan and Isolde* – not, of course, performed by himself, but as recorded by Kirsten Flagstad. I'd tried sometimes to imagine the scene: that enormous music, and Bobby somewhere in the lee of the gramophone, looking at Jane in what surely must have been a ventriloquial fashion: and Jane, a sensitive but also sensible woman from London, Ontario, adjusting to this splendid but alarming offer of a terminal sort of love. Bobby was convinced of the need to drive emotional implications out of the language of sociology, but in all other spheres he was committed to the idea that being up to your knees – perhaps up to your armpits – in emotion was a thoroughly good thing.

At one point my interviewee accused me of being helplessly addicted to the mere sound that words made. ('Mere' was his adjective.) Well, I said, that simply could never be the whole story, for a writer, but it was always part of the story. He swept on, angrily, and it was only later that I thought I might have quoted the verse I'd once written, invited to make one out of words that for their sound deserved a better fate than they enjoyed. I began with Hernia, who I'd always thought was plainly a Greek heroine:

Sweet Hernia on the heights of Plasticine
Sings to the nylon songs of Brassiere:
The very aspirins listen, as they lean
Against the vitreous wind, to her sad air.

I see the bloom of mayonnaise she holds
Coloured like roofs of far-away Shampoo!
Its asthma sweetens Earth! Oh, it enfolds
The alum land from Urine to Cachou!

One wild last gusset, then she's lost in night!
And dusk the dandruff dims, and anthracite!

Well, it was an uneventful life, then. Most of the weeks
of the year it made me an offer of two or more often deeply
interesting non-events, of a literary character. With those,
and the running amazements of the lives led by friends,
acquaintances and neighbours – and the enormous external dramas of which I read the most temperate accounts I
could find, in newspapers of large format – and the
occasional burglary – I thought my existence was as
fraught as I could easily endure.

14

'I'm afraid,' said the neighbour who'd picked us up at the
airport, 'that you have one or two problems to face when
you get home.' It was kindly said, but the vagueness of it
filled us with terror. The house had burnt down, fatal
accidents had disposed of assorted members of the family:
and on top of that, my general fear of being accused
of some appalling crime (probably murder) which I'd
undoubtedly committed but which had slipped my
memory, had turned out to be justified, and the police
were awaiting my arrival.

'You've been burgled,' said our neighbour.

Our natural inclination was to express dismay. It wasn't
as bad as we'd momentarily imagined, but it was bad
enough. However, we had with us our grandson Tim.
The spectacle of his grandparents dismayed would lead to
nightmares, a serious loss of security. 'Ha,' we said, lightly.
'Burgled! Ha, ha! Ah well!'

Tim said: 'Do you mean robbers?'

It would be ridiculous to pretend that we didn't mean robbers. It would be worse to attempt to suggest that robbers were welcome. 'Well, Tim,' said Kate. 'We'll see when we get there.' And to our neighbour: 'What did they take?'

It was certainly the hi-fi, he said, certainly the television – alas, perhaps much more: they seemed to have gone through everything. 'I'm afraid there's a lot of mess. Nothing that can't be tidied up, of course.'

It was one of those situations of a glum kind that cause people in their kindness to invent ludicrous reasons for your being light-hearted. 'You'll be glad to hear,' he said, 'that they didn't take the typewriter.' I was in fact sorry to hear that. I'd come to be at odds with the machine, the first electric typewriter I'd had: my technique, all trailing fingertips and knuckles, was hopeless with a machine that responded to the faintest touch. If I wrote excitedly, and often if I exercised painful care, there were three-letter words that would turn into ten-letter words. 'Oh good,' said Tim. 'Then I can use it when we get home. I *can* use it, can't I?' 'I don't think . . .' said Kate, and I knew she was about to tell Tim that one wasn't keen, in a freshly burgled house, to have someone continuing to compose his current novel (*Moonfleet*, by Tim Blishen) especially when the author was given to demanding collaboration from everyone within earshot.

'You *never* let me use the typewriter,' said Tim, flying in the face of the fact that he was *always* allowed to use the typewriter. But it was amiably said: I thought he had measured the loss of writing time against the dramatic gain of experience in respect of being present at or immediately after a burglary, and felt that he was winning.

It was our third burglary, and we knew what was involved, over and beyond the discovery of what, on this particular occasion, had vanished. There'd be, of course, the sensation of having been violated. It was curiously uncomfortable to know that strangers, altogether lacking in goodwill, had been through your things in the light of a heartless judgement of their being worth stealing or not. On our first burglary, many years before, nothing had been taken except, as it happened, my typewriter. I remembered the two kinds of wrath we'd felt: at being burgled, and at being disdainfully burgled. The burglar had been through everything and rejected almost everything. There'd been, all the same, that deep sense of violation. It was when we were living in a house shared with friends: and I remember Ben, who lived above us, being amused by my horror of the burglary as a form of intrusion. 'To me,' said Ben, 'a burglary would simply be an administrative matter.' From the earliest days of our association, at the grammar school, he'd regarded me as ridiculously over-emotional. ' "Feel" ', he'd said once, when we were in the sixth form, 'is your favourite word – do you know that? My favourite word is "think".' 'When you are burgled, Ben,' I said on this later occasion, '*you* will put on ludicrous displays of cerebration.' 'You don't have to hit back,' said Ben. 'I really do rather enjoy your emotional approach to burglary. But if I might be at hand to help you to keep emotion at bay when you meet the loss adjuster . . .'

At the crucial moment, when without entering I'd seen that somebody else had entered, Ben had been away. I'd called for support on my friend at the top of the house, who was undressing for bed. He'd dressed again and joined me on the verandah that ran round two sides of our ground-floor flat. Yes, yes, open window, footprints on sill. We'd go in, cautiously. At which point he'd uttered a cry of despair. Lying on the verandah, a pair of underpants. They were, he knew at once, those he'd been wearing that day. For a moment we reeled under the possibility that we were faced by a burglar who, whilst invisible, was capable of removing people's underwear without disturbing the rest of their clothing. In the gen- erally uneasy state of mind that burglary causes (except

225

in such as Ben) we were amazed, but not particularly surprised. Indeed, it seemed no less a cause of agitation when my neighbour remembered that, hurriedly re-dressing, he'd not bothered to put his underpants on. They'd clearly got caught up in his belt, and dropped out as we nervously prowled round the scene of what was to turn out to be such a disappointing crime.

For most of us, disorientation is one of the hazards that follow from sudden and unexpected events: disasters even so small in scale as burglary. I'd often wondered, side by side for so much of my life with my friend Ben, so close but temperamentally so distant, how he really responded when alone to such occurrences. There'd been more of them in his life than in mine. A signaller on a wartime destroyer, he'd once been required to row out, in an unfriendly Atlantic, to a German plane brought down by the ship's guns and, stepping onto the sinking thing, cut away one of the swastikas on its wings. The captain wanted to take it home as a souvenir. Ben said he regarded the errand as absurd, crazily trivial, and very dangerous. Moreover, he'd been chosen to undertake it on the grounds that he spoke German: which, since the only other German-speaker within miles, the pilot of the plane, had baled out and was now a prisoner on board the destroyer, struck Ben as infuriatingly beside the point. However, I easily imagine him, not being unafraid, but dealing brusquely with his fear, so mixed with irritation. He might even, as he plied his trembling knife, have thought of me as a pointer to states of mind of which, when cutting into the fabric of a fast-sinking plane in the middle of a hostile ocean, he would rather be free ...

More than forty years after that escapade of Ben's, we entered the house to find that over the decades we had progressed to being mildly burglar-worthy. Tim's robber had taken the easily renewed – hi-fi and television: he had also taken the irreplaceable – rings, for example, that had never amounted to much and had worn thin on the fingers of Kate's grandmother, my mother. I still hated it, and this time round detected in my distaste a connection – absurd, absurd! – with huger kinds of intrusion. BUR-GLARS MARCH INTO POLAND ... It wouldn't do. Being a burglar didn't make you a Nazi. Yet there was this willingness to invade and seize ...

I met the Higginses in Barley Wood's general shop. He was locally famous for making her, in her presence, the satirical target of any story he had to tell: and she was locally famous for seeming not to mind. 'Mrs H!' he cried. 'You can't tell her! Doors left unlocked, garage doors left open! Might as well drop the sods a line! "Going out Tuesday. Have a good time. The whisky's on the side-board."'

Mrs H laughed pleasantly: she seemed never to have taken the measure of the massive fury she caused in her husband.

15

Ben was now being phlegmatic in Sri Lanka, involved in the international support for the building of a great dam. When I was awarded a travelling scholarship, Kate and I went to see him and Marie. Not so much a highlight as a lowlight of the visit was the night we spent in a monastery: not Buddhist, but Benedictine. Marie had arranged it.

As she often observed, Marie had ideal expectations of all events: and all events, in her view, had from the beginning of her life set out to dash her hopes. George Straker had once taken her on her first visit to Kew Gardens, which she'd wanted to see since she'd read of it in an encyclopaedia in her childhood home in a French town. She'd imagined glorious weather, a kind of general effect of being inside a painting by the Douanier Rousseau, and a perfect conducted tour, since George claimed to know every inch of the Gardens. In fact it had rained horribly, there seemed an enormous amount of wet green between one floral marvel and the next, and George, as Marie told the story, had great difficulty in locating even the Palm House.

On this occasion in Sri Lanka she'd seen us in this monastery among clouds and mountains, spending a tastefully Spartan night amid, perhaps, a general, not too obtrusive, chanting. It would all be mistily courteous, with much bowing, a grave smile or two. Something of Benedictine fineness might rub off, even on us.

The first dismay was the monastery itself. It had been the residence of an Englishman from Shropshire who had taken the eccentric trouble to have erected at this altitude the country house he would have built if he'd continued to live in Shrewsbury. It was dizzying, to be so obviously in England when we were so obviously in Sri Lanka. We walked in the grounds, arms linked, and looked one way into exotic chasms and the other way at the homely façade. Then we went to our rooms, to be dismayed again. It was not possible, outside the worst of prisons, to be faced with beds more unrelated to notions of comfort. There were no visible nails: but these were still beds of nails. The bathroom was a small indoor flood. Its floor was inches deep in what was only partly water. No one was to be found who might be appealed to. Ben and I, drawing on our experience of having once lived together in that decayed Victorian house in Barley Wood, diagnosed a collapsed ballcock. In search of a means of fixing it in a more effective position, we discovered that the flowers in the dining room were artificial. We made the repair with the stem of a false rose; and then pinned to the door a notice declaring: THIS BATHROOM CANNOT BE USED – IT IS FILTHY. Later in the evening we were given to believe that an emergency spring cleaning was taking place. There were never any signs that this had happened.

The third dismay was the dining room, and what was offered in it. Round the walls stood a monk, the Assistant

Guest Master, and two or three boys, acolytes: and above them, on the warped Salopian pannelling, numerous watercolours and oils, the work of the wife of the original owner. She had clearly herself been confused as to where she actually was, and had painted the landscape around us as if, generally, it had been a sort of Long Mynd.

The meal began with a bad soup, coloured tepid water: and went on to a dish of rags of beef, fragments of potato and carrot and balls of what might have been soot, turgidly afloat in a greasy gravy. We called for salt, and one of the boys, an eager-eyed Tamil, darted here and there, struggling to open doors in wonderfully warped cabinets almost certainly purchased in Ludlow. He found a plastic object that had been exposed to the sun but could be made out to have been, at one time, a cruet. It was empty. Finally, a sweet came in plastic pots that had suffered worse even than the cruet: in this climate they'd become fearsomely carbuncular. There were off-cuts of the basic stuff out of which jellies are made that had never become jelly itself, afloat in a liquid that might once have been skimmed milk.

Ben and I thought rather a lot of whisky might be the remedy, from the bottle we had with us: but Marie said no, he was weak: and Kate said no, I must exhibit strength of character: and in the general context of incredulous amusement, Ben and I were sulky. Kate, who'd been known to become roaring drunk from a spoonful of sherry, sipped at the whisky and fell insensible. I could hardly sleep at all for the cruel bed and the fusty air of the room. Breakfast was worse than dinner. Fried eggs were waiting for us, and had been waiting, we calculated, an hour or so: each lay cold in a pond of coconut oil. They could not be eaten. Ben called for the Guest Master. He was absent, they said, in Kandy, but the Assistant Guest Master appeared instead. He and the acolytes made a guilty line. Ben said: 'I and my friends have never had a worse night – the food was inedible, the bathroom was disgusting, and

229

no attempt was made to welcome us or to tell us what we might do or where we might go.' It seemed awful, reprimanding boys so brightly willing. Ben said firmly: 'The boys were not at fault. They did their best in *impossible* conditions.' He then stalked out, and I followed: but the majesty of his wrath had made him blind, and he did not perceive that the lintel of the door by which we were leaving was horribly low. He struck his forehead on it and burst into laughter; and my own ready laughter was released. For fifty years Ben and I, in a variety of infuriating and, now and then, dangerous circumstances, had given way to amusement. Perhaps if I'd been with him when he was required to cut the swastika off the wing of that German plane, our laughter would have been fatal: we'd have caused the machine to sink under us.

Strange occasion! Such mysterious disgrace, all round, in the setting of ragged cliffs, immense valleys with rumpled floors! How different everything in the world was from the prior conception one had of it! Ceylon, Miss Baker had said in 1929; tea, almost entirely. Well, tea and temples. She'd not prepared me for discovering that the island was a kind of endless village street, aspiring to be a high street: and people walking, walking, walking, with an alert absence of mind, amid astonishing forms of brightness. She'd not mentioned the kites that were perpetually being flown in Colombo, on a green space close to the hotel Joseph Conrad used to favour, the air snapping with them – many of a kind I'd not seen elsewhere, like demented suspender belts. The air altogether clamorous, and full especially of that noise that in hot countries seems to be the noise of sunshine itself. A great clinking – from a universal conversion of old scraps of metal into new scraps of metal. A moon that I concluded must be peculiar to Sri Lanka: starting the night lying fat and blindingly golden on a bed of black treetops, and then skimming across the sky so fast you knew it wouldn't last the night out. And the Buddhas carved in the rock at Polonnaruwa,

230

the most profoundly moving objects I'd ever seen, of riveting serenity, and all the more marvellous because their true setting was not the one shown in the usual photographs – you stepped back a little and saw that these astonishments existed in a sort of meadow among grazing cattle and casual cattlemen.

And Miss Baker had not said that it was an island where the only creatures with road sense were elephants. Elephants looked right, looked left, and tucked themselves hugely into the side of the road. Cars, many of them Morris 1000s on their last wheels, were treated by their drivers as nudging and fidgeting extensions of themselves: the only rules being that you were bound to turn unexpectedly across one another's path, and must overtake if doing so offered a reasonable prospect of suicide. So that amid the wonderful dust and all those people walking, and a great trudging of cattle, there were cars and trucks behaving in accordance with their drivers' most abrupt and private whims. I noted that Ben, at home an unorthodox driver, had here improved upon his unnerving originality.

In the depths of the country, the endless odorous village street became an endless back lane. And one morning we were about at a time when the whole of Sri Lanka was on its way to school; and as in the smoky darkness before dawn our car passed a long line of a schoolgirls waiting for their cheeful ruin of a school bus, a grin ran along the line, like a flaw opening up in a dresserful of china. That was when we were on our way to a weekend with the owner of a tea plantation who, relentlessly generous, fed us meal after meal with things curried, even the dainties accompanying mid-afternoon tea being curried dainties, and our nights were given up to chagrin and explosion.

Miss Baker could not in 1929 have foreseen that being in Sri Lanka half a century later would cause one of her pupils to conclude that some of us in the West are now among an infinitesimal minority in human history who have lost understanding of how to treat with beggars.

Stop a car anywhere in Sri Lanka, in apparent wilderness perhaps, and within seconds there were hands, many of them children's, stretched out for alms. We drove, not far from the monastery, up a series of appalling hairpin bends. At the first bend was a child offering, in exchange for money, a Canna lily. It was not possible to stop on a bend so fearful, but at the next fearful bend, there she was: having scrambled up the virtually perpendicular bank in between. This story repeated itself, bend after bend: until we found her weeping, her lily lost, and desperately managed to stop: but by then, not all the money in the world could have staunched her tears. At one such halt Kate prepared to offer sweets from a tin, and was shaken by the hungry violence with which children took from her not only the sweets, but the tin; and almost took her hand, she said. In a bruising matter of seconds, everything had gone.

I tried hard to honour an intention of the scholarship that took me there – that it should lead to encounters with local writers. The BBC's World Service had supplied me with the names of entrants to their short story competitions. I met several of these, and became as sad as they were. Their sorrow sprang from the absence of a true local audience, and of a Sri Lankan literary market worthy of the name. 'I would like to write a novel, more than anything,' said one smilingly melancholy writer, 'or at any rate something longer than a short story, but –' It was a dismal 'but', covering the situation that virtually no one would risk publishing anything much longer than the short story for which room could be found in newspapers busy with obituaries.

Someone had told someone else that a travelling scholar was in the country. It was arranged that I should be interviewed on the air. Just before I left for Radio Colombo, I had a phone call from my interviewer. 'I have discovered who you are,' he cried. 'You are James Blish, and you write science fiction.' My dread of being self-

232

important made it perilously likely that I should assent to this, and be confronted in the studio with the frightful need to ventriloquise. But I managed to say 'No, not so', and to meet my interviewer in time to give him a rather unconvinced sense of there being some difference between Blish, SF, and Blishen, helpless autobiography. He turned out to be a journalist of resigned ferocity, who told me at length how he'd managed to keep his head above the turbulent local waters. And so I, a mild journalist who'd managed to keep his head above waters far milder, was quizzed about my mild work: and longed to be empowered to scatter, in every direction (and with half a dozen wry Sri Lankan men and women particularly in mind), travelling scholarships.

One thing Miss Baker had inadvertently prepared me for, simply by naming it: Kandy. I longed, for the sound of it, to go there. And it was as memorably fine as my nine-year-old self had imagined. Kate and I sat one early morning looking down on the misty square of the king-made lake that forms the heart of the town, and beyond it to layers of hill, one rare kind of blue after another.

Such a beautiful world! Such a muddle of feelings one lived in! Here we were, who in this seventh decade of ours had been in a canoe on that broad Canadian lake, had walked unremarked alongside the Remarkables, had scrambled with Agnes Mild up a hillside crammed with the bones of profoundly exiled Anglo-Saxons and French men and women: to Agnes, living bones. The atlas had opened up to us! And, as we saw things, a bad decade, too. We were grieved by the sharp-faced official Britain of the eighties, with the purring voice it had been advised to adopt because its natural voice was heartless. Civilisation, I thought, was a confidence trick carefully assembled over a long period to cause us to behave more generously than we might do if left to ourselves. Being essentially a trick, it was easily dismantled: it was necessary only for a run of powerful persons to refuse to subscribe to the benign deceit.

And it was a decade that offered, amid these continuing novelties and marvels of experience, and these social and political dismays, the increasing thought of its all being, for Kate and me, soon to be pinched out. Death, taking more or less time, would seize each of us between finger and thumb, and it would vanish.

I remembered how, in Cornwall once, my son Tom and I, climbing up from a lonely beach, had found the bones of an animal, too big to be a sheep, surely not a cow. We were amazed and delighted by the shapes of those bones: the winged shapes, the shapes stressed and massive at one end and at the other flowing to great fineness – a strong fragility. There were bones like Chinese pavilions, and others that offered portholes through which the world could be turned into circular pictures: ribs like swords and a jawbone light as air that was shaped like a ship, with three rattling teeth still sailing in it. It was an enchanting sort of mortality, and I wondered if the human skeleton, left in the weather, bleached and dried, would provide such an entertaining assortment. At seventeen, when I'd never considered I might be anything but immortal, I'd used the vocabulary of death to cut a dash in a poem, or simply in murmurings with friends. 'The skull beneath the skin,' I was given to sighing. Now Kate and I drifted into seeing a television programme about a young apprentice to undertaking. He was fat of face, nice, and moved among the horrors of the trade with buoyant interest. There they lay, the men in blue and the women in pink, the shrouds were like cheap dressing gowns: death had turned those wonderfully active objects, their hands and feet, into waxen rubbish. The apprentice was shown how to drain the sewage from a new corpse: it was all that now filled that once bright world of nerve and muscle, a pipeful of stench. And, after cremation, there were the charred

234

bones: the metal detector sorting out the nails and emergency joints from old operations: and at last the atomiser, and the final dust. The young man grew increasingly cheerful throughout his introduction to this trade. He thought he'd be suited to it, he said. And clearly he would be, growing into a man who'd never have difficulty in sleeping.

Our son Dan, Kate and I would sometimes recall, was puzzled as a child to distinguish between the written words 'Ahem' and 'Amen'. It struck us that we might end up in the same uncertainty.

16

'So it is a quite old thing,' said the guide. He was referring to a thirteenth-century church whose open tower, stuffed with bells, could be seen among the trees to our right. 'It was built after a disastering plague.' He blew into his microphone to clear it, and produced an impolite sound. We drove, laughing, towards two simultaneous seas: the nearer, a prairie of lavender: the further, the Adriatic.

Kate, the quite old thing at my side, asked if I'd noticed that, on this holiday, we'd read less than usual, because we'd slept more than usual. It was true. Sometimes, on this island of Hvar, we'd caught ourselves engineering very small exertions in order to justify very large programmes of recovery. 'But being asleep here,' said Kate, 'is like being awake anywhere else.' That, I thought, was because our window looked out across the small, wonderfully handsome, talkative harbour, a perfect stage for summer: it was like dozing in the stalls of such a theatre as was over there, on the further side of the water (but not at all far, for nothing here was far), the earliest surviving theatre in the Adriatic. That was another of the old things that added up to make the ravishing old thing that was the town square. To the right, at the end of that, the furthest building to be seen from our bedroom window, was the church, which regularly at sunset was subjected to alchemy, became a golden church, was melted down and, as the sun sank, slowly cooled and restored to its usual handsomeness: a façade painted on a stagecloth between two towers. In the early morning light it became the coolest bronze. I'd got Kate to photograph me sitting in one of the two valleys worn in the step at the main door: more feet than bottoms had been responsible for those in the past five hundred years, but I recognised the comic measure of my latterday largeness. The inside of the theatre was a little woodland of green-painted columns, everything delicate: a setting, you'd have thought, for a most fragile, whispering sort of drama. It wasn't only myself I felt was large, in there: there seemed a distance in dimensions between this place and the whole modern scene. The columns that made their way round the auditorium were sapling-slim, and I'd thought for a moment of the epidemic of porticos that had struck lately in Barley Wood, perhaps originating with George Straker. It was part of that restless activity of moneyed nomads, who'd gut and enlarge and go. The smallest doorways were inclined to opt for the largest canopies sustained by the most corpulent columns. Such clumsiness, compared with this! ... In the evening the square became the town's drawing room, making two seas again, this time of sound, the murmur and splash in the harbour and the murmur and splash in the square. In the very centre, a well, with a cap that seemed as delicate as the doileys my mother used to make, but was of seventeenth-century wrought iron: on it, the children swarmed, making a shrieking knot at the heart of the warm spread sound of the crammed square. I thought if I had a choice of place to die in, it might be there, some evening, in the heart of that hum that had been continuous for seven hundred years.

Except, of course, that Barton was where I belonged. I couldn't die in the middle of somebody else's drama, however exquisite the stage set! I'd have to stick to my original wish to perish in the Friar's Holt: possibly in the presence of old Charlie, who'd been a regular there for longer than I could remember, and who'd not even thought he might regard himself as being dislodged by the conversion of the pub into a mainly middle-class institution. Old Charlie, then youngish Charlie, was almost certainly there, in what would still have been the public bar, when Kate and I had sat in it with our nervous half-pints of bitter, three months after our return from Venice in 1948, and a day or so before our marriage. 'It would be terribly inexpensive, filming our life,' I'd said, thinking of this a few nights ago. 'The same few sets, over and over again.'

Well, dying! The week before we left to come to Hvar, old Charlie had caught my eye across the bar. He clearly had a need to talk: I'd smiled back, and he came across and said: 'I've just lost the wife. She said: "I'm dying, Charlie!" I said: "No, you're not, Annie!" She just went like that.' And I said how sorry I was and he went back to his seat and then I caught his eye again and he came across and said: 'This man flew to Ireland. "How was the flying?" they asked him. "All right," he said, "but it don't half make the arms ache!"'

Now we were on our way in a sightseeing coach to the island's oldest town: with our guide whose English was subject to occasions of syntactical breakdown. 'They collapsed over the night,' he said of buildings in some old earthquake. At times his pronunciation reminded me of myself, at my most unconfident moments in a studio at Bush House. The reasons for this or that were 'num -' (pronounced as if it were 'numb') '-erous'. Someone had added a wing to a building in a baroque style – 'a barrack wink'. A stream divided a village into two huffs. He told us, as was the practice, of the perfect character of political arrangements in Yugoslavia, and our liking of him, with his student's face, alternately solemn and amused, made us wish we could believe every word he spoke.

Indeed, happy, we leaned back in our seats and found in ourselves not the faintest stirring of disbelief. Nowhere in Yugoslavia was anyone to be found who was not completely in harmony with the system. The system was completely in harmony with itself. Vigorous attempts were being made to remove the few final flaws ...

Everywhere about us, great moles and dams and carefully heaped straggles of rock that kept the land from sliding away. And everywhere, dead villages. They were a consequence of tourism, which drew people to the towns. Our guide had something euphoric to say about that. I wondered what he'd have to offer in defence of that megalomaniac hotel back in the town of Hvar, luckily round the corner from the harbour, a *ziggurat* in concrete and glass, in which it was possible for holidaymakers to be immured without ever making contact with the real world. It was a vast Adriatic Dandy Lion. Or of the gap that for some reason had occurred in the square, and that had been filled in with a concrete beam or two, forming an elementary and, in the context, barbarous shop. Could Gobbling 'n Going ever make its way into that handsome scene?

We stopped to stretch our legs, and came across swans. She was nest-building, and padded about on those absurd galoshes, such unsuitable feet for a creature so lovely, picking up twigs, throwing them over the vague white width of her shoulders in the direction of the nest. She was simply pre-maternally restless. The male arrived with enormous decelerations, slappings of feet on the water and then a furious shutting down of wings: whereupon, instantly, he became the serene gliding swan of our common view of the bird.

Kate, undoubtedly moved by the mere vigour involved in being a swan, said of course if we were aware of ageing

238

it was in the setting of a determination to remain active and robust for as long as possible. I said this perhaps followed from my having these books with me, more slowly read than in the past, perhaps, but still read with relentless care, and all that obsessive making of notes, so that in two or three weeks I could face their authors and ask them ... Poor authors! said Kate. Expecting a shallow occasion and finding it had been converted by the interviewer into a sort of seminar! The term 'disturbance fee' hardly covered such a raid on a fellow writer's patience! Honestly, how much of each author's time was I likely to take up with questions and answers that couldn't possibly find a place on the final tape? *Touché*, I said. On the other hand, answers worth listening to in San Francisco, Sydney or Wellington (where we'd caught up with the programme during the trip round the world) might be better obtained in a context of excess than in a minimal context? Kate said, all the same, she braced herself for the figure I might, in the end, cut in the Yellow Pages: 24-Hour Reviewing: Books Read and Reviewed Same Day. I reminded her that in the 1920s and early 1930s I'd made my way every late afternoon to the local library, finishing the current book in order to be ready for its successor. The crisis of a narrative was still confused, for me, with the crisis represented by the question: Will I reach the library in time?

In Hvar, of course, as everywhere else in the world, and as happens to everybody, we'd met someone we knew. In this case, a noisy educationist who, to my intense relief, was at the end of his holiday. He was a man whose favourite phrase was: 'I am struck from time to time...' 'It has just struck me...' might be a variant. It was so much the thing he always said that you were amazed he was, or seemed, unaware of it. He had to be imagined as the victim of a remorseless bombardment by ideas. He lived under constant threat from mental meteorites. 'It strikes me forcibly...' he would say (and *had* said, here in Hvar). At times it must have struck him in the opposite fashion, glancingly: but oddly he had no word for such milder impacts. 'Has it ever struck you...?' he would inquire. 'I have a theory...' was a variation on that. 'An idea I have been brooding on for ages...' 'May I try this out on you?' That he was under siege from his own intellect was well-established: the odd thing was that nothing of this activity in the head, these collisions, all these long sittings on ideas as if they'd been eggs, all these trials and dummy runs and launchings, had ever had any practical issue whatever. I had known him for years as a central educational figure. I had never been able to associate him with a single educational achievement. Somehow he had come to believe that to say something was to do something. Meeting him out of our usual context, on this island, where (if I looked over his shoulder) hibiscus could be seen growing out of pinches of mortar, and the sea rolled in and out, light-splashed, and was blistered with islands: and those hopping leaves over there were sparrows: meeting him here, I was amazed at his emptiness, and that with it he should have travelled so far. It was like that other ambitious educator we knew, who spoke of education as if it had been some kind of cream bun. 'Oh my lovely lovely teaching!' seemed always to be what he was saying. 'Oh my scrumptious students! Oh my new beautifully cooked curriculum!' And so on.

Oh, synopses again, said Kate. Synopses ourselves, we moved among synopses! Some, dreadfully interrupted! Where was our ruined friend, Nat?

And we thought of a synopsis we'd recently seen, angrily inscribed on the floor of a Suffolk church; the life of Bridgett Applewhaite, in less than two hundred words:

After the Fatigues of a Married Life
Borne by Her with Incredible Patience
For four years and three quarters, bating three weeks,
And after the enjoyment of the Glorious Freedom

Of an Easy and unblemisht Widowhood
For four years and Upwards
She resolved to run the Risk of a Second Marriage Bed
But DEATH forbad the Banns
And having with an Apoplectick Dart
(The same instrument with which he had formerly dis-
patcht her Mother)
Toucht the most vital part of her Brain
She must have fallen directly to the ground
(As one Thunder strook)
If she had not been catcht and supported
By her intended Husband
Of which invisible bruise
After a struggle for above sixty Hours
With that grand Enemy to Life
(But the Certain and Merciful Friend
To helpless Old Age)
In terrible Convulsions, Plaintive groans or Stupefying
Sleep
Without recovery of Speech or Senses,
She dyed on the 12th day of Sept.
In ye year) of our Lord 1737
) of her own age 44

Did anyone, asked Kate, ever spend Eternity under a
better Synopsis?

Our guide said some of us might like to visit the summer
residence of a Croatian poet, Peter Hektorovic. He was a
quite old poet, lived 1487 to 1572, and it was a quite old
house. Down that street there, and march left, then march
right: please look for a house of some length, of the Middle
Age.

It was indeed a long house, and a plain one, part home
and part fortress: it didn't bristle with an intention of
keeping invaders at bay, but was nevertheless plainly on
guard. I thought it the best-mannered defensive house I'd

ever seen. Leading off the entrance hall, which after the watchful assertion made by the outside walls was light and open, there were rooms of a plainly humane kind: a study, a living room, a lavatory over the door of which the poet had inscribed a thought in Latin: the English of it being, 'When you know where you are, how can you be proud?' It seemed a long way from the enamel ovals screwed to the doors of lavatories back in Barley Wood, saying in facetiously floating letters, LOO. This was a house that, inside its courteous armour, united the outer and the inner: so that the garden was in no way an appendage, but a series of alternative rooms. You were among flowers, and then you were not among them. Against the general background of stone, any colour was an astonishment: every flower, a flag. And there was a fishpond, a sort of watery theatre, and in it mullet flickered like so many swimming quotation marks: no doubt about it, a writer's pond. The tradition of Petar Hektorovic's time was that the mullet were never caught: and in the five hundred years since his day, none ever had known hook or net. Among them, I was certain, there was a quite old mullet or two.

They said Petar Hektorovic was a sort of late Croatian Chaucer: or early Montaigne: a man whose poetry took heed of common life. The variety of human personality fascinated him. He'd written the first realistic poem in the language, called, with marvellous improbability, *Fishing and Talks with Fishermen*. I longed to read it.

I'd stumbled among the stones in the poet's house, and Kate said, as we made the return journey, that breaking our bones was, of course, something we must expect in the years ahead. A quite old bone was a bone quite easily snapped.

I thought of one of the pleasures we'd both known, sixty years earlier, tagging along behind our mothers as they shopped in Barton High Street. 'We shall be,' I said, delighted by the gentleness of the image, 'like a couple of bags of broken biscuits.'